00536

k is to be returned on or before
last date stamped below.

D0811509

*REGIONAL
RESEARCH
REPORTS 1*

Rural Development Issues in Industrialized Countries

EDITED BY
GYÖRGY ENYEDI AND JOEKE VELDMAN

CENTRE FOR REGIONAL STUDIES

1986

The *Regional Research Reports Series Editorial Board*
is composed of staff members at the
Centre for Regional Studies, Hungarian Academy of Sciences:

Eta Daróczi, Editor (Budapest)
György Enyedi, President (Pécs)
Sándor Péter, Member (Pécs)
Judit Timár, Technical Editor (Békéscsaba)
Lajos Tímár, Member (Budapest)

The Editor's Office
P.O. Box 48, 1251 Budapest 11

English text edited by
Éva Dessewffy-Pálmai
Brian O'Sullivan
Cover design by
Zsuzsa Murányi

Centre for Regional Studies,
Hungarian Academy of Sciences
P.O. Box 199, 7601 Pécs, Hungary

First published 1986

© Centre for Regional Studies 1986

HU ISSN 0237–3440
ISBN 963 01 6629 1

Printed in Hungary, by Akadémiai Kiadó és Nyomda, Budapest

CONTENTS

CONTRIBUTORS

Oedzge A. L. C. Atzema Department of Geography, Catholic University of Nijmegen
Berg en Dalseweg 105, 6522 BD NIJMEGEN

Dinny de Bakker Department of Geography, University of Utrecht
P.O. Box 80.115, 3508 TC UTRECHT

Györgyi Barta Regional Science Department, Centre for Regional Studies, Hungarian
Academy of Sciences
P.O. Box 48, 1251 BUDAPEST 11

Tjebbe F. de Boer Union of Dutch Municipalities
Nassaulaan 12, 2514 JS THE HAGUE

Bálint Csatári Settlement Research Unit, Centre for Regional Studies, Hungarian
Academy of Sciences
P.O. Box 261, 6001 KECSKEMÉT

Theo B. M. Dijkstra National Planning Agency
P.O. Box 90.618, 2596 BK THE HAGUE

Petr F. Dostál Institute for Human Geography, University of Amsterdam
Jodenbreestraat 23, 1011 NH AMSTERDAM

György Enyedi Centre for Regional Studies, Hungarian Academy of Sciences
P.O. Box 199, 7601 PÉCS

Hans van Ginkel Department of Geography, University of Utrecht
P.O. Box 80.115, 3508 TC UTRECHT

Jan G. Groenendijk Institute for Geographical Studies and Urban and Regional Planning,
Free University of Amsterdam
P.O. Box 7161 1007 MC AMSTERDAM

Paulus Huigen Department of Geography, University of Utrecht
P.O. Box 80.115, 3508 TC UTRECHT

Zoltán Kárpáti Institute of Sociology, Hungarian Academy of Sciences
P.O. Box 20, 1250 BUDAPEST

László Lackó Department for Architecture and Settlement Development, Ministry of
Building and Urban Development
P.O. Box 613, 1370 BUDAPEST

Jan D. Markusse Institute for Human Geography, University of Amsterdam
Jodenbreestraat 23, 1011 NH AMSTERDAM

Andries Piersma Department of Geography, University of Groningen
P.O. Box 800, 9700 AV GRONINGEN

Béla Sárfalvi Department of Regional Geography, University Roland Eötvös
Kun Béla tér 2, 1083 BUDAPEST

Marc de Smidt Department of Geography, University of Utrecht
P.O. Box 80.115, 3508 TC UTRECHT

József Tóth Centre for Regional Studies, Hungarian Academy of Sciences
P.O. Box 199, 7601 PÉCS

Joeke Veldman Department of Geography, University of Utrecht
P.O. Box 80.115, 3508 TC UTRECHT

LIST OF FIGURES

LIST OF TABLES

PREFACE AND ACKNOWLEDGEMENTS

This volume contains the revised papers of a Dutch-Hungarian workshop in "Consequences of rural settlement developments", held at Utrecht from 7–14 November 1983. The workshop was organized by the Working group on socio-spatial research in rural areas under the aegis of both the Netherlands' Organization for Pure Research (ZWO) and the Royal Dutch Geographic Society.

The workshop focussed on rural settlement problems in a cross-cultural comparative perspective. In the editorial introduction on "Key problems in rural settlement research" the general theme and specific sub-themes are elaborated in more detail. From a Dutch perspective this workshop succeeded the Anglo-Dutch seminar, held in Norwich in 1982 and published as "The Changing Countryside" (G. Clark, J. G. Groenendijk and F. Thissen, Eds., Geobooks 1984). Hungarian geographers organized workshops on rural geographical problems with their Polish (1980) and French (1984) colleagues. This type of conference on a bilateral base has turned out to be very fruitful and stimulating.

The Dutch editor of this book and chief organizer of this workshop, Joeke Veldman, died on 14th of June 1984, aged 59 years. He was the initiator of the Working group and the key-person in preparing this workshop. His work illustrates the renaissance of Dutch rural geography to which he contributed more than any other colleague.

The organizers should like to express their appreciation to ZWO for financial support, covering travel and hotel expenses for the Hungarian delegation. They wish to convey their tanks to the executive board of the Faculty of Geography of the University of Utrecht, acting as a host as well as giving financial support. The Working group, chaired by Frans Thissen, developed the key issues for this conference. The local organizers group consisted of members of this group. We are grateful to Ger de Rijk, senior lecturer in East European studies at the University of Utrecht and his assistants Bert van der Lingen and Jo de Viet for their advice and help.

GYÖRGY ENYEDI,
Vice President
of the Hungarian Geographical Society
1982–1986

MARC DE SMIDT,
President
of the Royal Dutch Geographic Society
1981–1984

Introduction

KEY PROBLEMS
IN RURAL SETTLEMENT RESEARCH
AND PLANNING

GYÖRGY ENYEDI AND JOEKE VELDMAN

KEY WORDS: *agrarisized* countryside; *agribusiness; agricultural* exodus; *area*-bound land-use; *asymmetrical* interdependence; *central* settlement development fund; *collectivization; contraction* of service points; *dichotomy,* ~ of peripheral versus peri-urban areas, rural—urban ~; *geographical* scale; *geography*, agricultural ~, economic ~, human ~, rural ~, settlement ~; *industrial* revolution; *infrastructural* development; *'key-village'* concept; *large-scale* farming; *outdated* technological—organizational system; *peripheral rural areas,* labour market in ~; *peri-urban* development; *rural—urban* complementarity; *rural* deprivation, ~ exodus, ~ industrialization, ~ public services, ~ settlement network, ~ sociology; *suburban* development; *urban* explosion; *urban—industrial* take-off; *urbanization* pattern.

The European countryside faced an impressive metamorphosis. Industrialization and suburbanization changed the morphology and socio-economic structure of villages. Even in remote areas people have undergone a cultural modernization. Small villages, however, lost services, and accessibility by public transport sometimes diminished. Each rural area constitutes a specific part of a mosaic. Rural geography has to paint a portrait of regions, tracing out which processes include policies carried out by different levels of government. It will be very interesting to compare the rural geography and planning of two nations with a different background in political economy. Moreover, there is the difference of a land-locked state, formerly integrated as an agricultural element in a vast imperial economy, and a seaborn, extremely open, economy of a densely populated country. Geographical scale and the dichotomy of periphery versus peri-urban can be seen as basic elements in dealing with a typology of rural planning issues.

Rural geography as a sub-discipline

In 1971 Piersma made a plea to replace agricultural geography with rural geography in the urban-industrial countries. A year after that, Clout published his *Rural Geography. An Introductory Survey* in Great Britain. Also in 1972, Enyedi established a Working Group on Rural Planning and Development within the International Geographical Union, for studying rural areas 'as multifunctional space' (Enyedi 1975). Piersma's argumentation was socially based. The mechanization of agriculture caused a tremendous decrease in the agriculturally active population. At the same time, in the 1960s, the necessity to leave the countryside (rural exodus) if one changed one's agricultural profession (agricultural exodus) came to an end. The enormously increased individual mobility and the establishment of a non-agricultural active population opened up the possibility for the non-agricultural active population to live and work in their own rural environment. Since this time, the 'agrarisized countryside' (Franklin 1969), which came into being as a consequence of the Industrial Revolution, has past forever. The village-communities, characterized by a territorially bounded spatial behaviour of the inhabitants, dissolved in a generally accepted national culture. Agriculturists lost their controlling role in the community. The rural areas now have to accomplish new functions for the living and open-air recreation of urban people and for maintaining ecological values and the amenity of the landscape. A rural—urban complementarity arises. Agriculture is a branch of trade like all others. The geographical specialization on agriculture is becoming a part of economic geography. The task of geography of rural areas now is to describe and explain the socio-spatial problems of rural communities with a view to contribute to shaping the land-use forms of the future. As such rural geography is a regionalized geography, just like rural sociology, rural economy and rural planning are regionalized branches of their disciplines. They are all engaged in a region-type, that is to say in parts of space which are homogeneous within a certain set of characteristics. By reducing reality in this way one is able to apply nomothetic statements valid for all those parts of space. For 'rural' activities the surface used is more important than location; for 'urban' activities it is the other way round. The foremost criterion for rural areas is that the physical-spatial structure consists of nearly uninterrupted area-bound land-use forms like agriculture and land left to nature. However, given the disappearance of an essentially innate rural form of community, the question arises of whether the socio-spatial problems of rural areas are significantly discernible from those of urban areas.

Pahl (1970, p. 88) states that in advanced industrial societies "any attempt to tie particular patterns of social relationships to specific geographical milieus is a singularly fruitless exercise." That would mean that the physical-spatial structure of rural areas has little relevancy for the sociological approach. "City and countryside are integral parts of the same social and economic systems" (Bryant et al. 1982, p. 5). The rural sociologist Warner (1974), however, speaking of small settlements amidst huge unbuilt surfaces, is of the opinion that the centralization of decision-making powers in city-regions leads to an asymmetrical interdependence between rural communities and the big cities. These communities will continue to distinguish themselves by the way in which they are involved in the processes and structures of the wider society. There will be a problem of spatial inequity in the future as there is one now. So rural geography remained a meaningful sub-discipline, although important changes took place in the subjects it studied and the way it was practised.

The first to recognize these changes were the British. British rural geography grew fast, covering themes like access and accessibility, key-settlement policy, rural deprivation and power structures. The developments in Great Britain heavily influenced rural geography in the Netherlands. Dutch rural geography developed out of agrarian geography as a regionalizing discipline which stands beside urban geography.

Modern Dutch rural geography covers a variety of fields like access and accessibility, migration, rural housing, rural employment, agribusiness, recreation, second homes, service provision, settlement planning and so on. A review of the development of rural geography in the Netherlands is offered by van Bemmel (1984).

The periphery versus peri-urban dichotomy

Many authors use the term 'urbanization' to describe the changes in rural areas. They differentiate between physical urbanization for growing urband land-use; mental urbanization for the changes in behaviour and ideas of rural people; and socio-economic urbanization for the desagrarization processes. These three forms of urbanization, however, are not always and everywhere co-extensive. Moreover, the endogeneous developments in rural areas are veiled by using urbanization in every respect (Mathieu and Bontron 1973). Rural research has been paralysed because of this for two decades. A more refined approach of rural change is used by Beckering and Huigen (1978). They distinguished four categories of rural change after the origin of causal forces.

They used two dimensions. The first dimension was agriculture as the paramount economic activity and land-user in rural areas; the second was a spatial dimension: regional versus extra-regional. In this way they discerned:

—agricultural—regional forces: the mechanization of agriculture as a cause of diminishing employment, out-migration and changes in the demographic structure in rural areas;

—agricultural—extra-regional forces: governmental and E.E.C. regulations for agriculture as a cause for termination and/or enlargement of farms;

—non-agricultural—regional forces: increase of the level of prosperity and increase of personal mobility changing the spatial behaviour, which put an end to the traditional village-community;

—non-agricultural—extra-regional forces: the increased spatial functions of rural areas for urban people: open-air recreation, suburbanization of living and of urban economic activities, commuting.

With this categorization of forces in mind one can define a difference between peripheral and peri-urban rural areas. In peripheral rural areas the changes predominantly originated from agricultural—regional and extra-regional forces as well as from non-agricultural—regional forces. In peri-urban rural areas on the contrary, the processes of change are predominantly caused by non-agricultural—extra-regional forces. Considered spatially, the peri-urban rural areas are practically located within the reach of city-region housing- and labour-markets. Hence they are the scenes of suburbanization, connected with the wish of urban people to live in the countryside. Also, many kinds of industry and servicing are established now in the 'city's countryside' (Bryant et al. 1982). Hence, the peri-urban rural areas are characterized by a relatively high rate of growth, a high level of prosperity and an over-representation of young people. Moreover, these areas have an important function for the open-air day-recreation of urban people. All this means a threat to landscape beauty and ecological values. The peripheral rural areas are located out of the daily reach of city-region housing- and labour-markets. Any form of suburbanization there is almost out of question.

The two region-types correspond to the physical-spatial structure. They contrast in almost every other respect: the land-market, public transport, services and village-communities. But the production milieu and the labour-market are right in the centre of this opposition. The peripheral areas have a narrow economic base, a quantitatively and qualitatively limited labour-market and often an inadequate infrastructure. There has been some industrialization and infrastructural improvements during the last boom. Nevertheless, the labour-market has some negative characteristics:

—the number of non-agricultural firms in the 'micropoles' (George 1977) is small, so that economic life is very sensitive to the business cycle; the possibilities for promotion for the workers are limited and there is a narrow choice of a career for school-leavers;

—unskilled labour is over-represented because well-trained workers cannot find suitable jobs in their residential area;

—unemployment is over-represented because, amongst other reasons, the old and the unskilled are also over-represented;

—female participation in the labour-force is under-represented because females have insufficient access to suitable jobs.

The peri-urban rural areas undergo an in-migration of people and firms, mainly originating from the cities. The labour-market offers a broad choice of a career for the school-leavers. Unemployment rates are relatively low for males as is the case for females. The supply of skilled labour matches the demand. The dynamism of the functional-spatial relationships within the city-region implicates the phenomenon that the qualities of space bear little weight in the interdependence between the social processes and the space used. Rural planning in this region-type guides the process of physical urbanization by protecting the rural physical-spatial structure generally. The urban pressure is strongest at the edge of the city and in the villages in the environment. The pressure is less, but unmistakable in the second zone of spatial conflicts: the frontier zone of the city-region, where peri-urban and peripheral rural areas merge.

The division of rural areas into peripheral and peri-urban areas was applied in planning the workshop's programme. It is thought to be a suitable way of grouping the socio-spatial problems for the use of all rural disciplines. This is especially so because the aims and means of rural planning are essentially different in both region-types.

Geographical scale in rural research and planning

Anotner difference made in planning the workshop's scheme is based on 'scale'. In this connection, scale is not comparable with the economic sense of the term as in 'economies of scale', but with the cartographic meaning: the reduction of reality increases as the map covers a bigger area. The scale of approaching a problem is necessarily connected with the level of abstraction of the terms used. This means that at a high level of abstraction the terms cover more individuals with a smaller number of characteristics, and at a low level of abstraction the terms contain less individuals with more characteristics. So at the national scale of rural research, planning and policy, the approach to problems is formulated in terms which are valid for all cases within the territory. The spatial units are mostly administrative units which are seldom coterminous with rural areas. Population development, prosperity and such are expressed in statistical averages. The pivotal problem at the national scale is regional economic inequality with non-agricultural employment as the main point. National rural planning- and policy aims are often put in general terms. This vagueness is unavoidable for an integrated approach to rural problems at this scale. At the local scale the spatial units are the villages and their surroundings. At this level the reduction of reality is least. The decision-makers are acquainted with the needs of the inhabitants from personal knowledge. The elements of research are the households, firms and individuals directly. The local economic situation is often fixed. So research and policy are concentrated most on sociological issues.

An important part of the policy-making powers is often found at the regional level. Here the conflict between (economic) efficiency and (social) equity in policy-making has its most acute character. The three levels of rural research, planning and policy should be effective as a system of telescopicly connected activities. That is less the case than is desirable. The differences between the three levels are too great for that: differences in problem-approach, differences in understanding the people's needs, differences in the level of abstraction, differences in planning goals, and last but not least, differences in executive powers (Cloke 1983, p. 334). That is why room was offered in the workshop's programme to consider both rural region-types at three levels: national, regional and local. De Smidt describes changes in the distribution of population and economic activities and changes in regional socio-economic policies. Subsequently he analyses the consequences of the slow-down of demographic and economic growth for urban and rural areas. The future problems for these areas are summarized.

Peri-urban rural areas

National policy should offer a framework for rural settlement planning in peri-urban and peripheral rural areas. For the peri-urban regions preservation as agricultural and recreational areas was the main objective. The strategy was therefore to restrict the population growth of the regions as a whole to zero (or even to a negative migration balance) and to concentrate the occurring growth in predetermined settlements. After reviewing national policy from 1977 on rural towns and key villages, Atzema and Dijkstra studied the impact of this policy. First they detected how national policy was implemented in regional plans. In the second place migration streams to and from peri-urban rural areas and between municipalities within peri-urban rural areas have been studied. The

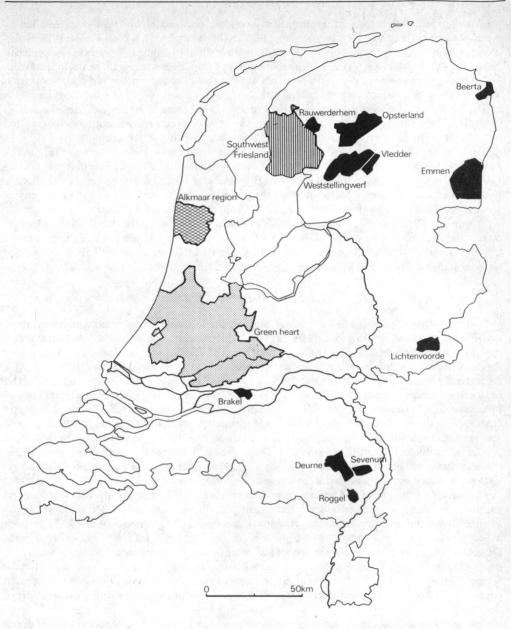

FIGURE 1 *Location of the research areas for the Dutch contributions*

peculiar spatial configuration of the Randstad created a peri-urban rural region surrounded by urban settlements (Figure 1). To keep this so-called Green Heart open has been a major objective in physical planning since 1966. Growth of the Randstad should be directed outwards or to urban settlements within the Green Heart. Despite these policy objectives many settlements in the Green Heart have grown substantially. Starting from Gibbs' stages of concentration and deconcentration of population in western urban industrial countries, van Ginkel describes the suburbanization process in the Green Heart in the period 1960 to 1980. Subsequently he has analysed the factors favouring suburbanization and the consequences for the settlement pattern, concluding that suburbanization did not alter but merely accentuated the existing settlement pattern.

The outward growth of the Randstad strongly affected the region around Alkmaar (Figure 1). Dostál and Markusse studied the effects of this outward expansion for the settlement pattern in this region. From a welfare geographical approach they analysed the relationships between changes in number and socio-economic composition of the population on the one side and the hierarchy of service provision on the other. Data were used from the 1960 and 1971 censuses and service inventories in 1972 and 1982; techniques like cluster analysis and partial correlation helped to clarify the researched relationships. They arrived at the conclusion that a population increase of above 2% had a positive influence on service provision and that the characteristic of a one-sided white-collar population had an additional positive effect.

Peripheral rural areas

Post-war physical planning in the Netherlands was predominantly concerned with problems of urbanization and industrialization. National rural settlement planning in peripheral rural areas, therefore, was primarily aimed at various forms of concentration of regional economic development funds. Problems of infrastructure and service provision due to loss of population and scale enlargement in the service sector received little attention. Regional authorities filled up this gap by formulating village plans in which the key-settlement option as a strategy prevailed. De Bakker and Piersma deal with the theoretical basis of key-settlement pattern in this province leaning heavily on central place theory. They describe the circumstances under which the policy was formulated, and analyse the effects for the distribution of the population over the settlements, and the pattern of service provision, in the period 1960 to 1980. They concluded that the policy had been successful in concentrating growth in key-settlements, but the social frictions which arose prove that key-settlement policy was not successful from a social point of view.

The nature of the settlement pattern in peripheral rural areas caused problems of access and accessibility. These became key-issues in settlement planning in these regions. Huigen developed a method to measure and standardize the concept of access, adopting a time-geographical approach as developed by the Lund-school and proceeding on Moseley's people—link—activity idea. Objective, plan and operation of the model are described in his contribution to this volume. He demonstrates the potentials of his model as an instrument to evaluate alternative strategies for the future development of the settlement pattern in terms of access by analysing the effects of a spatial contraction of services and employment for the access of inhabitants of the south-western part of Friesland.

Political geographical aspects have gained importance in the study of rural areas in recent years. The last contribution to this reader, from Groenendijk and de Boer, deals with the role of local governement in rural settlement planning. First they analysed the differential growth of settlements within Dutch municipalities for the period 1960 to 1971, concluding that major villages grew faster than other settlements. Subsequently they reported the results of a survey in a sample of Dutch villages in peripheral rural areas. The policy of the municipality with respect to the distribution of housing and infrastructure over the settlements within the municipality has been researched.

Changes in the settlement
pattern—a rural research perspective

By definition the settlement pattern is a regional phenomenon. The dynamism of the settlement pattern manifests itself in the pattern of growth, stagnation and decline of villages and hamlets. It finds itself at the regional scale of rural research, planning and policy. So the settlement pattern's problems are connected with local scale problems and with national scale problems at the same time. The connection is both positive and negative, that is to say, the changes inherent in the settlement pattern have consequences for national and local scale developments, and changes at the local or national scale influence the developments in the settlement pattern.

The pattern of rural settlements is the result of a now outdated technological—organizational system. A more spacious pattern is possible now and in certain respects necessary. Possible, because of the increased individual mobility, the developments in farming practice and the diminished agricultural employment; necessary, as a consequence of changes in the supply of central goods and services that people receive personally, as well as in the supply of address-bound goods and services, which are delivered. The increased quality of central services led to higher costs and so necessarily demanded a higher turnover. That implied a contraction of service-points in more central settlements away from small villages and hamlets in rural areas. Many shops, post-offices, schools and medical services closed down in these settlements. The address-bound goods and services (piped goods, cabled services, refuse-collecting, postal services and, more indirectly, public transport) are confronted with exceptionally high performance costs coupled with a poor turnover.

This picture is more true in peripheral rural areas than in peri-urban areas. First, in peri-urban areas the population in most settlements is growing so that the servicing problem there has relaxed or even is solved. Second, all settlements, the stagnating ones included, enjoy a relatively better public transport service. The main problem for rural planning and policy in relation to the settlement pattern in peri-urban areas is the maintenance of amenity and nature facing the threat of exuberant growth in urban land-use. The means to control urban expansion in general is to prevent non-agricultural constructions in rural environments; to guide the pressure of suburbanization to designated settlements; and to be very careful in planning the location of provisions for mass recreation and of massive infrastructural works. All these measures are directly connected with the national level of planning and policy. The local level is almost neglected. The villages liable to a restrictive population policy are confronted with problems comparable with those in peripheral rural areas.

In the peripheral rural areas the changes in the settlement pattern are much more connected with the local scale problems. The servicing problem is sharper. The stagnating and declining villages are more numerous. The intensity of the community-life tails off. Rural deprivation here is a problem in all villages and hamlets. In fact, rural deprivation here is a regional problem, too. Shaw (1979) defined rural deprivation as a situation in which rural people have less possibilities in relation to a combination of housing, working, education and recreation. At the root of rural deprivation is the lack of individual mobility, especially for those who have not a car at their disposal: aged people, teenagers, house-wives, the sick and the poor. A more spacious settlement pattern aggravates the rural deprivation problem.

The stagnating and declining villages experience a languishing community-life. This finds material expression in a diminishing and ageing number of inhabitants and in a slow decay of houses. The immaterial signs are the continuing dissociation of village-associations. Church-, school-, club- and neighbourhood-organizations have serious difficulties in continuing their work. A more spacious settlement pattern will hamper their functioning still more.

Cloke (1983) in his book on rural settlement planning gives advice to achieve some realism in the prescription of rural policy-alternatives (p. 332):
—different types of policy for different types of area are necessary;

—the policy at the national scale has to offer a framework only.

Within this framework, specific problems at the regional and local scales can be tackled by special initiatives. He indicates two roads down which to go, namely a better use of existing resources amongst which is self-help, and activating new resources, amongst which is urban-rural resource allocation. In our opinion Cloke's advice is very useful.

Characteristics of the Hungarian setting

Despite some substantial basic features common to the whole European industrialized countryside, there are important differences between the Hungarian and the Dutch rural scenes. Due partly to these differences, partly to the limited effects of Anglo-Saxon geography, Hungarian rural geography has its own individual trends. It is these differences both in the rural countryside and in rural geography that are reflected by the Hungarian papers.

Rural geography has deeper roots in settlement geography and in rural sociology than in agricultural geography. The latter was part of sectoral economic geography, and focussed on the location of single agricultural products, or tried to delineate agricultural regions (Bernát—Enyedi 1977). Rural geography formed a part of human geography which developed under strong German and French influence in the first half of the century. Hence the strong interest of rural geographers in classifying the different morphological forms of rural settlements. Because of our historical development, rural settlements in the Alföld (the Great Hungarian Plain)—which covers half of the country's territory—differ both morphologically and socially from the rest of country. Rural sociology, which was especially strong in the 1930s, also recognized the close interrelationship between the form, geographical location and social characteristics of rural settlements (Erdei 1974, Vágvölgyi 1982). Rural geography suffered serious setback in the postwar period. Urban enthusiasm shadowed the substantial changes which started in the countryside, at least till the middle of the 1960s. The last 10–15 years have witnessed a rapid development in rural research, partly due to the changes provoked by the collectivization of agriculture, and partly as a consequence of the growing concern about the still existing rural-urban dychotomy.

Special rural problems in Hungary have come from the late urbanization, and from the social consequences of collective large-scale farming. The industrial revolution and urban explosion started in Hungary in the last third of the 19th century, but it was limited in depth, in length and in geographic terms. Budapest, the Hungarian capital, followed the Western European urbanization pattern, and a number of small and medium-sized cities in western Hungary joined the mainstream of urbanization. The Great Plain remained almost untouched by industrialization. Its agriculture remained traditional; it was unable to accumulate enough capital for industrial take-off. Nevertheless, in this period, Hungary was approaching the European core area. This development was interrupted for a long time by World War I, and by the dissolution of Austria–Hungary. Regional urban centres as well as mining and heavy-industrial regions were incorporated into the neighbouring states by the Trianon peace treaty. The interwar period was characterized by continuous crises and stagnation. Budapest, the only real modern city, housed one fifth of the country's population. The 1930 census registered only two provincial cities with more than 100,000 inhabitants—both huge rural market towns in the Alföld (Szeged and Debrecen) with a pre-industrial social structure. After World War II, a new industrial take-off started which resulted in a new phase of urban growth. Actually, it was the continuation of the original urban-indutrial take-off interrupted for decades. This post-World War II phase had some special features:

(i) The whole process was regulated by comprehensive central planning, where, up to the 1960s, industry got absolute priority. Settlements which were favourable for industrial location received the overwhelming majority of the central settlement development funds. Hence the growing neglect of rural areas.

(ii) Though industrialization attracted a large part of the population into the cities, modern industrialization had a more moderate effect on urban concentration than that of the last century. The leading sectors of the industry—the chemical industry had the fastest growth—were less labour-intensive than the classical food and textile industries; transport facilities in so small a country made commuting general, so professional changes provoked residential changes to a lesser extent.

In the last period of the industrial take-off, industry moved out from the cities to rural areas. The main reason for industrial relocation was the cheap manpower still available in rural communities. Rural industrialization was facilitated by the fact that Hungarian rural communities generally have a large population: the national average is 1,800 inhabitants, which reaches 3,000 inhabitants in the Alföld. In the early 1980s, the rural manufacturing industry is employing as many workers as the Budapest industry, a tremendous shift in industrial location in 20 years (see Barta's paper).

Industrial take-off actually ended by the late 1960s, early 1970s. This period of socio-economic modernization was a condensed one, it finished before a substantial part of the rural population would resettle into the cities. Consequently, a stage of relative deconcentration was reached with a still high rural population ratio (47% in 1980). This is not a symptom of underdevelopment, as some Hungarian urbanists suggest; it simply follows logically from our late development. It means that rural development has much more social importance than in the European core area where the rural population represents a small fragment of the society.

(iii) Socialist economic development has been characterized by a constant neglect of infrastructural development. Investments have been excessively concentrated in the sphere of production. It was supposed that the growth of production would lead to significant capital accumulation which would create favourable condition for infrastructural development later. But capital accumulation turned out to be less favourable than was expected, and production's appetite for further investments has not diminished. By the end of the last century, during the first industrial take-off, some 60% of the investments were going into the infrastructure; this proportion has diminished to less than 40% today. Investments lag behind need constantly, and in fact are concentrated in the ever-reproducing bottlenecks.

This situation has been especially unfavourable for rural areas. Government housing, road construction, the development of telecommunication etc. has been channelled mostly to urban areas. Rural backwardness, very serious in pre-war Hungary, has not diminished at an adequate rate. No doubt, the living conditions of the rural population have changed greatly, especially their housing conditions, and their income level has improved enormously in the 1970s. At the same time, rural public services were concentrated in northern and south-western Hungary where small villages dominate the rural scene. Settlement planning worked along the 'key-village' concept here, which did not prove adequate, due to the lack of good transport and telecommunication facilities. The development of the last 15 years has speeded up the differentiation within the rural sphere. The social problems of the peripheral rural areas have become sharper, as these territories lost their economic dynamism and the improvement of living conditions slowed down remarkably (see Tóth's paper).

In sum, the urban—rural dichotomy still exists in Hungary, and the rural—peri-urban—urban continuum has developed but in few areas and to a limited extent. The repated criticism of the urban-centered government settlement policy led finally to the reformulation of this policy (see Lackó's paper).

Concerning the rural part of the settlement network, collectivized agriculture has certainly had its impact on rural development. At the time of collectivization, it provoked an important out-migration from the countryside, but later it became an important stabilizing element of the rural areas. The special features of rural development due to collective large-scale farming are as follows:

(a) The Hungarian model of socialist agriculture combines the capital-intensive, highly productive large-scale operation with a labour-intensive, high value producing small-scale family operation. This model has been successful so far, and has assured a decent income for the farming population.

(b) The largest, strongly capitalized and well-managed farms have been able to compete with food industry and the state trading companies in organizing the agribusiness. Actually, a large part of the agribusiness—food processing, marketing, different types of servicing connected to modern agriculture—is organized by the large farms themselves, which has contributed to the multifunctional character of rural settlements, and has increased rural employment. Large-scale farms have set up different types of service industries for supplying the whole rural population: they have invested in rural tourism, contributed to the modern reconstruction of rural settlements, etc.

In the early 1960s, when collectivization was finished, urban planners envisioned the substantial reconstruction of the rural settlement network, which would concentrate the rural population into large 'agricultural towns' with more than 3,000 inhabitants. Actually, the official plans for reconstruction failed; collectivization did not change the basic pattern of the rural settlements, except for speeding up rural depopulation in the poor agricultural areas. The stability of the rural settlement pattern can be explained partly by the still existing great importance of private farming activity, partly by the fact that the majority (two-thirds) of the rural population has a non-agricultural occupation, so agricultural changes have no definitive impact on rural settlements. Later, a spontaneous settlement-forming process started which created, almost totally unnoticed by urban planners, a number of new clustered villages, particularly in the zone of the scattered farmsteads (the problem is discussed by Csatári and Enyedi).

Suburban development was also late, and had a special mechanism in Hungary. Suburbanization started around Budapest at the turn of 19th and 20the centuries. The agricultural population of the neighbouring villages started to commute into the city, where they performed unskilled work in industry, in the building industry and in some of the tertiary sectors. These villages were transformed gradually into mixed agricultural—blue collar suburbs. Between the two World Wars, the first signs of the white collar suburbs appeared: mostly lower-middle-class people moved there, because of the very high housing and rent costs in the city itself. This development was interrupted for long time, and it is just a recent phenomenon that some of the suburban communities with an attractive environment on the right bank of the Danube have become upper-middle-class residential areas.

Suburban development actually started around some large provincial cities 20 years ago, and is still limited in scope. The suburbs are practically blue collar residences continously receiving in-migrants from distant rural areas, people who seek work in the central cities, but for whom it is easier to settle in suburbs. Part-time and auxiliary farming is still important in these suburbs. Peri-urban development, thus, has a different mechanism than in Western Europe; peri-urban areas have rather a blue collar character, and they have conserved many of their earlier agricultural features, as is discussed in Sárfalvi's paper.

The Netherlands has belonged to the European core area of modernization for many centuries. The forms and social processes of modern urbanization and, consequently, rural transformation diffused from the core to the southern and eastern periphery of our continent. The eastern periphery—including Hungary—followed a different (socialist) way of modernization than the southern. Thus, modern rural settlement patterns showed up later in the eastern periphery, and their social content has had some special features. Nevertheless, processes of a similar nature are going on, and decision-makers have to face comparable problems.

Bibliography

BECKERING, S. E.—HUIGEN, P. P. P. (1978) *Boer, zijn burgers buitenlui?* (The Attitude of Farmers to Recreational Use of Agricultural Land), (Utrecht: Department of Geography).

BERNÁT, T. (1984) "Marginal Agrarian Regions in Hungary". In: *Geographical Essays in Hungary 1984* (eds.: Enyedi, Gy.—Pécsi, M.), (Budapest: IGU Hungarian National Committee—Geographical Research Institute): 217–228.

BERNÁT, T.—ENYEDI, GY. (1977) *A magyar mezőgazdaság területi problémái* (Regional Problems of the Hungarian Agriculture), (Budapest: Akadémiai Kiadó).

BRYANT, C. R.—RUSSWURM, L. H.—MCLELLAN, A. G. (1982) *The City's Countryside. Land and Its Management in the Rural-Urban Fringe,* (London: Longman).

CLOKE, P. J. (1980) "New Emphases for Applied Rural Geography in Advanced Industrial Society", *Progress in Human Geography* 2: 181–218.

CLOKE, P. J. (1983) *An Introduction to Rural Settlement Planning,* (London: Methuen).

CLOUT, H. D. (1972) *Rural Geography. An Introductory Survey,* (Oxford: Pergamon Press).

ENYEDI, GY. (1974) "La location optimale de l'agriculture hongroise", *Bulletin de la Société Géographique Languedocienne* 97, no. 2: 155–171.

ENYEDI, GY. (1975) *Research Problems in Rural Geography,* (Budapest: IGU Working Group on Rural Planning and Development).

ENYEDI, GY. (ed.) (1976) *Rural Transformation in Hungary,* (Studies in Geography in Hungary 13, Budapest: Akadémiai Kiadó).

ERDEI, F. (1974) *A magyar falu* (The Hungarian Village), (Facsimile Edition, Budapest: Akadémiai Kiadó).

FRANKLIN, S. H. (1969) *The European Peasantry. The Final Phase,* (London: Methuen).

GEORGE, P. (1977) "Réflexions sur quelques aspects actuels d'un vieux problème: l'exode rural", *Norois* 24, no. 1: 99–107.

KOSTROWICKI, J. (1984) "Types of Agriculture in Europe. A Preliminary Outline", *Geographia Polonica* 50, (Warsaw: PWN).

MATHIEU, N.—BONTRON, J. C. (1973) "Les transformations de l'espace rural. Problèmes et méthode", *Etudes Rurales* 49/50, no. 1: 137–159.

PAHL, R. E. (1975) *Whose city? and Further Essays on Urban Society,* (London: Penguin Books).

PIERSMA, A. (1971) "Agrarische versus rurale geografie" (Agrarian versus Rural Geography), *Geografisch Tijdschrift* 5, no. 1: 25–32.

SHAW, J. M. (1979) "Rural Deprivation and Social Planning, An Overview". In: *Rural Deprivation and Planning* (ed.: Shaw, J. M.), (Norwich: Geo Abstracts).

VÁGVÖLGYI, A. (ed.) (1982) *A falu a mai magyar társadalomban* (The Village in the Hungarian Society Today), (Budapest: Akadémiai Kiadó).

WARNER, W. K. (1974) "Rural Society in a Post-Industrial Age", *Rural Sociology* 3, no. 3: 306–318.

CHANGES OF URBAN
AND RURAL AREAS IN THE NETHERLANDS

MARC DE SMIDT

KEY-WORDS: *deconcentration* policies; *Green Heart; horticulture* districts; *Integrated Structure Plan* for the Northern Netherlands; *key-village* approach; *new towns; Physical Planning*, Second Memorandum on ~, Third Memorandum on ~; *policies*, regional socio-economic ~; *Randstad*, ~ Green Structure, ~ Metropolis; *Report* on Rural Areas; *sand-soil* regions; *Structural Outline Sketch* on Urban Regions; *Urbanization* Report; *West* European Nucleus Area.

People's behaviour in time and space is largely dependent on personal characteristics such as age and place in the household, level of education, occupation and income. In fact, these indications changed tremendously in recent decades, as did functional organizations during the process of industrialization and the blossoming of the welfare state. As a consequence of these structural tendencies as well as of increasing car-ownership, people's field of mobility was altered and this called for an adjustment in the spatial configuration of activities. The changing face of the built-up environment and increasing claims on land were also indications of this specific evolution of the human habitat. In a densely-populated country like the Netherlands there is a need for physical planning. In a capitalistic economy—mitigated by the collective sector of the welfare state—planning differs fundamentally in scope and intensity from socialist economies. In capitalist economies economic planning does not play the central role. Physical planning—and recently environmental regulation in a broader sense—has offered a framework for a type of conditional and consultative planning.

When people and functional organizations are confronted with spatial problems, different levels of scale must be taken into account. The formulation and implementation of physical planning is bound up with specific levels of the execution of government. In daily life, most people are concerned with a field of action that does not exceed the boundaries of a city region. Though many functional organizations operate within a much broader field—even on a world-wide level—it has been found that the local organization of production requirements such as labour, land, infrastructure and environmental control is of crucial importance for the efficiency and continuity of these organizations.

The Netherlands is characterized by an extremely open economy which acts as a gateway to Europe. Within this international framework the changing structure and distribution of both population and economic activities in the Netherlands will be discussed, followed by a short account of the implications of the slow-down of demographic and economic growth. This will involve a reconnaissance of the human habitat in urban and rural areas. Changing ideas on planning will be dealt with at the various levels of execution of government.

Population, economic activities
and regional disparities

The Randstad Metropolis is one of the cornerstones of an urbanized mega-region known as the West European Nucleus Area which is characterized by a tremendously high concentration of population (in most regions over 500 inhabitants per square kilometre), and a high level of gross regional product and market potential. Socio-economic structures of the regions involved are comparable to a high degree, and may be considered to be at the same time both complements and competitors. Both interaction and interdependencies between these regions are on the increase. Though differences do exist, the regions concerned pass through more or less the same stages of socio-economic development. Urbanization and industrialization have reached their climax. There has been suburbanization and even desurbanization. Recently, tendencies towards re-urbanization have been observed. The office boom in the cities and the rush to the coast of heavy industrial activities have changed the economic base. The phenomena have even reshaped the skylines of these urbanized mega-regions.

The Randstad Holland passed three phases in its participation in the economic evolution of this Nucleus Area. Up until the Second World War, the main emphasis was on traffic and trade directed to the German 'hinterland'. In the 1950s, the emancipation of the Netherlands as a manufacturing country was the most important tendency. The 'rush to the coast' of basic metallurgic and chemical industries in the booming 1960s underlined this economic change. However, these characteristics and changes are in themselves not sufficient to place the Randstad in the category of a true metropolis, even though the population base is six million and population density surpasses 1,000 inhabitants per square kilometre. To qualify as a metropolis other qualitative indications are called for.

The functional role of a metropolis can be characterized by inter alia concentration of dicision-making and R&D activities on the one hand and the filtering down of light, programmed, industrial activities on the other hand. The office-boom of the 1960s in the Randstad retarded the autonomous deconcentration of population and economic activities in the Netherlands in general. Headquarters of companies are concentrated in the four main urban regions of the Randstad, in the non-manufacturing sector to the extent of 80 per cent.

In fact the urban field is far larger than the Randstad Metropolis. A half-way-zone of southern and eastern urbanized regions should be included. If the Alkmaar—Arnhem line is taken as a boundary, it can be found that the south-western half of the country is populated by 11 million persons and the north-eastern half by just 3.5 million. This sparsely populated half of the country contains 180 persons per square kilometre and the main urban centres of the northern region are located within 200 km of Amsterdam. By Western European standards, therefore, this area cannot be labelled as a periphery. Moreover, regional disparities are limited. Income disparities between regions within the European Economic Community are much greater (30–180, E.E.C. average 100) than within the Netherlands (80–120, Dutch average 100).

This semi-periphery of north-eastern regions was based predominantly on agriculture and agro-industrial activities. Manufacturing industries, in particular some large domestic and foreign companies, established branch plants in these areas in order to use labour pushed out by farms. In the southern regions industrialization was fostered along the same lines in order to offer jobs for a fast-growing population (in the 1950s the region had one of the highest demographic growth rates in north-western Europe).

Regional socio-economic policies were part of a national industrialization strategy in the 1950s and early 1960s. Later, regional policies broadened their scope to include the tertiary sector (for example, in the 1970s, relocation of governmental services from the Hague, or later, from the western regions in general, to five cities outside the Randstad). More important for these areas, however, was a tendency to integrate socio-economic, socio-cultural and physical planning goals and their implementation, the so-called integrated regional plans (Integrated Structure Plan for the Northern Netherlands, ISP, and Perspective Memorandum for Limburg, PNL).

At the end of the 1960s and early 1970s regional socio-economic policy became adjusted to deconcentration proposals, starting with the Second Memorandum on Physical Planning (1966) and culminating in the Selective Investment Regulation (SIR 1975). In the second half of the 1970s and early 1980s, in a period of growing economic crisis, regional disparities, in particular in unemployment, decreased. Fostering of the growth of regions with high economic potentials, located in or near the Randstad, is advocated. In 1983, the SIR was abolished and high investment premiums for peripheral regions were reduced. A new category of regional socio-economic policy, the so-called development potential policy, was introduced for the Randstad regions, although implementation has not yet started. Deconcentration policy on the macro-level is no longer a heated issue in physical planning in a period of recession with no major congestion problems. In the three volumes of the Third Memorandum on Physical Planning (1974–1977) deconcentration has been advocated for the sake of reducing regional arrears and inequalities. This goal involves two main elements since there are socio-economic disadvantages and problems of accessibility. However, more and more concentration becomes the new issue in a period of slowing-down of demographic and economic growth.

Slowing-down of demographic and economic growth

Population forecasts in 1965 estimated that in the year 2000 the Netherlands would number 21 million inhabitants, a growth of 8.5 million people within 35 years. In fact, between 1965 and 1983 there was a growth of only two million inhabitants. These 14.5 million people will be augmented with about another one million by the end of the century. Only 35 per cent of the forecasted growth will become a reality. Deconcentration policies focussed on precautionary measures to prevent congestion, shortages of housing space and industrial premises in a period of expected high growth rates for both population and economy. In the second half of the 1960s, some autonomous deconcentration tendencies could be observed but, in fact, this government policy was never successful. Migration flows before 1965 were directed from peripheral regions (north, south-west) towards the large urban areas in the western provinces. Migration losses of these Randstad cities after 1965 became tremendous, comprising an overflow of population (not so much of jobs) to adjacent eastern and southern regions with high living amenities. There was rapid growth of long-distance commuting. On the macro-level the urban field of the Randstad widened while on the meso-level the urban sprawl surpassed the boundaries of the cities and traditional suburban rings. The Green Heart of the Randstad Metropolis was invaded by upper-class families looking for detached residences in a quiet, green, environment. Recently the high rates of housing and labour mobility have slowed down. As a matter of fact the growth of suburbanization has decreased tremendously.

In the recent Structural Outline Sketch on Urban Regions (1983) the Randstad is no more than four main urban regions and some medium-sized urban areas (Figure 2). Three alternative views (concentration, selective sprawl and railway-linked ring development) have been developed for the Randstad—the concentration alternative has been chosen—but no concept of the international role of a Randstad Metropolis has been proposed.

On the macro-level, deconcentration of economic activities is no longer a realistic expectation. Low-risk locational attitudes have intensified, favouring the large urban areas. In the long term the increasing average age of the Dutch population will decrease mobility rates both on the labour and housing market. During the last two decades, the immigration of 700,000 people from Mediterranean countries and the West Indies to a large degree quantitatively compensated the regional migration losses of the western provinces, filling up the lower strata of the labour and housing market in the main cities. A new dimension, the minority problem, has been added to the long list of urban problems. In an era of demographic and economic stagnation for most regions, redistribution of population, economic activities and welfare becomes far much difficult. Funds for stimulating such redistribution policies, also in a spatial sense, are either no longer available or have been cut.

The Sketch on Urban Regions (1983), just mentioned, underlines the stabilization of the spatial pattern of population and employment on a macro-scale. Even an economic recovery will not

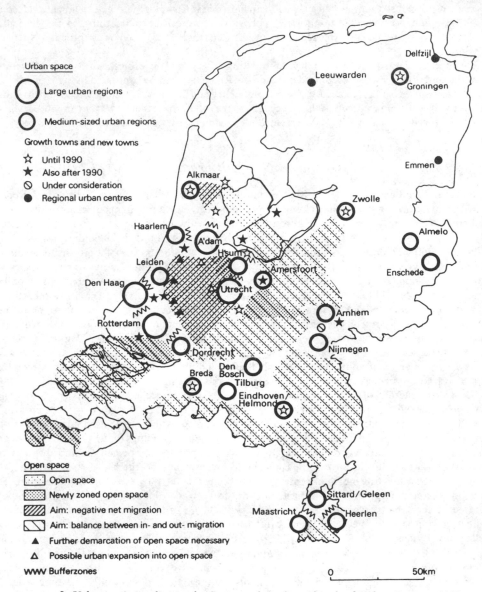

Urban space

⬭ Large urban regions

○ Medium-sized urban regions

Growth towns and new towns
☆ Until 1990
★ Also after 1990
⊘ Under consideration
● Regional urban centres

Open space
▦ Open space
▨ Newly zoned open space
▧ Aim: negative net migration
◹ Aim: balance between in- and out- migration
▲ Further demarcation of open space necessary
△ Possible urban expansion into open space
WWW Bufferzones

0 ————— 50km

FIGURE 2 *Urbanization policy in the Structural Outline Sketch of Urban Regions 1983*

change this, and distribution policies are no longer seen even as an issue. The Urbanization Report (1976) re-emphasized the traditional view in physical planning that population and activities must be spread more equally over the Dutch territory, in particular to foster growth in the Northern Region.

However, the growth centre policy, stimulating large housing projects in four main centres (Groningen, Breda, Zwolle, Helmond) outside the Randstad, will be continued in the 1980s for the two first-mentioned cities, partly for Zwolle, but Helmond (Eindhoven region) will loose this status as a growth centre. The impact of these recent changes will be discussed now from an intra-regional policy perspective, looking first at the urban areas and later on at the rural areas: a meso/micro-level approach.

Recent problems of urban areas

In the first volume of the Third Memorandum on Physical Planning, the Orientation Report (1974), some early signs of policy changes were indicated. Further urbanization according to the principle of concentrated deconcentration of urban development was advocated with a stronger accent on concentration. Improvement of the residential environment in the old urban areas and environmental differentiation of functions and amenities in all quarters of a city-region required stimulation. As a follow-up, the Urbanization Report (1976) pointed out two main issues: 1. congestion and imbalanced urban development should be avoided, and 2. the growth of mobility should be retarded. Three sets of alternatives (scenarios) were formulated. The first alternative, a steady home—work balance within reasonably small urban regions, could no longer be seen as realistic for large city-regions. A second alternative took account of an urban daily system of a size adjusted to the possibilities of city-region public transport. This alternative is favoured in order to prevent tendencies already present and enumerated in the third alternative. In this third scenario, physical planning must adjust to the possibilities of individual transport (cars) and is therefore characterized by strongly interwoven home—work relationships over large areas.

The second alternative has been chosen. New residential areas needed to be planned at a distance (by public transport) of no more than 25 to 30 minutes from the cities. New towns and extensions of already existing small cities got the opportunity to realize plans with 35 to 45 dwellings/hectare. New towns have been responsible for a programme of about 20,000 dwellings in the 1980–82 period, one third of the building capacity realized in the three western provinces. Formerly, planned extensions located at a greater distance from the central cities were struck off the list of special funds.

This tendency towards more concentration has been stimulated by the economic recession. The cities started with large building projects in order to keep their inhabitants. These projects were located in the urban fringe and even in the city itself, making use of open spaces and former industrial quarters. In the brand new Structural Outline Sketch on Urban Regions (1983)—a follow-up of a comparable Sketch in the Urbanization Report of 1976—the idea of concentration is obvious. The concept of new towns is not abolished but reformulated into a transitional concept. Some new towns located at 20–35 km from the donor cities are confronted with a slowing-down in their programmes. Building in high densities in or near the major cities as well as urban renewal are the two top priorities to a much greater degree than is indicated in the Urbanization Report. Urban renewal had already been stimulated in the mid 1970s, starting with the demolition of old private housing stock and later shifting to rehabilitation of social housing projects. The recent trend is to maintain small business establishments at the urban renewal sites and no longer to push them out as was normal practice (migration to suburbs or liquidated). Subcentres, in particular based on railway stations in the main cities, get full attention for the location of offices and other public-orientated facilities (shopping and socio-cultural centres). Two main topics could be distinguished as basic factors for the extension of urban areas. The CIAM planning concept of a functional city, comprising specific locations for each function (residential areas, central business district, commercial subcentres, industrial estates, freeways, etc.), has enlarged the urban built-up environment at the cost of vast expanses of agricultural and recreational land, and brought about long-distance trips (e.g. commuting), mainly by car. This concept supported autonomous spatial tendencies of functional organizations to combat congestion. This tendency was already altered by a high-density policy in the Urbanization Report (1976).

A second topic of crucial importance for the extension of urban areas has been the process of decrease of the number of persons comprising one household (1965: 3.3; 1980: 2.7), which has had a tremendous impact on the amount and composition of housing demand. Families become smaller for demographic reasons and the growth of one and two-person non-family households is quite obvious, in particular in the cities. Youngsters and old people have their own household. The number of dwellings has consequently grown rapidly. Though these units may be smaller, urban space consumption per dwelling is not so much lower.

Cities have to fight with a wide range of social problems, sometimes labelled as social disintegration and deprivation. The minority problem has already been mentioned, spatially expressed in a high concentration of immigrants in old urban quarters, causing problems of segregation. Push factors to leave the city have also been intensified by congestion, the inadequacy of the housing supply and the loss or insufficiency of amenities. New initiatives, financially supported by the national government, to revitalize the cities recently seem to be successful. The economic crisis decreased the growth of an effective housing demand and urban space will be used far more intensively in the coming years.

Recent problems of rural areas

A rural geography of the Netherlands would discern three major regions. First there is the (semi)-periphery of the northern and south-western regions, characterized by vast tracts of agricultural land and some large recreational projects. Decision-making in Brussels, arrived at in meetings of the Common Market officials on agriculture, is crucial to their future. Urbanization, let alone sub-urbanization, is not an issue. In these sparsely populated regions (by Dutch standards) the accessibility problem is a major one. In this connection the planning proposals for a rationalized settlement system are relevant. This rationalization started as procedure for distributing service elements of the welfare state over rural areas. Regional plans took care to maintain a key-village approach. At the same time the process of rising thresholds for commercial or semi-public services (shops, P.T.T., etc.) was taken into account. Public transport companies have rearranged their schedules, for financial reasons, with the same effects. Planners did not want to allocate new building permits at the bottom of this settlement hierarchy. Action groups of villagers protested against this rationalization, afraid that the quality of life in their villages would be severely threatened. Recently, some provinces have changed their regional plans in order to enumerate local initiatives.

A second major zone of rural areas consists of southern and eastern sand-soil regions which have a higher population density due to intensive units of small farms. Although some of the settlement hierarchy problems just mentioned are also relevant for this zone, there is a more specific problem of conflicts in land use between (intensive) agriculture and natural environment within the context of a very attractive landscape of small lots of farmland intermingled with woods. In the Report on Rural Areas (1977), a volume of the Third Memorandum on Physical Planning, some guidelines were given for specific regions with a different mix of functions such as agricultures, recreation and conservation of nature. Intensification of agriculture is at the same time controlled by new laws for environmental protection. Economic crisis causes several problems. Industrialization and services will no longer provide labour opportunities for people leaving agriculture, so a new tendency to (labour) intensification may be demonstrated. Funds for landscape conservation, partly as a compensation for restrictions on farming, will no longer be available to such an extent. Most of these areas must be protected by physical plans (regional plans, land-use plans). A maximum of 200,000 hectares will be included in the special conservation funds (first stage 100,000 hectares). These areas are not situated only in the second zone but also in some specific part of the third zone of rural areas.

A third zone of rural areas consisting of some horticulture districts with an international reputation and vast tracts of meadow-land of the so-called Green Heart region is situated around the Randstad cities in between the wings of the Randstad. This last characteristic is also relevant for the River District, centrally located in the Netherlands. The horticultural regions, linked to the urban markets in medieval times, could be saved from (sub)urbanization to a large extent. Acquisition for urban housing plans became too expensive. Suburbanization in the Green Heart region culminated between 1965 and 1975. Accessibility to this region is very good compared with rural areas in the northern region, several urban labour-markets and service centres being situated within a 30-minute drive by car. Private housing projects were welcome by local governments. Their financial contributions to land-use plans compensated the losses caused by social housing projects in these villages. Some vital thresholds could also be surpassed by this growth of both autochthonous and allochthonous population. Suburbanization, recreation and intensification of dairy farming had a negative impact on the environment of these polders.

Recently, a decrease of suburbanization, influenced by the economic crisis, urban planning and environmental control by regional plans, as well as initiatives for a Randstad Green Structure (recreational landscaping) have offered a new perspective to the transitional zones between the cities and the Green Heart region. Since the end of the 1950s, the Green Heart of the Randstad Metropolis and the adjacent River District have been earmarked in official physical planning reports for preservation from (sub)urbanization. These open areas are a characteristic feature of the geographical image of the Netherlands. Some of these polders consist of landscapes of outstanding natural beauty and high ecological value. Protection by physical plans, reservations and conservation funds to some degree guarantee the specific intermingling of agriculture and nature. The dunes along the western coast are also important conservation areas which are confronted with claims for drinking-water storage and as a recreational area. Plans for 10,000 hectares of forests have been proposed for the Randstad city-regions.

Conclusion

Redistribution of population and economic activities is a phenomenon on the meso-level, namely the expanding city-regions (in particular of the Randstad). The slowing-down of demographic and economic growth in recent years has decreased mobility rates, at the same time limiting the locational range of tolerance of both population and economic activities. Urban planning has been reformulated, becoming more and more orientated toward concentration rather than deconcentration on the meso-level, let alone on the macro-level. Fostering of urban renewal, growth of new towns and intensification of urban land-use plans are the main elements of this policy. Rural planning differs for the peripheral, intermediate and peri-urban regions. In the peripheral regions agricultural dominance in land-use is clear. Employment opportunities and accessibility problems are priorities in regional plans. In intermediate regions, the complex mosaic of farmlands and landscapes of outstanding beauty causes planning problems as does the intensification of agriculture. In peri-urban regions there are horticultural complexes with high land value as well as vast expanses of pasture-land, the latter being more subject to the influence of suburbanization.

THE PLACE OF VILLAGE DEVELOPMENT IN THE SETTLEMENT DEVELOPMENT POLICY OF HUNGARY

LÁSZLÓ LACKÓ

KEY-WORDS: *infrastructure,* social and technical ~; *rural regions; settlement* system; *settlement development,* ~ policy, ~ plans; *urbanization,* stages of ~, process of ~; *village* development, ~ policy.

The process of urbanization and efforts aimed at influencing it in recent years have raised several issues for which science cannot answer appropriately. Therefore, the understanding of the essence of the process, as well as possibilities for efficient management, are limited. These problems include the relationships between urbanization and general socio-economic development and their characteristics, respectively, or the stages of urbanization; the degree of determination, and 'freedom' of urbanization from socio-economic phenomena. The clarification of standpoints, the real verification of several hypotheses, has not taken place, the effect of fashionable ideas is strong, and these do not strengthen the positions or the acceptance of the scientific and practical activities associated with settlement development.

(i) These problems, in the author's view, include the question of whether it is necessary and at all possible to formulate and follow a separate village development strategy and policy. It is unexplored, unjustified scientifically, yet at the same time of fundamental significance. Not only in Hungary, presumably, are experts divided into two sharply conflicting groups in this respect.

One opinion holds that the announcement and implementation of a separate village development policy is absolutely necessary, stressing the elimination of social inequalities and injustices in this way. The general trend of urban development—at least up to a certain level—shows also the out-migration of population from villages and the deterioration of those rural regions having unfavourable natural and economic conditions. The notion of settlement development is covered in most languages and countries by the term urban development, the higher level, while the latter generally refers to the town. Of course, confronting problems of town and village is much easier with those countries where the level of infrastructural supply is generally low or where the internal disproportions of the settlement system are great.

In professional literature and public life, the relationship between town and village is portrayed as that between the distinguished, rich, relative and the poor one. Of course, in addition to the factors mentioned, it would be possible to mention several other factors in the system of relations. The author cannot accept the necessity of a separate village development policy and practice but joins the other group of opinions maintaining that a given state or development of the settlement system can be achieved only if it is regarded as an integral whole.

(ii) The role of the town and the village within the settlement system, its relationship with the philosophical part—whole concept, can be explained by its dialectics. Considering the settlement stock of a given country or region as a whole, both towns and villages form a part. And what is perhaps most important is that the whole cannot be understood without the part and that the part cannot be interpreted without the whole.

In the course of the application and interpretation, respectively, of the dialectic interaction between the part and the whole, it is necessary to pay attention to a few fundamental theses. The whole can never be reduced to the parts because the whole would then become meaningless. However, it is a frequent mistake that town/urban development is identified with settlement development. To view the whole in its entire complexity is very important, taking into consideration the relative independence of the individual elements and parts, because the individual peculiarities of these may differ from the ones characterizing the whole. To analyze the individual parts, it is necessary to know (even if only preliminarily) the nature of the whole and vice versa, the studying and interpretation of the whole must be based on a knowledge of the components' properties.

Settlement development policy, besides the comprehensive tasks and objectives, necessarily contains elements differentiated by category, type, etc. The detailed character of these obviously depends on whether it relates to a country, to a part of a country or to a regional unit. In Hungary, the national concept contains principles, objectives and categories which are valid for the entire country while the settlement development plans of the counties comprise the tasks valid for them.

The arguments of the last two or three years produced the thought that both the national concept and the county plans have neglected the problems of villages and, simultaneously, that they have given too much prominence to towns. Therefore, as if to correct 'mistakes', there are those who want the country to have a village development policy. The thought is echoed by many, starting from several points of view, such as anxiety for the village, the danger of depopulation and the interests of agricultural production.

Without disputing the reality of the motive, the author holds the opinion that it would be unnecessary to announce a separate village development policy from the point of view of the national, local, production and supply requirements; the villages, owing to their position, character and endowments, exist together, intertwined with the towns. They are simply inconceivable if separated or torn apart. The problems of villages cannot be solved by their being separated (and the separate village development policy also points in this direction), but by the making of more balanced proportions, mainly the proportions of distribution of development funds, by intensifying relations between town and village and by the creating of cooperation among all settlements as partners. Linked to this is the necessity to change the classification of a town involving honour, advantage, superiority. The obligations of towns to their surroundings should be stressed much more strongly than they have been.

Thus, development of the village can be evaluated only in the entirety of the settlement stock and not separately. Only in this way are we able to think appropriately in the long term unless we want to commit ourselves to developments which might be regretted soon. Of course, all this does not mean that it is not necessary to bestow much more care on the development of villages than earlier. And, in the course of this, special attention should be paid—besides the very backward ones—to the stable main group of villages which are viable and developing in every respect. Moreover, it should not be regarded as a tragedy but as the manifestation of a natural life-cycle of a village ceasing to exist. This should not receive more attention than the new settlement parts coming into being which develop day after day all over the country, on the outskirts of existing core settlements, only they do not receive a separate name plate. The real objective for regional and settlement development is that regions should not become depopulated, that instead of the change of the number of population of the administrative or statistical settlement—concerning which data are available—it would be much more important to follow with attention and to plan the problems and development of minor regions. Probably, this requirement will increase more and more in the future.

(iii) Despite all this, it is not in dispute that the two, characteristically, different, fundamental elements of the settlement system are the town and the village, of which the diverging paths of development are characteristic, and for which the functions, development objective and means are different.

This is proved by the latest publication of UN ECE which, in the chapter concerned with settlement development, reports on the trend of rural regions. The study says that, practically, the significant differences in the conditions of life between the urban and rural regions still exist even today. It continues: "The scattered character of the rural population makes the supply of villages with proper social and technical infrastructural facilities and service facilities difficult and expensive. This problem was aggravated by the concentration process that took place in the service sector which raised the population threshold to a considerable extent, below which the functioning of certain services became uneconomical." In the 1970s, a significant economic advance took place in the rural regions due to the improvement of the industrialization of agricultural production and its supply with technical infrastructure. And it is also generally true that the rural population increasingly resembles the urban way of life in which telecommunications have an important role. Concerning the East European socialist countries, the study stresses the fact that several state and cooperative farms were established in the rural regions and became a forerunner to the combined agricultural and indutrial plants.

These statements, of course, are valid for Hungary as well. What must be added to this is, primarily, the combination of cooperative agriculture and individual farming taking several forms, moreover the especially rapid development in Hungarian villages in the 1970s, and the comment that, before World War II, a great part of agrarian regions in Hungary—measured by West European standards—were especially backward and poor.

(iv) It is also true that essential problems have arisen in the development of villages. The most characteristic among them is perhaps that an intensive differentiation has taken place; there are villages developing dynamically and villages declining rapidly. Today it is still unusual to acknowledge and assert in planning that the village is no more equal to the scene of agricultural production and that peasants are no longer in majority within the population of villages.

The problems and the importance of the village issue are also indicated by the fact that in 1982 the Hungarian Academy of Sciences organized a conference entitled "Development problems of rural settlements in Hungary". At these discussions—although villages were on the agenda—both the evaluation of the situation and the formulation of the future tasks took place in a calm atmosphere free from exaggerations and with the consideration of the entire settlement system.

The notion of village—even in Hungary—covers a great variety of settlements. Their endowments are different not only in the order of magnitude but also in the natural environment, transport conditions, social composition, the economic and cultural supply and administrative functions. The differences among the various types of villages are increasing in the course of present socio-economic processes, they are greater than those between large villages in the process of urbanization and underdeveloped small towns. This creates special circumstances for villages situated in the immediate attraction zone of towns. The more developed towns promote the proportionate, more rapid development, urbanization of villages near towns by the location of some functions in nearby villages, and by the stimulation of cooperation between town and village. On the other hand, towns developing too rapidly take away resources, population and manpower from the development of villages. In this case, location on the urban fringe hinders village development or causes retrogression.

On one extreme there can be found villages performing minor central functions, attracting both agricultural and industrial manpower, involved in the urbanization process and, moreover, privileged by rural recreation. On the other extreme there are the small villages without endowments for economic development, conserving a backward infrastructure, declining because of their rapidly decreasing population, thus being in a disadvantageous situation in all respects. Medium-sized villages, with 1,000–3,000 population, deserve special attention because their destiny decides where and to what extent the general decrease of rural population can be retarded. Many of these settlements have declining population, mainly due to out-migration, and drop from the category of medium-sized villages into that of small and very small villages. This incessantly increases the number of small and very small villages and places their population in a more disadvantegous situation.

The settlement system has changed regularly in the course of history. There will be more rapidly developing, dying and newly-born settlements among villages in the future, too. Some villages in regions where there are no towns and which have exceptional economic conditions develop into small towns. On the other hand, the decline of some very small villages cannot be stopped because their development conditions have ceased to exist. There are, however, such declining villages which can be saved by proper development policy while, at the same time, new and very small settlements come into being beside profitable large-scale farms for the workers of these, growing into villages with a more modern, more urbanized, infrastructure than the older ones. With a certain delay, the settlement network accommodates the new socio-economic conditions.

(v) It is probably not necessary to prove the fact that, for example, the settlement—whether it is taken into account as a technical or social or geographic formation—can be understood only in relationships, in internal and external relations. By the application of the system concept and approach, respectively, the condition within the settlement—moreover the interaction, the coexistence of the ensemble of the settlements—becomes more understandable. The settlement stock of the country is such a closed spatial system which is divided into subsystems both horizontally and vertically; multilateral relations, mutual determination exists both among the elements (settlements) and the subsystems. (The characteristically different settlement types of the various regions of the country can be regarded as horizontal subsystems while the vertical subsystems can be formed on the basis of the categories of the number of population and the functional ensembles).

Geographers and settlement scientists abroad and in Hungary have attempted for several years to explore the internal relationships of the settlement stock, and in the last few decades regional economists also joined them. Much important knowledge has been acquired by means of theoretical and analytical works of library size. Yet, what is lacking is the exact knowledge of the processes and relationships. It is frequently repeated that the situation and development tendencies of the settlement system can be explored thoroughly only by the joint consideration of the physical geographic, economic, social and technical factors. Thus, there is still much to be done in scientific and practical activities. However, it should be noted here that the obviously necessary progress depends to a considerable extent on the depth and exactness that economic and sociological approaches are able to achieve.

(vi) Considering all these, too, the main trends and endeavours of Hungarian settlement policy can be summarized as follows:

(1) The new policy is based on the realization that the concentrated urbanization development stage—characterized by the dynamic growth of industry—is followed by a development stage of more deconcentrated character, affecting a larger number of elements of the settlement network and unfolding the peculiar local development energies better than previously. The objective of the new development policy is not a gradual approximation of the settlement network conditions, generally considered to be ideal, but the optimization of the next urbanization development stage—characterized by the more deconcentrated transformation of the settlement network—by the intensification of agglomerations. Such policy takes into account the intensification of agglomeration and intends to support the positive effects of this and to reduce the sources of tension of it, respectively, by solving the problems accumulated in the previous development stage simultaneously. It also takes into account the new inequalities which may develop in the next long term due to the difference in the pace of development of settlements belonging to an urban region (being in a favourable position from the point of view of the multiplying effect of development energies) and the settlements outside the urban region.

(2) The settlement development policy should be asserted on three levels (national, regional and local) in a consistent manner. An essential characteristic feature of the decision mechanism is its

accommodation to the appropriate competence level. The decisions should be made on those levels where the responsibility for the implementation of the decisions lies. All those who are affected by consequences of the decisions must take part, directly or indirectly, in the decision-making. Under Hungarian conditions, this will facilitate the decentralization of the decisions, and it makes necessary the strengthening of democratic decision-making. As with other significant spheres of socio-economic development, it is necessary to decentralize the management of settlement development because this is a condition of the possibility that the objectives formulated by the central management and the interests of the local communities should meet more successfully. This is a condition also of the inclusion of the resources of the population which will become more significant in the next development period. This is accompanied by the growth of democracy.

(3) On a national level, the new policy regards as its main objective the regulation of the settlement development processes and not the calling into being and realization of the actual developments. Following on from this it does not allocate development priorities to certain settlements (regions) in the long term but intends to promote the accelerated development of that development component valid for the entire settlement network which can activate the other components. In the future, central management will act decisively to influence effect mechanisms. Thus, with indirect control, it does not want to interfere with the processes directly.

In the use of central resources, a guiding principle is that they should serve as far as possible the stimulation of the coordinated development of settlement associations and to support those settlement infrastructure developments which, respectively, are of national or macro-regional significance and which exert a favourable effect on other—more complex—development processes (e.g. transport network development). The regional level of settlement development policy has a mediating role primarily in the direction of the local (regional) interests and the central objectives, while the preparation and realization of the actual developments are, for the most part, the task of the local development policy. Development policies at the national and regional level must promote the far-reaching realization of the local initiatives.

(4) A change, compared to the development policy of the past period, is that the subject of the next long-range development policy will be not so much the stimulation of the development of the individual settlements but rather the development of the regions. Namely, at the present level of Hungarian socio-economic development and in the next stage of urbanization, the pledge of the development of the individual settlements will be the intensification of the division of labour among settlements, and the enrichment of functions of settlements and among settlements within the individual regions of the country.

Bibliography

"A magyarországi falusi települések fejlesztési kérdései c. konferencia összefoglaló ajánlásai" (1982) (Conference on the Development Questions of the Rural Settlements of Hungary. Summary and Recommendations), *Településtudományi Közlemények* 31, (Budapest: MUT—BME—VÁTI): 74–77.

ENYEDI, GY. (1980) *Falvaink sorsa* (The Prospects of Our Villages), (Budapest: Magvető Kiadó).

"Human Settlements—Key Factor in Economic and Social Development", (1983) *Economic Bulletin for Europe* (The Journal of the United Nations Economic Commission for Europe), 35, no. 1.

LACKÓ, L. (1982) "A településfejlesztés holnapjáról" (The Settlement Development of Tomorrow), *Területi Statisztika* 32, no. 1–2: 8–14.

RURAL INDUSTRY IN HUNGARY

GYÖRGYI BARTA

KEY-WORDS: *auxiliary* industrial activity; *'branch-plant-character';* *industry,* agricultural cooperative and state farm ~, dispersion of ~, location of ~; *industrial* wages; *labour* demand, ~ shortage, composition of the ~ force, ~ force released from agriculture, available ~, rural ~; *parent* company; *regional* development policy, ~ planning; *rural* branch plants of large scale industry, female workers in ~ industry, ~ industrialization, ~ infrastructural development, ~ living conditions, ~ services; *settlement* development policy.

Introduction

Rural industry gained greater importance twice in the course of modern industrialization in developed countries. The first instance was during the Industrial Revolution, when a great number of small, rural, industrial units came into being for the purpose of exploiting and processing the local raw material. In this period, the industry of the cities and that of the country differed strongly in character and structure.

The second important period of rural industrialization coincided with the increasing, extending, continuous period of industrial development, the general boom of economy. This period lasted throughout the 1960s until the beginning and middle of the 1970s both in the developed capitalist countries and in Hungary. (Lonsdale 1979) At this time, industrial enterprises opened many branch plants in poorly urbanized areas on the basis of various economic motives. When looking for the reasons of rural industrialization, the causes and circumstances can be grouped in three categories: (Davin 1969, Townroe 1975, 1979, Enyedi 1980)

—Taking advantage of those favourable endowments able to be provided by rural area for the settling industry;

—Assistance for settling industrial plants, which is of local or state origin, depending upon what kind of interests were served by the location of industry;

—Relocation of industrial activity from cities, which was enforced by the rising costs of those conditions necessary for its functioning or by the lack of them, or the spatial development policy which aims at the slowing-down of city growth.

Though the causes which brought about West-European rural industrialization—more precisely the order of importance of these causes—differed from Hungarian practice, it can be demonstrated that rural industrial location belonged nowhere directly to settlement development intentions. The origin of these processes was always determined by the interests of national industry.

In Eastern and Central Europe centralized industrial control—mainly in favour of the compensating purposes of regional policy—settled industry in the economically underdeveloped regions but, following the growth-pole theory, was concentrated mostly on particular cities. Enterprises gained greater independence in Hungary as a result of the economic reform established in 1968. Rural dispersion of industry arose from the spread of city-seated bigger enterprises in the country. However, from a territorial point of view, the rural industrialization of the 1960s–1970s was a spontaneous process because the choice of a settlement by enterprises for new locations was not orientated by central planning. In Hungary the abundant source of the labour force (parallel with the increasing shortage of labour in cities) was decisive in attracting industry into the villages. All other aspects (e.g. cheapness of labour force, moderate costs of investment and operation, offer of cheap tenements) were of secondary importance.

This paper will concentrate on the rapid rural spread of Hungarian industry during the 1960s and the 1970s. This expansion came to an end by the late 1970s; the 1980s mark the beginning of a new era in Hungarian industry as well as in rural industry.

Conditions of rural industrialization in the 1960s and 1970s

POTENTIAL INDUSTRIAL CAPACITY OF THE RURAL REGIONS

The opening and continuous operation of industrial plants have their conditions. First of all the desired number and composition of the labour force, the infrastructure (transport and telecommunication, electricity, water system, gas, canalization system etc.) belong to these conditions. The absence of these conditions can usually be accepted but this seriously increases the cost of investments. So, when choosing the location of an industrial plant, aside from special cases, these conditions and the endowments of the region and the settlement are taken into consideration. Mostly cities possess these fundamentals. This can explain why industry has strong links with cities, though local raw material, energy, favourable geographical position, cooperating possibilities and traditions influence the choice of settlement for industrial location.

RURAL POPULATION AS A PART OF THE INDUSTRIAL LABOUR FORCE

The increased labour demand of the post-World War II reconstruction and the accelerated industrialization of the 1950s was solved by the labour force being released from agriculture. This source of labour was quite abundant at that time mainly because of the pre-war over-population in rural areas[1] and because industry had a greater attraction than agricultural work[2] and finally, agricultural collectivization (being shocking for many people) multiplied the number of those who engaged themselves in industry.

But industry—aside from its branches needing local raw material—settled and expanded in the cities. This went hand in hand with the influx of previous agrarian population to the towns. Most of the village people getting jobs (mainly industrial ones) in cities and towns also made efforts to move there. Settlement policy which concentrated its forces nearly exclusively on town development merely confirmed this. Owing to the various difficulties of resettlement (city housing shortage, lack of favourable flats, great expenses, administrative restrictions, etc.) commuting became predominant by the 1960s. Most of the commuters were village people employed in town industry.

The phenomenon of labour shortage first appeared in Budapest in the middle of the 1960s. From the beginning of the 1970s, industries of all large cities also had to struggle with it. It became increasingly obvious that manpower reserves of extensive industrialization were being exhausted.[3] (The first reason for this was the re-arrangement of the economic structure: the unappeased hunger of industry for the labour force and the increasing proportion of the tertiary sector. The insufficiency of manpower supply can also be explained partly by unfavourable demographic processes, for example, fall in the birth-rate.) But the switch to a programme of intensive development is not smooth. And it is obvious that, under present Hungarian circumstances, enterprises strive to gain a new labour force as long as they can have the smallest chance of getting it. This is why a part of the rural area became a scene of industrialization, especially from the 1960s onwards when organizational mergers and acquisitions of industrial plants were frequent. Still, very soon agriculture could not spare a large number of workers, and even the attraction of industry lessened.

Activity rate figures by settlement categories in 1980 proved clearly that not even in the villages was there a notable available labour (Table 1). After 1980, even the number of workers employed in

TABLE 1

RATIO OF THE ACTIVE AND INACTIVE EARNERS FROM THE WHOLE POPULATION
ACCORDING TO SETTLEMENT CATEGORIES (%)

	1949		1960		1970		1980	
	Active	Inactive	Active	Inactive	Active	Inactive	Active	Inactive
Budapest	48.2	5.4	54.5	9.0	55.5	18.1	50.0	25.1
Towns	41.2	4.4	46.6	5.5	49.0	12.6	48.0	18.0
Villages	44.6	1.3	46.2	2.3	45.2	12.3	45.8	20.6
Hungary	44.4	2.8	47.8	4.4	48.3	13.5	47.3	20.6

Source: 1980. évi Népszámlálás 22. kötet, KSH, Budapest, 1981 (Population Census 1980, Volume 22, Central Statistical Office, Budapest 1981)

TABLE 2

SIZE DISTRIBUTION OF HUNGARIAN VILLAGES IN 1980

Size groups	Villages		Population	
	Number	(%)	(1,000 persons)	(%)
20,000–	1	0.0	21.4	0.5
10,000–19,999	44	1.5	576.8	11.5
5,000– 9,999	142	4.7	976.2	19.4
2,000– 4,999	543	18.0	1,620.6	32.3
1,000– 999	708	23.4	1,004.9	20.1
– 999	754	24.9	554.3	11.1
– 499	833	27.5	253.7	5.1
	3,025	100.0	5,007.9	100.0

Source: 1980. évi Népszámlálás, 30. kötet, KSH, Budapest, 1982 (Population Census 1980, Volume 30, Central Statistical Office, Budapest 1982)

rural industry began to diminish. The mere existence of a labour force is of course not the only condition necessary for industrialization, it must also be available in a spatially concentrated form (the possibilities of commuting being limited by the access and the expenses going with it—paid either by the employer or the employee). The obstacle to rural industrialization is generally the latter. Hungarian villages show a special population distribution pattern (Table 2). In the various regions of the world, sporadic villages with only a few people are more frequent. The cause of the vast differences in the size structure of villages is that, while settlements of particular regions could develop continuously in the course of history and retain their traditions and achievements, in other regions war ravages wiped off—in many cases—hundreds of settlements. This is why Alföld, the Great Hungarian Plain—consisting of more than one-third of the country's area—became nearly uninhabited after the 160-year Turkish rule in the 17th century. The inhabitants, seeking safety and defence, settled down in the bigger villages here which—owing to their function—did not develop into towns for many years. The world of scattered farmsteads around these enormous villages came into being at about this time and some of them survived until the present time.

In Hungary, mainly larger villages have been industrializing, the average population of industrialized villages was about 4,000 souls. Population number 2,000 meant a certain threshold, hardly any industry settled in villages smaller than that. (This was naturally modified by a number of other factors, for instance, in the neighbourhood of towns, and along transport lines new industrial plants were opened in smaller villages, too.)

During the acceleration of industrialization in the 1960s, the rural labour force consisted mainly of unskilled people inexperienced in industrial work. At this time, their mass employment still met the demands of new rural industrial working places. Namely, industrial enterprises spreading in the country took especially simpler jobs to their remote branch plants for the completion of which greater physical strain was needed. They could not find enough workers for this in Budapest or in other large cities. But the efficiency of the production of enterprises can only increase if the standard of production grows high also in their country plants, an essential condition of which is the improvement of professional standard and competence. Therefore, enterprises quite often take over the headache of their workers' professional training and organize the courses 'indoors'. Rural industrialization, created by the opening of plants, naturally accelerated the process of professional training in the beginning. Of course, the support of schooling, the formation of professional training conditions, are not autotelic activities and go just as far as to meet the plans and interests of the enterprise. So this method of industrial professional training (having close connections with the activity of the enterprise, usually reaching a mid-level) can be rather unilateral, which delays the workers' future professional mobility and is an obstacle to structural transformation in industry.

INFRASTRUCTURAL SUPPLY OF VILLAGES

Hungarian settlements can be best distinguished by the differences in the standard of provision. It is a fact that, after 1945, economic policy permanently affected villages disadvantageously. Investment goods were distributed mostly at the expense of villages. In the 1950s, the heavy expenses of the forced-stroke industrialization were financed mainly from the produce of agriculture. Industrial production, without an extension of infrastructural background, could not start while traditional agriculture could function even under primitive conditions. This was the reason for the postponement of agricultural and (almost parallel with this) rural infrastructural development. Nevertheless, by the beginning of the 1960s and in the mid-1960s even such highly important investments as the electrification of villages and the connecting of all villages with transport were realized.

The prominence of agriculture and its increasing role from the 1960s onwards was not immediately accompanied by a change in regional and settlement policy. For nearly another two decades—to the beginning of the 1980s—settlement development was practically restricted to town-planning.

During the 1970s, a detailed survey of about 850 villages was carried out at the Geographical Research Institute. Those features and conditions of the villages were analysed which could influence or exert an attractive or repulsive effect on industrialization or on the location of new plants, in other cases on the loss of industrial activity or on the basic transformation of it. Village characteristics which affected industrial activity were divided into the following groups:

(a) labour force situation of villages (number of inhabitants, activity rate, female activity rate, degree of commuting, occupation structure etc.);

(b) education of rural population;

(c) infrastructural supply of the village (electricity, running water, canalization, gas, dwelling conditions, state home-building, supply of health and education institutions, services, electricity consumption of the population);

(d) technical infrastructural conditions in the village (the needs of new industrial plants for fresh water and energy);

(e) industrialization of the village (industrial backgrounds of the new plant);

(f) investment expenses of the new industrial plants;

(g) average industrial wages in the villages;

(h) geographical and transport situation of the village.

From among the above groups (c) (d) and (h) contain the data of infrastructural supply while (b) (e) and (f) have indirect connections with local circumstances.

The purpose of the survey was:

—to show the characteristics of an 'average village';

—to find any deviation from the average in particular factors;

—to rank—with the help of factor analysis—the listed factors of industrialization;

—to establish regional types of industrialized villages by relying upon local features which promoted industrialization.

Two periods (1970–72 and 1972–75) and two groups of villages (the ones where industrial plants were newly opened and others where they were closed) were examined. The intention was to show the effect of village endowments on the location of an industrial plant, on the closing of it, and also to compare the effects of urging or restricting industrialization during periods characterized by economic boom and later by the economic situation becoming harder and harder.

The most important conslusions of the research referring to the role of infrastructure are the following:

—Industrialized villages belong to those which are the most prosperous economically or the best supplied with infrastructure;

—Infrastructural supply of villages chosen for new industrial location fell behind compared with those villages where plants were being closed (in other words, the most important cause of a plant closing cannot be found in the underdevelopment of infrastructure);

—New industrial developments are taking place in villages with less and less favourable infrastructural supply;

—The water and energy consumption of new plants is increasing, and it is increasingly exceeding the average level for villages;

—New plants are located further and further away from towns, especially from the capital;

—Differences among villages are sharpest in the level of education, in investment expenses of industrial plants, in the geographical and transport situation, and in the infrastructural supply.

These conclusions, of course, show merely the differences among those villages represented in our sample. Other studies (Enyedi 1981) show that there is a diminishing difference between rural and urban living conditions. A certain levelling off can be observed in the quality of rural housing stock. The supply of water, canals, and bathrooms of homes built in the country show a smaller shortfall today from similar town indices than earlier. But, in respect of some basic provisions, differences grew higher between village and town, namely: in the consumption of electricity and water of the households, the quality of district medical treatment, retail trade supply, and canalization of settlements.

Infrastructural development is a burning issue in villages today, too, and not only because of industrialization. This is even more demanded by modern large-scale farming production. It is also urged by the growing dissatisfaction which originates from the disharmony between the inhabitants' needs supported by a strong purchasing power and the weak development of rural services (and, in many cases, it becomes the cause of out-migration).

Regional development policy
and rural industrialization

The regional development policy of the 1960s outlined the form of spatial equalization in the moderation of regional differentiation of economy and in the accelerated development of underdeveloped regions. The only means of reaching this aim in this period was industrialization. The three main targets of the regional development policy were to help to industrialize underdeveloped regions and to support the relocation of industries from the capital into other parts of the country. Above all, these targets referred to the development of towns (the towns of the underdeveloped regions such as Alföld or South Transdanubia). In some cases, however, they also concerned the villages (since most of the closed coal mines were in villages).

Regional spread of industrial productive forces in the 1960s–1970s and the industrialization of villages occasioned debates even among experts concentrating on regional development. They argued that the strong deconcentration of productive forces may lead to an over-dispersal of the investment goods. But regional planners failed to consider a very important aspect: plants based in villages were mostly not independent but came into being as the outlaid industrial units of town-seated industrial enterprises. They function like this even today. Investments in branch plants, in fact, increased the assets of the planting middle and large parent companies. The production of these plants formed part of the large-scale production.

In all, we can state that the strong spatial spread of industry appeared neither among the targets of regional planning nor even among its suppositions. From this point of view, it was basically a spontaneous process. The debate has, however, been forgotten about because, on the one hand, most of the available rural labour force has been expended and, on the other hand, production decline caused by economic recession affects the process of enterprise expansion, too.

Size and qualitative characteristics of rural industry

Various forms of industrial activity were formed in the villages. One of them is the auxiliary industrial activity which is becoming increasingly important in the agricultural cooperatives and state farms and which is included in the statistics of the agricultural sector. The objective of auxiliary industrial activity in the beginning of the 1960s was, first of all, to solve the permanent and continuous occupation of cooperative members and a steadier and improving waging of them.

TABLE 3

THE PROPORTION OF INDUSTRIAL JOBS WITHIN
THE TOTAL NUMBER OF JOBS IN VILLAGES (%)

	1960	1970	1980
Agriculture	69.2	53.7	43.8
Industry and			
construction industry	19.7	26.2	28.2
Others	11.1	20.1	28.0

Source: Területi Statisztikai Évkönyvek (Spatial Statistical Yearbooks); 1980. évi Népszámlálás, 33. kötet, KSH, Budapest, 1983 (Population Census 1980, Volume 33, Central Statistical Office, Budapest 1983)

Later, the role of auxiliary industrial activity changed: industrial activity has become very important in the profitable functioning of quite a lot of agricultural cooperatives and state farms, which compensates for the losses of farming and animal husbandry and provides a remarkable source of basic activity investment. Today, out of about 800,000 agricultural workers, nearly a quarter is engaged in the auxiliary branches and 100,000 to 120,000 are in industry. Nevertheless, agricultural cooperative and state farm industry provides only a small portion, 5–6% of the country's industrial production. And, although auxiliary production of agricultural farms is of a decisive importance in certain industrial sectors—especially in food processing—, in other cases it is a stop-gap, and its major role is to support the functioning of agricultural organizations. Auxiliary industrial activity is a specific feature of Hungarian agriculture and has an important role in the successful development of farming. The subject of this paper is, however, not auxiliary industrial activity but that proportion of the *large-scale industry* which settled in the villages. This is more than one-fifth of national industry with regard to the number of employees and the value of fixed assets. Industrial plants employing at least ten workers are located in about one third of Hungarian villages. Three quarters of industrial jobs in villages belong to large-scale industry, so this study deals really with the most frequent phenomena.

Finally, private small-scale industry, represented by 10,000 to 15,000 workers altogether, has an insignificant and diminishing proportion within the industries of villages. The servicing activity of self-employed artisans has, however, a stop-gap function in the provision of rural population.

All in all, industry has until now increased its role in the economy of the villages and, together with the tertiary sector—considering the number of jobs—it already dominates the economic structure of villages (Table 3).

BRANCH PLANTS OF LARGE-SCALE INDUSTRY LOCATED IN VILLAGES

Since 1975—following the country-wide tendencies with a five-year time lag—the number of employees decreased also in the rural branch plants of large-scale industry by 9% until 1981. We must add, however, that this decrease is, on the one hand, slower-paced than that of the country's whole industry thus village industry—considering the number of jobs—has an increasing proportion (16.7% in 1960; 21.9% in 1970; 26.3% in 1981). On the other hand, the decrease in the number of rural industrial workers did not originate mainly from the regression in industrial staff but from the dwindling of the number of villages which came about in the meantime. (Since 1970, nearly 40 villages—of course, the most populous and most developed economically—became towns.)

The value of industrial fixed assets doubled in villages between 1970 and 1981. Investments have been increasing continuously though at a pace falling behind the national average, consequently the proportion of village industry stagnated at about 21% within the country's total industrial fixed assets. The proportion of machines within the fixed assets increased remarkably between 1970 and 1980 (from 39.7% to 46.2%). In this period, the motorization of village industry improved considerably and its capacity increased. This indicates, to some extent, a closing-up process which shapes the development of parent companies and their branch plants (in other words the development of urban and rural industry). In case the parent company has long-range plans with its established unit, it is by all means in its interests to draw the technical standards of the unit closer to those of the whole enterprise.

STRUCTURAL CHARACTERISTICS OF RURAL INDUSTRY

Rural industry, in essence, refers to the *location* of units of town-seated enterprises. In 1980, only 7.2% of rural industrial plants were independent enterprises. Considering the industrial plants employing more than ten workers, this proportion reached 16%. 'Branch-plant-character' strengthened in past decades and determines the possibilities of the development and restructuring of rural industry. From this arises the similarity between the structure of rural industry and the national industry and its regional concentration around large cities. The branch-plant-character also explains, at least to some extent, the relatively poor technical standards of rural industry as well as its position in the division of labour.

Branch plants seem to be more unstable economic units than independent industrial enterprises. (Between 1970 and 1975, about a quarter of all village branch plants stopped functioning and about a third of them opened.) This instability has many causes. Big enterprises, in the struggle for a new labour force, have more favourable chances than small and middle-sized ones. They often gained a new labour force by incorporating small and middle-sized plants. In many cases these smaller enterprises themselves showed only weak resistance or demonstrated a firm interest in joining, in the hope for greater security and development possibilities. Another manifestation of the concentration arose from the drop in the density of industrial service network. Physical winding up, the total liquidation of activity, concerned only the small-sized plants (employing fewer than 20 workers). Bigger plants were mostly reorganized, incorporated, or changed their profile. They very rarely ceased for good.

Mining and heavy industry played the main roles in the structure of rural industry in the 1970s. More than 56% of the employees, and nearly 76% of the fixed assets were from these two branches. This shows a remarkable similarity with the national sectoral structure of industry. Nevertheless, industrial sectors which are connected with raw material production or processing (mining, the building material industry, food processing) are over-represented in rural areas, while the machine industry which demanded a more qualified labour force and a higher level of infrastructure has remained of less importance. In the course of rural industrialization the labour force supply consisted mostly of women who were unskilled and previously housewives. Since 1970, the proportion of women employed in rural industry (45.9% in 1981) has exceeded the national average (44.1% in 1981). The number of female workers in rural industry began to decrease only after 1975 while the decrease of the active men has been going on since 1970. The slow decrease of the number of active women also shows that the labour force supply became exhausted in villages, too.

Rural industry has an uneven regional distribution. Most industrialized villages are still to be found in those regions which are the most developed industrially. This is in spite of the fact that industrial progress of the past 15–20 years decreased remarkably the economic differences between counties and regions. Rural industrial plants, because of their branch-plant-character and due to a lesser concentration of population, have smaller sizes than the national average. The average number of the employed staff in 1981 was 121 to one plant (nationally 166) and, while the national average did not change in the past 10 years, a remarkable concentration came about in the rural industry: between 1970 and 1980, the average size of a plant, with regard to the number employed, increased by 14%. Naturally, plant sizes vary by branches (for instance, nearly ten times more people work in one mining unit than in one of the food processing industry). In rural industry, the number of quite small plants with fewer than ten workers is very high. Their proportion is nearly 40% but they only employ about 1.0–1.5% of the total number of active earners in rural industry. Plants with more than 500 workers (representing 7% of all rural industrial plants) have more than a half of the people employed in rural industry. Strong and continuously increasing concentration is a process to be found not only in the spatial distribution of rural industrial labour but of the fixed assets as well.

QUALITATIVE FEATURES OF RURAL INDUSTRY

The branch-plant-character of rural industry and the vertical division of labour between parent companies and their outlaid units decrease the need for a skilled, not speaking of a highly-qualified, labour force. Parallel with this, the strong dependence of branch plants on their parent companies also means that there is no need for a large group of managers and directors, some middle-level managers are enough. Branch plants, primarily, have production functions. Managing functions demanding skill are possessed mostly by the headquarters. The proportion of the skilled workforce was especially low in newly-opened units. With the time passing, the share and number of the skilled workforce also increased in branch plants. The proportion of skilled workers is small among women. The lower level of the skilled workforce in rural industry originates not only from the demands of these plants but also from the fact that villages provide the labour force. According to our case studies, 70–80% of the rural industrial workers completed elementary school but the number and proportion of those who finished vocational training or secondary school was very small.

At the end of the 1970s, industrial wages paid in villages—though varied according to sectors—fell below the town wage standards of the same sector by 14–15%. The greatest shortfall was in light industry and in the food processing industry. Our case studies proved that the shortfall of rural industrial wages can be mainly explained by the lower wages paid in provincial units of enterprises. Lower wages paid in villages are, on the one hand, the consequences of the demand and supply proportions of the labour-market, which differs according to regions, and on the other hand, they originate from the smaller productivity of rural industry, from its less favourable sectoral structure and from the lower level of technical standards.

Technical standards, expressed in the value of fixed assets per one worker, is a highly indicative feature of industry. It is worth mentioning that the considerable rural industrialization realized during the 1960s resulted in technical standards of rural industry falling increasingly behind national standards mostly in light industry. The capital of enterprises for the development of branch plants was limited, thus new units were often placed in old buildings built for quite different purposes and equipped with old-fashioned machines which were out of use in the parent companies. Case studies, though, show the fact that, after five or six years, the technical standards of units came generally closer to the enterprise level.

EVALUATION OF RURAL INDUSTRIALIZATION

Extremely different views on rural industrialization emerged among experts depending on whether they evaluated the results of rural industrialization from the point of view of national industry or from the aspect of rural development. The negative criticism which enumerates the unfavourable effects of the spontaneous regional development of rural industrialization is not groundless. Undoubtedly, a great number of out-of-date, badly-equipped, plants came into being during rural industrialization among which cooperation could be only accidental. In the beginning, an unskilled labour force, unfamiliar with industrial work, was only able to function on a low level. The proliferation of multi-plant enterprises led to a regional dispersal of production processes and as a consequence of their spatial separation the transport demands of production increased considerably.

However, rural industrialization cannot be evaluated apart from the economic or industrial development of the country. The diffusion of industry into small town or village regions was a process dictated by the Hungarian economic conditions and mechanism as well as by the established directives of the time. Growth was vital for Hungarian firms but funds (first of all the development fund created from the enterprise profit) were limited, labour was cheap, the aspects of rentability were unimportant and efficiency immeasurable due to the deformed price system etc. All this determined the development of the industry in these years.

Rural industrialization was linked with the development of national industry, above all it served the interests of industrial companies. And, though the industrialization of villages contributed to a more balanced regional development, it was not the regional development policy which initiated the location of industries into villages. Social aspects (providing jobs, for example), did not play an important role in moving industries into rural areas.

Experts dealing with regional and settlement development emphasize the decisively favourable effects of rural industrialization. There is no doubt that new village industry played an important role in the improvement of the living conditions of the rural population, in the infrastructural development of villages and, more than that, of the socio-economic balance of the country. A great number of villages (nearly one-fifth of the industrialized ones) became small growth poles thanks to industrialization. The enrichment of village functions is one of the conditions for keeping the population on a certain level. But, unfavourable effects also showed themselves during the period of functioning of newly-located industrial plants (four or five years). The fact that industry has no roots, it is unstable, it strongly depends on the decisions made in remote headquarters, reduces the possibilities of industrial development started in villages.

The 'golden age' of rural industrialization seems to have ended. The most important source of extensive development—the available labour—was exhausted. Although, at present, only the signs of a slow shortfall can be traced: the number of employees has decreased and more than 200 industrial plants in villages were closed in the past five years. For the time being, however, there is no danger of a sudden drop in rural industry. Not even the worsening economic conditions could force industrial enterprises to a more effective use of labour until now (for instance, there is no apparent dismissal of superfluous labour force), or to modernize the production structure. (Even today most of the enterprises do not evaluate the efficiency of work in their branch plants.) The companies are not interested in doing so because they can include their entire, increasing production expenses in the prices of their products.

Notes

[1] In 1930, for instance, the majority of the agrarian population consisted of agricultural proletarians and small land-owners whose position stood near to that of the proletariat. Their proportion (within the agrarian population) exceeded 80% or without peasants with 5–10 *holds* (1 *hold* = 1.42 acres) 66%. (Andorka—Harcsa—Kulcsár 1975, p. 309)

[2] At that time industrial wages well exceeded agricultural income. Average monthly wages of state farm workers reached only 59% of industrial workers' wages in 1950 and 79% of it in 1955, and wages of peasants in co-operatives amounted to 76–80% of state farm workers' payment. The value of individual farmers' comsumption only exceeded that of the cooperative peasantry by 20–25%; consequently, it was also far behind that of the industrial workers. (Andorka 1979, p. 165)

[3] Industrialization is extensive when the quantity of inputs (additional labour and capital investments) plays a decisive role in the increase of production. In this case the efficiency of labour and the return on capital decrease. Accordingly, the source of intensive development is the increase of labour productivity and a better exploitation of production bases.

Bibliography

ANDORKA, R. (1979) *A magyar községek társadalmának átalakulása* (The Social Transformation of Hungarian Villages), (Budapest: Magvető Kiadó).

ANDORKA, R.—HARCSA, I.—KULCSÁR, R. (1975) *A társadalmi mobilitás történeti tendenciái* (Historical Tendencies of Social Mobility), (Statisztikai Időszaki Közlemények Vol. 343, Budapest: KSH).

BARTA, GY. (1979) "A falusi ipar területi problémái" (Regional Problems of Rural Industry), *Területi Statisztika* 29, No. 4: 377–390.

BARTA, GY. (1979) "A falusi ipari kutatás fontossága és időszerűsége" (The Importance and Timeliness of Research on Rural Industry), *Területi Kutatások*, no. 2: 35–52.

BARTA, GY.—ENYEDI, GY. (1981) *Iparosodás és a falu átalakulása* (Industrialization and the Transformation of the Village), (Budapest: Közgazdasági és Jogi Könyvkiadó).

BARTKE, I. (1980) "A területfejlesztés irányai és irányelvei Magyarországon" ((The Directions and Directives of Regional Development in Hungary), *Területi Statisztika*, No. 1: 1–8.

BARTKE, I. (1979) "A gazdaság területi szerkezetének átalakulásáról" (On the Transformation of the Spatial Structure of the Economy), *Gazdaság*, no. 4: 66–82.

DAVIN, L. (1969) "Les facteurs de localisation des industries nouvelles", *Revue économique*, sept.: 10.

ENYEDI, GY. (1980) *Falvaink sorsa* (The Prospects of Our Villages), (Budapest: Magvető Kiadó).

ENYEDI, GY. (1977) "A korszerű falufejlesztés elvei és legújabb tendenciái" (The Principles and the Latest Tendencies of Modern Village Development), *Területrendezés* 24: 11–15.

ENYEDI, GY.—VÖLGYES, I. (1982) *The Effect of Modern Agriculture on Rural Development,* (New York: Pergamon Press).

FODOR, L. (1982) *Lépéskényszerben a magyar ipar* (Hungarian Industry under Pressure of Change), (Budapest: Kossuth Könyvkiadó).

FODOR, L. (1973) *Falvak a nagyváros árnyékában* (Villages in the Shadow of the Large City), (Budapest: Kossuth Könyvkiadó).

GALASI, P. (1976) "A községekben élő ipari-építőipari munkások mint a munkaerő sajátos csoportja" (Industrial and Building Industrial Workers Living in Villages as a Special Group of Labour Force), *Közgazdasági Szemle,* no. 2: 154–175.

HEGEDŰS, A. (1970) *Változó világ* (Changing World), (Budapest: Akadémiai Kiadó).

INZELT, A. (1978) "A vállalati centralizációról" (On Enterprise Centralization), *Gazdaság,* no. 2: 58–77.

KULCSÁR, V. (ed.) (1976) *A változó falu* (The Changing Village), (Budapest: Gondolat Kiadó).

LADÁNYI, J. (1977) "Községekben élő munkások" (Workers Living in Villages), *Szociológia,* no. 1: 28–41.

LAKI, M. (1982) "Megszűnés és összevonás" (Liquidation and Amalgamation), *Ipargazdasági Szemle,* no. 1–2: 242–248.

LAKI, M. (1980) "A háttéripar fejlesztése" (The Development of Technical Infrastructure in Industry), *Gazdaság,* no. 3: 61–74.

LONDSDALE, R. E. (1979) *Agro-Industrial Employment and Demographic Change in Rural U. S.,* (Paper prepared for Symposium of IGU Commission on Rural Development, Szeged, Hungary).

MÁRKUS, I. (1980) "Az ismeretlen főszereplő, a szegényparasztság" (The Unknown Protagonist: the Peasant Poor), *Valóság,* no. 4: 13–40.

RÁNKI, GY. (1964) "A kisipar szerepe a magyar kapitalista fejlődésben" (The Role of Small-Scale Industry in Hungarian Capitalist Development), *Történeti Szemle,* no. 2: 423–451.

ROMÁN, Z. (1978) "A magyar ipar szervezeti rendszere" (The Organizational Structure of Hungarian Industry), *Ipargazdasági Szemle,* no. 3: 7–50.

ROMÁNY, P. (1975) *A területi fejlesztés: gazdaságfejlesztés. Területi fejlesztés a szocialista országokban* (Regional Development—Economic Development. Regional Development in the Socialist Countries), (Budapest: Közgazdasági és Jogi Könyvkiadó).

STARK, A. (1967) *A helyiipar Magyarországon* (Local Industry in Hungary), (Budapest: Kossuth Könyvkiadó).

SZABÓ, B. (1972) "A helyiipar fejlesztéséről, a kis- és középüzemek szükségességéről" (The Development of Local Industry, the Need for Small and Middle-Sized Plants), *Valóság,* no. 4: 9–21.

SZEGŐ, A. (1976) "A területi érdekviszonyok, a központosított újrafelosztás és a területi igazgatás" (Regional Interest Relationships, Centralized Redistribution and Regional Administration), *Szociológia,* no. 3–4: 420–442.

TATAI, Z. (1975) "Az ipar fejlődése falun" (Industrial Development in Villages), *Földrajzi Közlemények,* no. 3–4: 283–295.

TOWNROE, P. M. (1975) "Branch Plants and Regional Development", *Town Planning Review* 46, no. 1: 47–62.

TOWNROE, P. M. (1979) *Industrial Movement Experience in the US and the UK,* (Farnborough: Saxon House).

VÁGI, G. (1975) "'Mit ér' egy község; 'Mit ér' egy megye? (A tanácsi fejlesztések intézményi szerkezetéről)" (What is a 'village worth'? What is a 'county worth'? (On the Institutional Structure of Council Investments)), *Közgazdasági Szemle,* no. 7–8: 882–899.

NATIONAL POLICY
AND SETTLEMENTS IN PERI-URBAN REGIONS

OEDZGE A. L. C. ATZEMA AND THEO B. M. DIJKSTRA

KEY-WORDS: *compact* city; *concentrated* deconcentration; *interweaving* of rural and urban functions; *liveability; migration* balance; *policy* impact analysis, ~ of spreading, ~ of structuring, national ~, anti-suburbanization ~, restrictive ~; *regional* plans; *Report* on Rural Areas; *suburbanization; Urbanization* Report; *zoning.*

The Netherlands is a highly urbanized country. Besides four large cities (Amsterdam, Rotterdam, the Hague and Utrecht) there are many medium-sized cities. In the last 25 years, the most striking phenomenon of the urbanization process is deconcentration of city-population over the rural areas surrounding the cities. The peri-urban regions have a large population growth by in-migration of urban people, particularly from 1960 to 1975.

National policy, in general terms, is aimed at affecting spatial changes in order to minimize the prospective conflicts between spatial claims. The state, by means of mapping out objectives and making use of instruments to realize these objectives, directs structural changes in peri-urban rural areas. In the 1970s one could see a growing governmental concern in population changes of settlements in peri-urban regions. The main objective from the beginning was the reduction of residential suburbanization.

In the research on the governmental influence on the spatial structure, one can discriminate between the evaluation of the policy and the effects of policy. By the evaluation of the policy is meant the manner in which the objectives are mapped out, the justification of the objectives, how objectives are translated into instruments for the realization of the formulated objectives. In the research of the effects of policy, objectives and instruments are seen as data and what matters is the research into the consequences of the governmental policy with regard to the spatial lay-out of the areas with which the policy deals. In this article we shall confine ourselves to the effects of the national government's policy with respect to the dispersion and population growth of settlements in peri-urban regions. Our contribution deals with policy impact analysis. The framework of the article is limited and the analysis is primarily descriptive. A broader approach is necessary to measure policy effectiveness, one which not only measures the degree to which the policy goals have been reached, but which also examines the means employed in the light of the formulated goals and evaluates the theoretical possibility as to whether the selected means can reach the intended effect (Glasbergen and Simonis 1979).

In the Dutch case, there are three interconnected policy levels (national, provincial and municipal). Policy impact analysis takes into account the interdependency of the three policy levels as well as the specific possibilities of each level separately. We shall restrict ourselves to the national policy level.

Firstly, we shall discuss the formulation of objectives in national reports. We shall look at both the Urbanization Report (1976) and the Report on Rural Areas (1977), as well as the so-called Orientation Report containing general policy objectives. Secondly, we shall deal with the influence of national policy on regional administrations. We shall trace to what degree national objectives have been transferred to regional plans made after 1976. Moreover, differences of opinion on the proposed settlement policy have been examined on the basis of the notes of the discussions between the national government and two regional administrations. Concrete form has been given to this settlement policy by influencing regional migration streams and concentration of population growth in one or more places within peri-urban regions. This is why we shall dicuss the course of both, in the third part of our article, illustrated with migration and population figures for the period 1976–1981.

National policy

In the mid-1970s, the government underlined the planning for the quality of life. The emphasis on well-being implies that for small rural settlements a policy be focussed on the improvement, or at least the maintenance, of liveability. It was assumed that the liveability of settlements in peri-urban regions was in danger because of the extensive in-migration of people from the cities. In the operationalization of the concept of 'liveability' by Groot (1972), this boils down to the fast extension of the physical living environment/built-up environment (new building tumours) and the interference of the social living milieu through tensions between autochthones and allochthones. One can wonder whether such a relationship is real, particularly with regard to this last aspect. Recent research points out that one has to guard against a too determined relationship between population growth and social disintegration. The growth rate appears to be of little importance for the integration of autochthones and newcomers (Ostendorf and Vijgen 1982).

However, the main arguments in support of the anti-suburbanization policy refer to the many negative consequences of suburbanization for the cities. So, with respect to peri-urban regions, there is a mutual coherence between spatial developments in urban and rural areas. The national government has, however, made a conscious distinction regarding the objects of physical planning between urban areas on the one hand (the Urbanization Report in 1976) and rural ones on the other (the Report on Rural Areas in 1977). The reason for this distinction—the rough scope of the policy-items at hand—is of a practical nature. The distinction has been generally accepted even though there are warnings from the political and scientific world against a separate treatment of problems in both types of areas. Information from both reports are required to describe the national policy on peri-urban regions.

In the policy for rural areas, a zoning of the Netherlands is prominent, a zoning based primarily on the quality of landscape. Within these zones, a choice is made for separation or interweaving of urban and (mainly) rural functions (agriculture, nature, recreation). In naming the peri-urban area in the spatial national policy, two categories of districts must, in our opinion, be distinguished politically: firstly, at the level of city-regions, the areas with non-urban use of land within an urban influence and, secondly, on a national level, the open areas and the areas tending to become densely populated.

The policy of structuring in city regions is aimed at preserving living conditions—for example, by means of urban renewal—in the urban areas, a concentration of the growth of population and restriction of mobility. The concentration of the growth of population concerns the central towns of the city regions and, if this is not feasible, a concentration in growth centres.

The policy of structuring for rural areas within an urban influence is directed at interweaving the functions of urbanization and those of agriculture and nature. The rural areas near towns must be structured in such a way that a halt is called to the many threats to these rural areas but, at the same time, the utility of green space needs to be enhanced for the inhabitants of the towns.

Besides the rural areas, within the (especially morphological) urban influence, the open areas and the areas with a strong population growth (because of a large positive in-migration) can be called peri-urban areas. Open areas have already been mentioned in the Second Report (1966). These are rural areas at a national level for which it is considered wise not to include them in urbanization and for which, to counter this process of urbanization, rural functions must be intensified. The policy of structuring for open areas depends on zoning. Depending on the zone code, either the separation of functions—for example, mainly agriculture or mainly nature—or their interweaving is emphasized. The policy of spreading is formalized in the choice between concentration or spreading of the

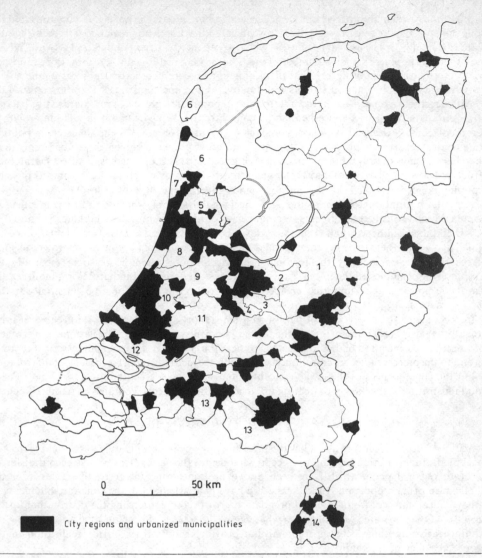

City regions and urbanized municipalities

1 Veluwe
2 Gelderse Vallei
3 Utrechtse Heuvelrug
4 Kromme Rijnstreek
5 Droogmakerijen/Waterland

6 Kop van Noord-Holland
7 Noord-Kennemerland
8 Haarlemmermeer
9 Utrechts-Zuid-Hollands Veengebied
10 Kleine Ring

11 Waardengebied
12 Voorne-Putten/Hoekse Waard
13 Kempen
14 Zuid-Limburg

FIGURE 3 *Peri-urban rural areas in the national policy*

population growth in the areas in question. The realization of both the policy of structuring and the policy of spreading is generally left to the provincial authorities who formulate it in their regional plans. Generally, this is also valid for areas which experienced a strong population growth. Within the categories of policy stated, a number of areas have been mentioned where strict conditions are set for further elaboration in regional plans. These areas are chosen on the basis of the state's responsibility for coherent policy of distribution over urban and rural areas. These directives—the so-called restrictive policy—comprise a restriction of population growth (a zero or negative balance of migration in the district concerned) and a concentration of the district's population growth in certain places to be designated in the regional plan. The directives are presented as essential political statements, that is to say provincial administrations are expected to implement them. There are no coercive measures to prevent these directives being neglected because there is no direct hierarchical structure between the national spatial plans and those of the province. If the state wants its physical planning policy to be carried out it must convince governments at a lower level by well-founded arguments; it cannot enforce measures. We consider these areas, which tend to become densely populated, and so-called 'open' areas, as the peri-urban regions in the Netherlands (Figure 3).

For all these regions, it is valid that the state authority advocated a restrictive population policy aimed at a zero or negative migration balance and at concentration of population growth in some places to be determined by the regional authorities. For pragmatic reasons (especially the restructuring of municipalities in 1982), we will not consider Southern Limburg. For some areas, the restrictive policy is also supported on the basis of natural or scenic quality (materially spatial characteristics).

In 1983 the national government published a new report about the policy on urban areas. No great differences were found in it from the former policy just mentioned. The national government stresses the concentration of developments in or near the cities. The national policy set out to make an end to the process of deconcentration. An amazing aspect of the report is the lack of information about the consequences of the urban concentration policy on (peri-)urban regions. This seems a good illustration of the danger of treating urban and rural problems separately in national reports.

National—provincial policy

National ideas concerning the policy of spreading must be realized mainly in regional plans and local plans. In this section we want to trace to what degree the national ideas have been transferred to those regional plans which have been drawn up concerning the restrictive areas after the publication of the Report on Rural Areas. We have paid attention to the concrete statements of policy concerning the size of regional population growth and concerning the distribution of this growth. At the same time we shall see to what degree differences of opinion have arisen during the administrative meetings between national and provincial authorities on the realization of the proposed policy of spreading.

First we looked at whether the regional plans refer to the national policy concerning the dispersion of population in rural areas. Only in a very small number of cases did we find references to the restrictive policy advocated by the national authorities. On the basis of this knowledge it seems justifiable to say that the provincial authorities emphasize the specifically regional problems and solutions in drawing up their regional plans and pay little attention to the directive of the 'higher' national authorities. The remaining three items pertaining to our analysis deal with the contents of policy. Generally speaking, it appears from the latter that the political intentions of the national authorities have become the common property of the provincial plans.

(1) In most regional plans, the policy is in accordance with the restrictive policy of the Report on Rural Areas with respect to the reduction of net migration to a zero or negative level.

(2) In all regional plans, places of concentration have been allocated. At this point, the overlap between urbanization policy and rural area policy, mentioned in the last section, becomes

prominent. Several of the places mentioned in the regional plans are situated in city regions and urbanized municipalities. Thus they do not belong to the rural areas as is mentioned in the Report of Rural Areas. The places of concentration have already been mentioned in the Report on Rural Areas (Part 3A, p. 87) where it is stated that they need not be situated in the restrictive regions. Also, as a result of this division in which most remaining (rural) municipalities are considered as one group, one can hardly speak of a policy aimed at the concentration of population growth within rural areas.

(3) With respect to population growth allowed in small places it is significant that, although a restriction of growth is advocated in all regional plans, the definition of the increase of housing allowed differs in each area. In the demographic definition of the increase allowed (constant population, increase equal to natural increase) and in the definition on the basis of the supply and demand of houses different criteria are used in the regional plans.

We have also traced the transfer of national policy to regional policy in another way. The national and provincial authorities discussed the Report on Rural Areas in 1978. One of the items of discussion was the policy of dispersion as it had been proposed. Looking at the discussions between the state and the province of Zuid-Holland which seems to differ from the restrictive policy in the Report on Rural Areas, and the province of Noord-Brabant which seems to agree with the national policy, there appears to be no difference of opinion—that is so say theoretically—on the dispersion policy to be executed. The only item of discussion is the manner in which the policy should be realized. The provinces assume that there is a need for a general directive concerning the distribution of houses while the national authorities are of the opinion that there are sufficient possibilities within the limits of the present legislation and, moreover, that there is no need for a general directive on a national level because the situation is different in each municipality or in each province.

Population growth in peri-urban regions 1976–1981

The restrictive policy in the Report on Rural Areas in the peri-urban regions set out to reduce population growth by the diminution of urban in-migration. Considering the coherence between national policy and population changes in peri-urban regions we have made a review concerning population growth in the years 1976–1981. Figure 4 shows the annual average population growth in 1976–1981 for the peri-urban regions and in Figure 5 the share of migration within total population growth has been shown.

There is no general tendency for the peri-urban rural areas as a whole. Some areas still have strong population growth. On the other hand one region (Noord-Kennemerland) showed a light decrease of population. There are regions with a strong positive net migration and regions with a negative or very small positive net migration. In spite of the clustering of the peri-urban areas in 7 larger regions (Table 4), the differences still exist. There are peri-urban regions where the net migration has risen strongly in the last three years.

At first sight there is little coherence between national policy and population growth in peri-urban regions. In order to get a better view of the developments in migration we have distinguished the out-migration and in-migration for 1976 and 1981 and we have looked at the origin of the in-migrants and the destination of the out-migrants. For the sake of clarity we have united the figures of all the peri-urban rural areas (namely the first 13 regions of Figure 3). Before we try to get some conclusions from these figures, some explanation will be necessary on the basis of an example. In 1976, 77,882 people settled in the 13 peri-urban rural areas. 28% of them originated from a rural area, exclusive of those migrating within one of the 13 peri-urban rural areas.

Moreover, as background information, we can mention that in 1976, 42.3% of the total population lived in rural areas, 50.3% in city regions and 7.4% in urbanized municipalities. In 1981, these percentages were 43.3, 49 and 7.7 respectively. From Figure 6 it is clear that the in-migration

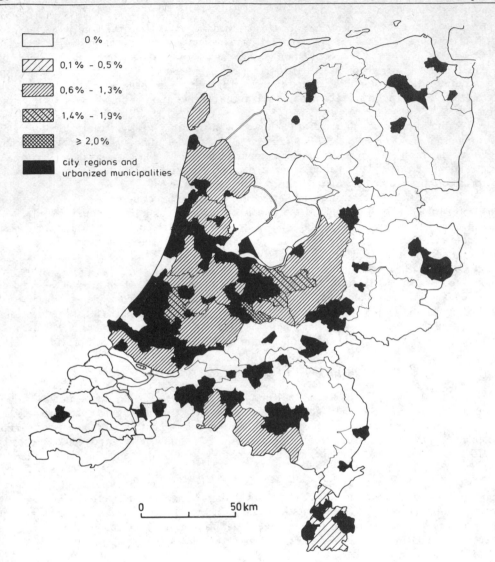

FIGURE 4 *Annual average population growth 1976–1981*

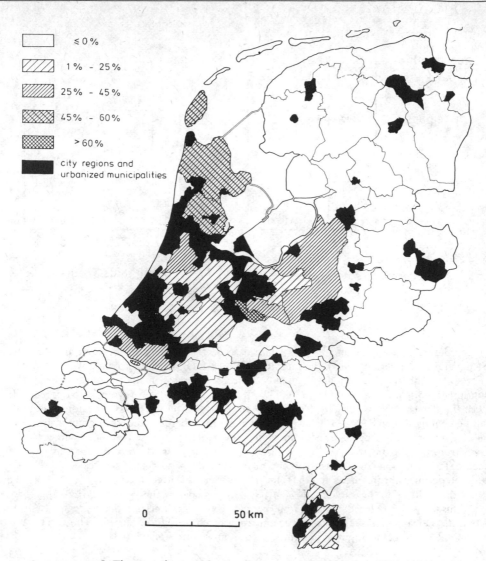

FIGURE 5 *The contribution of migration to population growth 1976–1981*

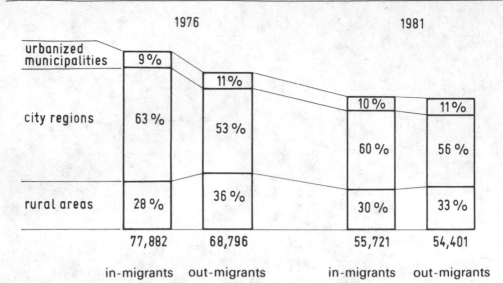

FIGURE 6 *Migration in peri-urban rural areas*
(excluding foreign migration)

to, and the out-migration from, the peri-urban areas decreased, the latter however at a slower rate. At the end of the period (1981), the migration for the total peri-urban region was balanced.

In spite of the two former developments, little has changed in the statistical distribution of migrants by origin/destination. In 1976, 63% of the in-migrants came from city regions while in 1981, this percentage was 60%. In 1976, 53% of the out-migrants left for a city region while in 1981, this percentage was 56%. Nevertheless, the flow of migrants between the peri-urban rural areas and the city regions has changed strongly. In 1976, 13,000 more people settled in the peri-urban rural areas from city regions than vice versa; in 1981, the figure was reduced to approximately 3,000 people. The migration flows between the city regions and the peri-urban rural areas are mostly those between peri-urban rural areas and the four big city regions (Utrecht, Amsterdam, the Hague and Rotterdam). In 1976, the outgoing flow surpassed the incoming flow by nearly 12,000 people. In 1981, this figure was reduced to nearly 2,500 people. Both migration from the city region to the peri-urban rural areas and migration between rural areas has been reduced sharply. This can be seen by looking at the place of origin of migrants to rural areas in 1976 and 1981.

Concentration of population growth

In Holland there is no national registration of the population change per settlement. Only censuses (the last one was held in 1971) give national information on the numbers of inhabitants per settlement. This is why use has been made of figures per municipality.

The degree of concentration is expressed in the concentration index of population growth between January, 1, 1976 and January 1, 1982. The index is the quotient of percentage population growth per municipality and percentage population growth of the region. Since a small number of municipalities per region have only a limited information value on their own, some of the peri-urban rural areas have been joined together (see the seven districts in Table 4). The municipal concentration indices have been mapped out in Figure 7. The concentration municipalities featuring in the regional policy and located in the rural regions cannot clearly be recognized by high

TABLE 4

NET MIGRATION 1976–78 AND 1979–81 (INCLUDING FOREIGN MIGRATION)

		1976–78	1979–81
1.	Veluwe/Gelderse Vallei	5,014	7,551
2.	Kromme Rijnstreek/Utrechtse Heuvelrug	904	3,247
3.	Kop van Noord-Holland	8,455	– 41
4.	Noord-Kennemerland/Waterland	3,565	901
5.	Utrechts-Zuidholland Veengebied/Kleine Ring/Waardengebied	2,144	1,330
6.	Voorne-Putten/Hoekse Waard	1,185	1,120
7.	Kempen	806	– 109

concentration indices. On the other hand, there are various municipalities with concentration above 200 which have not been specified in the policy. Concerning the concentration municipalities referred to in the policy and situated outside the rural regions, those that have been especially designated as growth centres in the national urbanization policy have shown remarkable growth (for instance Hellevoetsluis with 83%, Spijkenisse 50% and Hoorn 46%).

On the basis of this development, it can be concluded that the principle of concentrated deconcentration on a level that extends beyond the borders of the rural regions—thus including the growth municipalities within urban regions—is effective as far as the concentration of population growth is concerned. Whether this also implies a concentration of suburbanization cannot be concluded from this material. However, considering the results from Figure 6, it can be expected to be the case. The urban regions contain more inhabitants than in previous periods. One can hardly speak of concentration of population growth in rural regions, at least according to the lines that have been laid down in the regional plans. An explanation for this development can be found in the inertia of the regional housing programming. The regional plans drawn up relatively recently reflect a policy that will be implemented not earlier than during the 1980s. The municipal local plans contain housing programmes that have been drawn up in a previous period and that cannot be drastically reduced from one day to the next by drawing up a regional plan. In this sense, the analysed period cannot be seen as indicative of quantifying the effectiveness of policy on the concentration of population growth.

Conclusions

The restrictive policy of the national government was at one time defended on the basis of assumed problems in cities and rural regions that are caused by extensive suburbanization. This line, in the present revision of the urbanization policy, is extended by the inclusion of the concept of the compact city. The arguments for the rural regions are within the fields of protection of ecological and natural values, reduction of mobility and the maintenance of the 'liveability' in rural settlements. This final arguments originates from a relationship between the settlement of numerous new-comers and the decrease in 'liveability' in rural settlements. It is unwise to proclaim an urban concentration policy without considering the consequences of this policy for peri-urban regions.

It is not clear whether the concentration policy is a reinforcement of the restrictive policy in peri-urban regions or if it makes that policy superfluous. If the return of ex-city dwellers to the cities is the aim, one should take into account its consequences for the places in the peri-urban areas. The matters must be clarified in a revision of the structural outline plan for rural areas. However, the revised plan will not be published before 1988.

What about the effectiveness of national policy on the settlements in peri-urban regions? The goals of national policy are adopted by regional authorities. There is some discussion about how to realize the dispersion policy. The results of the policy, with regard to population growth and

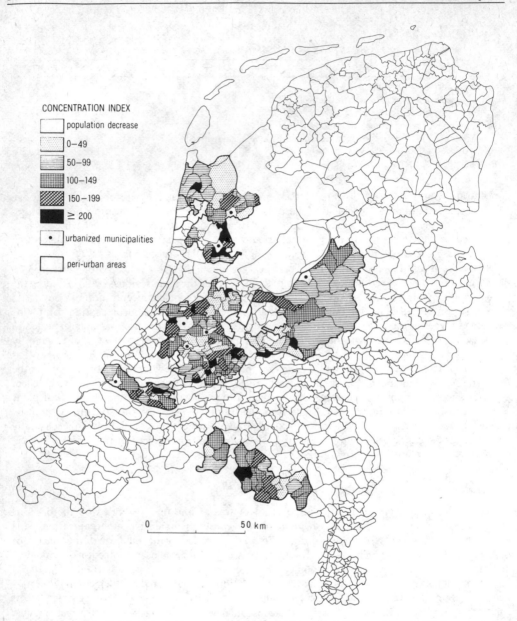

FIGURE 7 *Municipal concentration indices of population growth 1976–1981*

population concentration, are not clear. There remain peri-urban areas with a high net in-migration. On the level of large urban regions, including peri-urban regions, there is a concentration in accordance with the urbanization policy. The peri-urban regions as such are too small for a concentration since the policy is aimed at enabling the autochthonous population and the socio-economically committed population to live in all places. With regard to a decrease of suburbanization, such a policy option implies that there is hardly any scope for concentration in the future. It is clear that the future developments are directly linked with developments in the (free) housing market. At present, many rural municipalities are experiencing more and more difficulties in setting aside houses for the autochthonous people because of the collapse of the expensive free housing market. Moreover, cities are favoured in the distribution of the ever-diminishing quotas of social housing in connection with the urban concentration policy. One might think that the scales have been tipped in favour of the cities. In former days there was little policy, so that the peri-urban areas were growing too quickly; at the moment there is such a strong concentration policy that the peri-urban regions may not able to provide housing for their autochthonous population.

Bibliography

GLASBERGEN, P.—SIMONIS, J. B. D. (1979) *Ruimtelijk beleid in de verzorgingsstaat; Onderzoek naar een beschouwing over de (on)mogelijkheid van een nationaal ruimtelijk beleid in Nederland* (Spatial Policy in the Welfare-State; Study of a Contemplation on the (Im)Possibility of a National Spatial Policy in the Netherlands), (Amsterdam: Kobra).

GROOT, J. P. (1972) *Kleine plattelandskernen in de Nederlandse samenleving* (Small Rural Communities in the Dutch Society), (Wageningen: Veenman).

NOTA LANDELIJKE GEBIEDEN (1977) (Report on Rural Areas), ('s-Gravenhage, Staatsuitgeverij).

ORIËNTERINGSNOTA (1973) (Orientation Report), ('s-Gravenhage, Staatsuitgeverij).

OSTENDORF, W. J. M.—VIJGEN, J. "Segregatie en sociale integratie. De spreiding van bevolking binnen dynamische stadsgewesten" (Segregation and Social Integration. The Distribution of Population within Dynamic Metropolitan Areas), *Geografisch Tijdschrift* 16, no. 4: 368–380.

STRUCTUURSCHETS VOOR DE STEDELIJKE GEBIEDEN (1983) (Structural Outline Sketch for the Urban Regions), ('s-Gravenhage: Staatsuitgeverij).

VERSTEDELIJKINGSNOTA (1976) (Urbanization Report), ('s-Gravenhage: Staatsuitgeverij).

THE BUDAPEST AGGLOMERATION

Changing Spatial Connections Between Home and Workplace

BÉLA SÁRFALVI

KEY-WORDS: *agglomeration* zone; *attraction* zone of the capital; *commuting; concentrations* of workplaces and residences; *disintegration* of place of residence and of work; *drop* in local jobs; *employment re-stratification; industrialization; industrial* jobs; *labour* force, ~ supply; *large-scale* farming; *multicentric* structure; *new* employment centres; *peri-urban* ring; *regional* subcentres; *satellite* settlements; *settlement* network pattern; *spatial* pattern, ~ sprawl, stages of ~ expansion; *suburban* ring, ~ settlements, ~ zone; *transport* facilities.

(i) The literature on the Budapest agglomeration has grown richer during the past decades. These works represent a quantitative growth; at the same time, the scope of the disciplines exploring the processes of change taking place in the agglomeration has also broadened considerably. An especially great number of studies have been published in urban planning, sociology and economics, investigating primarily the development and spatial sprawl of the agglomeration; the relations between the central town core and the suburban ring; migration processes; and the impact the changes in the Budapest agglomeration have had on population's lifestyle. As a result of the research carried out so far, we have come to some understanding of the main features of the development, of spatio-structural changes in the whole region, but further investigations of the expanded settlements network of the various elements of the agglomeration, and of the qualitative changes are still needed. The aim of the present paper is to describe the process, and to identify the causes which have contributed to the emergence of the new tendencies within the capital's agglomeration ring, and to outline the modifications of the raltionships between the various settlements.

(ii) The Budapest agglomeration started to develop about 100 years ago. Four characteristic stages of spatial expansion can be distinguished during this period:
—from the beginning to 1950;
—from 1950 to the mid-1960s;
—from the mid-1960s to the mid-1970s;
—from the mid-1970s to our days.

PRE-1950 PERIOD

In the last quarter century, a suburban ring began to develop around the core town of the time, i.e. within the contemporary administrative borders. As a consequence of rapid industrialization, industrial enterprises in need of space settled on the outskirts; concurrently with this process, the housing estates of the continuously arriving labour force also concentrated here, where plot prices were much lower than within the capital. The external ring of the agglomeration took an increasingly definite shape: large concentrations of workplaces and residences were formed both in the north and south, mainly along the Danube. Of these concentrations, seven settlements developed into independent towns during the first half of the century. Seven new housing settlements went up a little farther from the Danube, each of them on what was then the eastern fringe of the city. Nine old agricultural settlements comprised the third part of the contiguous suburban ring: more and more industrial workers from remote settlements settled here to commute to their workplaces in the capital.

1950 TO THE MID-1960S

The suburban ring had developed by stages along with the capital, both the workplace concentrations and the housing estates, to become almost an organic part of Budapest. The internal ring of the agglomeration was, thus, merged with the capital in 1950: there were now 22 districts instead of the previous 14. The external agglomeration zone remained outside the new boundaries of the enlarged Budapest administrative area; population concentration continued here at an accelerated pace. The pace of in-migration to the areas which joined the capital in 1950 was more modest: this was due partly to administrative regulations, partly to restrictions on the sub-division of the existing lots and on their sale, all of which made for a rapid increase in lot prices.

In the new wave of industrialization of the 1950s, the labour force demand of the capital had to be met from ever farther a field. The occupational mobility of the former agricultural population of the commuting ring settlements accelerated, as people in great numbers were funnelled into industrial and service sectors located in the capital. The additional labour force coming from more distant agricultural areas also accumulated in these suburban settlements, so that it was this agglomeration zone that experienced the most rapid population increase.

MID-1960S TO MID-1970S

The deconcentration of the capital's industry has come into the limelight since the mid-1960s. As a result, the new industrial job concentrations were located in the external ring of the agglomeration, and the increase in industrial employment in Budapest slowed down. However, the majority of new concentrations were closely connected to the capital, and labour force movement continued to be centripetal: the workplace concentrations became more sprawling, as a result of decentralization, but that was all (Figure 8). As a matter of fact, the new employment centres did not narrow the attraction zone of the capital, but provided for their labour force needs from more distant regions, thus expanding the area in which the agglomeration had a suction effect considerably.

MID-1970S TO THE PRESENT

Satellite settlements continued to grow and increase in the agglomeration region, and there was an acceleration in the development of regional subcentres on the fringe of the attraction zone. Industrial jobs were located in local centres which performed significant service functions, too (Figure 9). As a consequence, the old monocentric agglomeration was gradually replaced by a multicentric structure. But however great the development of the centres around the capital was, it did not reach that of the capital, and it only contributed to a change in manpower flow within the agglomeration region. The local centres have had two conspicuous effects: new workplace concentrations on the outskirts have made for a modest out-commuting from Budapest to its environs; and the labour force supply of the employment centres within the capital has reached a new phase. There has been a slight decrease in the number of workers commuting to Budapest during the last decade, though the commuters now fill a larger proportion of the available jobs because of the overall reduction in the industrial jobs in the capital. Concurrently, some new tendencies in the spatial structure of the capital's labour force attraction have become evident. While the rate of commuting from a number of settlements on the outskirts has grown, the great majority of them being clearly dormitory settlements, there has been a drop in the rate and number of workers commuting to Budapest from those satellite settlements in which new workplaces have

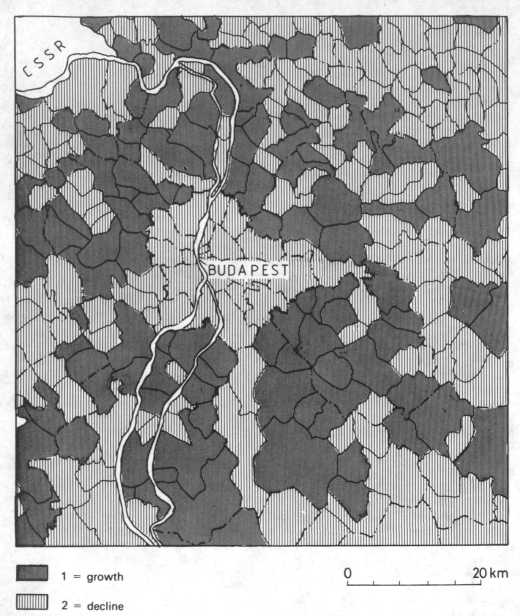

1 = growth
2 = decline

0   20 km

FIGURE 8 *Change in the number of workplaces
in the Budapest agglomeration 1970–1980*

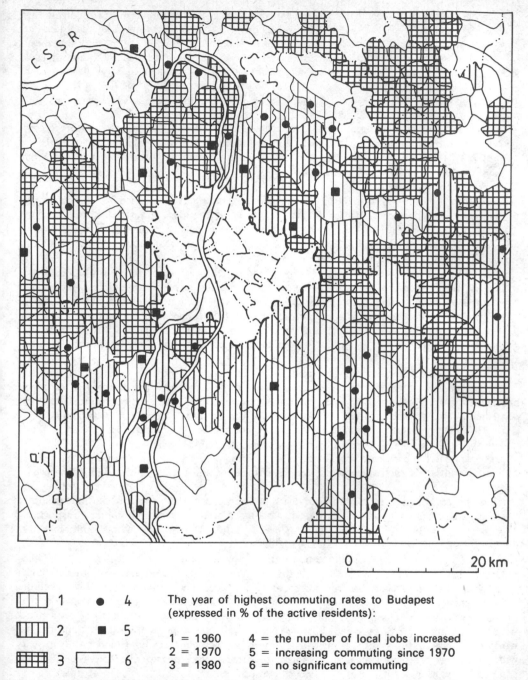

0   20 km

1	● 4		
2	■ 5		
3	6		

The year of highest commuting rates to Budapest
(expressed in % of the active residents):

1 = 1960   4 = the number of local jobs increased
2 = 1970   5 = increasing commuting since 1970
3 = 1980   6 = no significant commuting

FIGURE 9 *Change in the intensity of commuting and the number of local jobs*
in the Budapest agglomeration

been concentrated (Figure 9). These new local centres offer a wide range of jobs requiring high quality labour and have relatively favourable transport facilities; thus, they can compete successfully with the capital's attraction. As a consequence, the possibility of meeting Budapest's labour force demand from the local centres zone has considerably lessened, and the commuting field of the capital has been enlarged substantially from the mid-1970s, which involves an increase of travel time for the long-distance commuters to the capital. At present, some 6% of the workers commuting to Budapest arrive from 70 distant settlements. In 1960, these same settlements had no or very few commuters to Budapest.

(iii) While the overall number of commuters to Budapest has decreased somewhat during the past decade, in the outer ring of the capital which includes more than 200 settlements, the number of commuters has grown, by 50%! On the national scale, an increasing proportion of the active population living in rural settlements commutes to work. At the same time, population has decreased in the majority of these settlements.

Two complex developments in the Hungarian economy have played a particularly important role in shaping the settlement network pattern of the last decades: industrialization, and the establishment of socialist large-scale farming. More or less concurrent developments, they have contributed to the radical abolition of the traditional spatial unity of the place of work and of residence, and have had mutually reinforcing effects.

The rapid, and for quite some time extensive, industrialization involved the multiplication of industrial employment. Although more and more regions have become industrialized, the traditional industrial centres have preserved their leading role, and industrial jobs continue to concentrate in a relatively narrow area. During the three decades between 1949 and 1980, industry absorbed as many as 1,300,000 agricultural workers. Large-scale, technologically advanced farming neither needs nor attracts the masses of the rural labour force, to say nothing here of the difficulties that attended socialist collectivization in agriculture.

Due to this rapid employment re-stratification, the number of jobs in rural settlements has decreased by half on an average. The spatial unity of residence and the place of work which characterized rural settlements in the past has disintegrated, and has undermined the rural settlements' ability to retain their populations. The drastic drop in local jobs which took place during a short period of time has had a quick and effective response.

The challenge has been answered by rural settlements in three basic ways:

(a) settlements have increased local labour opportunities by providing for non-agricultural, i.e. industrial and service, activities on the cooperative farms, and by launching affiliated industrial projects;

(b) settlements have been able to preserve a significant part of their population if industrialized centres or the developing job concentrations were made accessible through public transport;

(c) people have been obliged to migrate if neither local job opportunities were improved nor adequate transport facilities were made available.

Naturally, the above three possible responses never appear in any given settlement as pure types, but combined; however, in every case one of them generally comes to dominate. We can distinguish three types of rural settlements according to which one does. Their distribution shows a definite spatial pattern taken all in all. The majority of the settlements where local jobs could be stabilized or increased were located along the important transport lines. A large proportion of the settlements with a commuting rate of over 50% for the economically active population lay around the big workplace concentrations. Settlements with a diminishing population can be found mainly in areas with poor transport facilities; or, where adequate transport facilities are available, then they are situated in the neighbourhood of underdeveloped centres.

Although the tensions resulting from the far-reaching disintegration of place of residence and of work have lessened gradually, in different ways and to different degrees in the various regions, some new contradictions have come into being as a result:

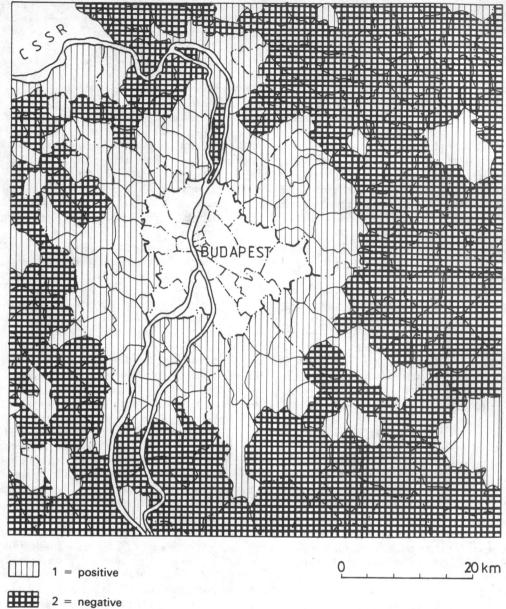

☐☐☐☐ 1 = positive

▦▦▦ 2 = negative

FIGURE 10 *Net migration in the Budapest agglomeration 1960–1980*

(a) the urban settlement network is too uneven to act as a catalyst for regional development, even important centres proved to be unable to satisfy the demands of their rural hinterlands (lack of jobs, housing and services);

(b) local workplace development in rural settlements has been realized at a very slow pace, due mainly to their lack of an independent economic administration, but also to the negative effects of migration (e.g. the young and educated population has left);

(c) insufficiently developed transport networks between the centres and their atraction areas have not been able to insure smooth socio-economic interactions.

(iv) In the environs of Budapest, rural settlements have also developed in one of the three ways mentioned above:

(a) In settlements no more than 15 to 20 km distant from the capital, the population keeps growing; but the larger the distance, the more modest the population increase. Growth has been especially rapid in the peri-urban ring close to the Budapest administrative border. This ring includes settlements with considerable local job concentrations and good transport conditions used by 50 to 60% of the active residents to commute to their workplaces in Budapest. There is a continuously increasing commuting rate of the active residents in the dormitory settlements; while in the majority of settlements that have increased the number of local jobs, there has been a drop in the rate of commuting to work to Budapest since 1970. In satellite settlements within the region of agglomeration with significant job concentration, commuting to the capital has been decreasing, and to local centres has been rapidly increasing since 1960. Settlements of this inner ring had positive net commuting in 1960 and 1980.

(b) Settlements with a stagnating population do not constitute a contiguous ring outside the 20 km zone. Equilibrium could be established only by more extensive commuting on the part of their active population partly towards the capital, partly to the minor local centres. In this area, the proportion of commuters has increased continuously. A few settlements could be mentioned which have increased local employment opportunities to a modest extent. Settlements with a stagnating population, almost without exception, closed the period between 1960 and 1980 with a migration loss (Figure 10).

(c) The majority of the settlements situated in the most external ring have a decreasing population, and only a very few have been able to stabilize, let alone increase, their population. Their net migration is also negative, but out-migration has been able to lessen local employment tensions only in part; increasing commuting became dominant. This zone also includes settlements where the number of commuters to the capital has been growing rapidly during the last decade, despite the long distances. This is due to the lack of adequate job opportunities in the minor centres situated much closer. Nevertheless, this situation is probably transitional, and would change rapidly in case of the spatial modification of jobs.

(v) Until the mid-1970s, population growth in the agglomeration ring around Budapest was wave-like a process well-known elsewhere as well, starting from the city centre and progressing towards the periphery. Until the last third of the past century, it was in the historical city that the population increased the most; from then on, outstanding growth was realized in the surrounding fringes which constitute the outer districts of Budapest nowadays. Population increase in the suburban ring settlements around the present administrative borders of Budapest has accelerated gradually. Between the two World Wars, it surpassed the city's growth rate, and, from the 1950, it has even surpassed the rate of population growth in the outer districts of the capital. At present, the inner suburban zone of the agglomeration, adjacent to the border of the capital, can be considered the most rapidly growing zone where population concentration is based not so much on the attraction of workplaces in the capital, as on the rapidly developing satellite settlements of the agglomeration region.

Bibliography

BERNÁT, T.—VISZKEI, M. (eds.) (1972) *Budapest társadalmának és gazdaságának száz éve* (Hundred Years of Budapest's Social and Economic Life), (Budapest: Közgazdasági és Jogi Könyvkiadó—Kossuth Könyvkiadó).

DARÓCZI, E. (1984) "The Population Dynamics of Functional Urban Regions in Hungary, 1870–1980". In: *Geographical Essays in Hungary*, 1984 (eds.: Enyedi, Gy.—Pécsi, M.), (Budapest: IGU Hungarian National Committee—Geographical Research Institute): 69–86.

ENYEDI, GY. (1980) *Falvaink sorsa* (The Prospects of Our Villages), (Budapest: Magvető Kiadó).

SÁRFALVI, B. (1981) "The Budapest Agglomeration", *Annales Geogr. Universitatis de Roland Eötvös* B. XIII.: 62–79.

VÖRÖSMARTI-TAJTI, E. (1971) "A munkahely és a lakóhely közötti térbeli kapcsolat alakulásának tendenciái a budapesti agglomerációban" (Tendencies in the Spatial Link between the Place of Work and the Place of Residence in the Budapest Agglomeration), *Földrajzi Értesítő* 20, no. 2: 131–151.

POPULATION GROWTH
AND SETTLEMENT PATTERN
IN THE GREEN HEART
OF THE RANDSTAD

HANS VAN GINKEL

KEY-WORDS: *autochthonous* people; *desurbanization; Green* Heart area; *housing,* non-subsidized
~, social ~, subsidized ~; *maxurbanization; population concentration,* evolution of ~;
Randstad, ~ ringform, urban ring of ~; *ruralization; rurban* stayers; *rurbanization; suburban*
movers; *suburbanization,* dispersed ~, genuine ~, hidden ~, planned ~, real ~, residential ~,
stages of ~.

Introduction

After an initial period of post-war reconstruction and growth of the large cities, suburbanization developed widely in the Netherlands, reaching its peak in the late 1960s and early 1970s. In some of the large cities in the western part of the country, negative net migration even exceeded natural growth by that time. The three largest agglomerations (Amsterdam, Rotterdam, the Hague) entered the stage of desurbanization (Klaassen 1979), as population losses in the respective central cities exceeded population gains in the remainder of these agglomerations.

The widespread suburbanization was favoured by the modest size of the country, the high population and settlement density and the excellent transport facilities which make relative distances really short. This was particularly true in the Green Heart area (Figure 11), surrounded as it is by the large cities of the Randstad. Since 1958, however, a major goal of Dutch government's spatial planning policy has been to prevent the development of a disorderly urban mess throughout this area. It has attempted to do so by:
—trying to limit the growth of the large cities on the Urban Ring of the Randstad, and to maintain greenbelts with a width of at least 4 km between these cities; and
—trying to preserve the central open area of the Randstad, the so-called Green Heart, as an agricultural and recreational area on a regional scale.
The efforts to set bounds to the population growth in both the large cities of the Urban Ring and the Green Heart implied the diversion of future population growth to outlying areas. Besides, in order to keep the Green Heart open, it was necessary to concentrate the population growth which occurred even then, mainly in existing urban municipalities, such as Gouda, Woerden, Alphen aan den Rijn, and in some 'new towns' like Zoetermeer, Nieuwegein and Houten (Borchert and van Ginkel 1979).

This contribution examines the relationships between population growth and settlement pattern in the Green Heart between 1960 and 1980. This seams the more interesting, even on an international level, not only because the Green Heart has been a keystone in Dutch spatial planning for such a long time, nor because of the small scale and the high population and settlement density of the area, nor because of the characteristic ringform of the Randstad, but particularly because the housing market in the Netherlands is largely government-controlled. In principle, this provides the government with a great opportunity to implement its own spatial planning policy.

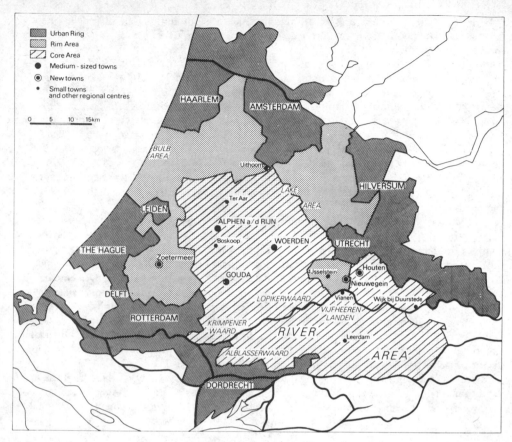

FIGURE 11 *The Green Heart in the Randstad*

In the following chapters, the population growth that has actually taken place in the Green Heart will be compared first with the theoretical stages in the evolution of population concentration as distinguished by Gibbs (1963). Then, some specific factors which favour suburbanization in the Netherlands and, more particularly, in the Green Heart will be investigated. Next, the processes leading to population growth in the area will be analysed and a comparison will be made between what are called the suburban movers and the rurban stayers. This means those people who were born outside and those who were born inside the Green Heart. When, in this way, more insight is given into the processes that have been going on, the attention will be focussed on the stages that can be distinguished in the population growth which occurred during the decades studied. In a concluding chapter, the relationship between population growth and settlement pattern in the Green Heart will be outlined and some planning implications will be explored.

The evolution of population concentration

In the process of concentration and deconcentration of the population that has been occurring in the western urban-industrial countries since the Industrial Revolution, J. P. Gibbs (1963, pp. 119 ff) theoretically distinguished five successive stages.

In the *first stage*, although cities were developing, the rural population was still growing at least as fast as the urban population. But, in the course of time, important improvements in the food and transport situation brought about an acceleration of the urban growth. This acceleration was realized through a growing rural—urban migration as well as the resulting migration-effect. In the *second stage*, the urban population was growing faster than the rural population.

In a *third stage*, the continuous drain of predominantly young people with a high fertility rate resulted in such a decline of the natural growth in the rural areas that the negative net migration was no longer compensated. As a consequence, the rural population declined in absolute numbers. Following this decline of the rural population, the rural—urban migration soon diminished as well. Therefore, in a *fourth stage*, a migration from the smaller towns, offering fewer opportunities, to the larger and eventually the largest cities developed instead (*maxurbanization*, cf. Ottens 1976, p. 79). As a consequence of this migration from small towns to large cities, these towns began to experience an absolute population decline. In the Netherlands this was generally the case in the second part of the 1950s.

In the course of time, however, the communication facilities improved so much that the process of maxurbanization came to an end before the whole population was concentrated in one large urban complex. In this *last stage*, a very high degree of concentration is no longer necessary to maintain all the advantages of large cities. New and diffuse patterns of population distribution, in which new growth and concentration points continuously emerge, come into existence. Eventually, this development results in an absolute decline of the population in the large cities and even in the large urban agglomerations as a whole, in favour of the contryside which, incidentally, loses part of its rural character through this process. Where, after the Industrial Revolution, rural areas some distance from the large cities were characterized by a negative net migration, these now begin to experience a surplus of arrivals over departures. In our country, this situation began to manifest itself during the 1960s and became the general rule in the 1970s (Table 5).

In view of the degree of detail with which Gibbs theoretically analysed the first stages in the evolution of population concentration, it seems appropriate to detail his fifth stage in the same way. At the very least, it seems desirable to differentiate between a *(fifth) stage* in which populatión loss is

TABLE 5

POPULATION IN THE CITIES OF THE URBAN RING AND IN
THE GREEN HEART OF THE RANDSTAD 1960–82

	Percentage of the population of the West			Population on January 1, 1982 (x1,000)
	1960	1970	1982	
1. Nine cities of the Urban Ring*	55	48	39	2,502
of which the four largest	45	39	31	1,958
2. Green Heart	13	15	20	1,293
of which the Rim Area	7	8	11	671
and the Core Area	6	7	10	622
The West** percentage	100	100	100	100
absolute (x1,000)	5,429	6,014	6,350	6,350

Source: Central Bureau of Statistics, the Netherlands
  * Nine cities of the Urban Ring: Amsterdam, Rotterdam, The Hague, Utrecht, Haarlem, Dordrecht, Leiden, Hilversum, Delft; the four largest: Amsterdam, Rotterdam, The Hague and Utrecht.
  ** The West: the provinces North Holland, South Holland and Utrecht.

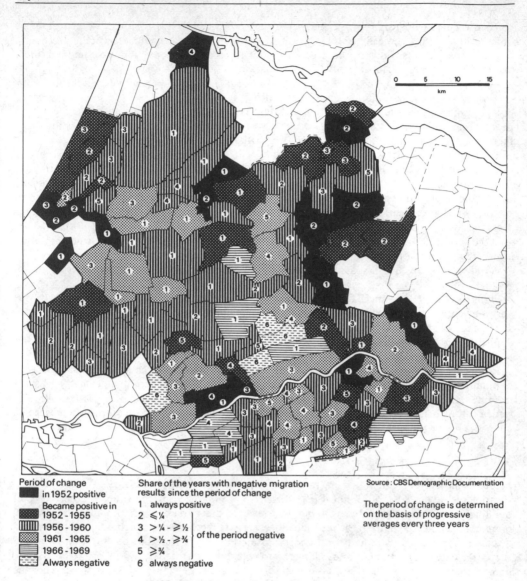

Period of change

in 1952 positive

Became positive in
1952 - 1955
1956 - 1960
1961 - 1965
1966 - 1969

Always negative

Share of the years with negative migration
results since the period of change

1 always positive
2 ≤ ¼
3 > ¼ - ≥ ½
4 > ½ - ≥ ¾   of the period negative
5 ≥ ¾
6 always negative

Source : CBS Demographic Documentation

The period of change is determined
on the basis of progressive
averages every three years

FIGURE 12 *Period in which the migration results changed
and continuity of the in-migration surpluses*

still outweighed by natural growth, and a *sixth stage* in which this is no longer so and in which mortality can even become higher than natality. Eventually, it could be further useful to distinguish a *seventh stage* in which not only the largest cities but also the smaller ones (in the Netherlands those having 50,000 to 100,000 inhabitants), lose population to the countryside. In this way, the nebulous structures, which Gottmann (1961, a.o. pp. 5 and 736) thought to be characteristic of the large urbanized areas of the future, begin to materialize.

But, just as the ultimate concentration in only very few large cities or even one true metropolis never came about, a complete dispersion of urban population is not likely. As cities are given increasing opportunities for renovation, they will again prove to be a desirable residential environment. In the process, their accessibility will remain an important advantage. In the meantime, it will become clear that the population in the countryside will not be evenly distributed. Instead, population growth will focus there in some nodes. The economic situation, government policy and population selection (e.g. concentration of single persons or families, older or younger people) will have a decisive influence on differential population growth patterns. For the Green Heart at least, it could be shown that:

—in the period 1950–69, various municipalities changed from a negative to a positive net migration at different points of time, and a few of them did not change at all (Figure 12);

—in only a few cases did the balance remain continuously positive after this change in migration (Figure 12);

—in the peak period of suburbanization (1960–76), the population growth in the Green Heart was very unevenly distributed between the various municipalities: it was concentrated in municipalities at the edge of the large cities and along highways, in medium-sized or small towns like Gouda, Alphen aan den Rijn, Vianen and Wijk bij Duurstede, and in 'new towns' like Zoetermeer and Nieuwegein.

From this evidence it can be tentatively concluded that there has been a relationship between population growth and settlement pattern in the Green Heart over the period under study. In some instances, the population growth has brought about modifications in the existing pattern. We will return to this matter in the concluding chapter. First, we will turn our attention to some specific factors favouring suburbanization in the Netherlands and, more particularly, in the Green Heart.

Special factors favouring suburbanization

It is a well-known fact that housing in the Netherlands is strongly controlled by the government. In principle, about 80% of all houses constructed are subsidized by the state. Furthermore, all building plans need official approval and they must be put into effect on building sites that are prepared by, and bought from the municipalities. Despite these regulations, the spatial patterns of dwellings constructed over the period under consideration have stimulated suburbanization to a very large extent. The number of dwellings constructed in the cities fell considerably short of the numbers needed. But, perhaps even more importantly, the large majority (about 80–90%) of the new dwellings in the cities came in the form of apartments. Given the population's outspoken preference for one-family terraced houses, a move out of the cities was to be expected. This expectation was based on the ample availability of these terraced houses in the small municipalities and their relatively low price; a consequence of the fact that the preparation of building sites and other infrastructural costs in these municipalities were considerably less than in the cities on the Urban Ring. The ringform of the Randstad, combined with the short distances and excellent transportation facilities, brought almost every municipality in the Green Heart within sub-urbanization distance (Figure 13). It should be kept in mind here that the ringform keeps the slow in-town traffic at a minimum, whereas the length of the city edge is maximized. At the same time, the necessary east—west and north—south connections between Utrecht and the Hague and between Amsterdam and Rotterdam open up a major part of the Green Heart to those travelling by private

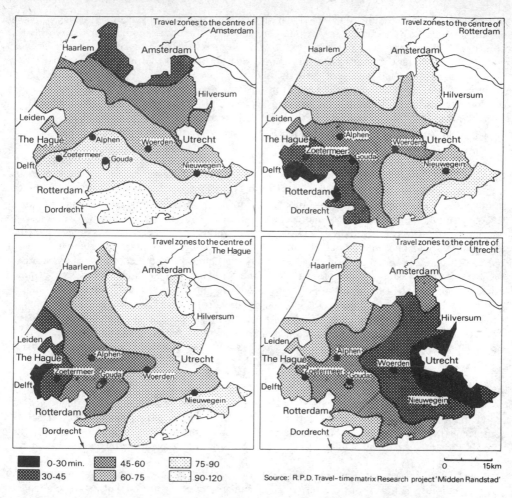

■ 0-30 min.	▨ 45-60	░ 75-90
▨ 30-45	▨ 60-75	░ 90-120

Source: R.P.D. Travel-time matrix Research project 'Midden Randstad'

0   15km

FIGURE 13 *Travel-time zones in the Green Heart*

car, as well as to those using public transport. Only a few municipalities, mainly for topographical reasons and especially in the Rivers Area, remained comparatively isolated. In some cases this was done deliberately—by not giving direct access to the highway system—so that these municipalities would retain their rural character. But, in general, the transportation network in the Green Heart is very well developed. And in view of the division of functions over the cities of the Urban Ring (for example, The Hague: seat of government; Amsterdam: commerce and banking; Rotterdam: port and industry) most enterprises have a strong preference for the Green Heart over the outlying areas, when they have to re-locate outside the central cities. In response to this general trend, many families looking for a suburban home prefer the Green Heart as well in order to reduce the daily journey to their workplaces.

The construction of relatively large numbers of the strongly-desired terraced houses in the 'green' in many small municipalities, quite in opposition to the officially agreed upon spatial planning policy, was possible for two reasons: *first* to be mentioned is the relative autonomy of the municipalities in the Netherlands and the wish of many municipal authorities to improve, or at least maintain, the social and commercial services present in their municipality, as well as to guarantee adequate housing to the autochthonous population. Under existing economic conditions a growing population is needed to maintain and improve services. To supply adequate housing for the autochthonous population, primarily low-cost (social) housing is needed because of the relatively low socio-economic status of this population. In the Netherlands' system, part of the cost of social housing is paid for by the owners of non-subsidized dwelling through land-pricing of the building sites prepared by the municipalities. Each social housing project, therefore, needs to be combined in some way with the construction of non-subsidized dwellings. Besides, in order to keep the loss of interest on land in the hands of the municipalities as low as possible, building sites have to be occupied as soon after their preparation as possible. As a consequence, the municipal authorities have frequently stimulated the arrival of allochthonous people. The predominance of housing interests over spatial planning interests is the *second* reason. In the late 1960s and early 1970s, in particular, there was not enough space within the urban municipalities to build the large quantities of dwellings needed, certainly not in the form of terraced houses. Besides, in the designated growth-municipalities, it took some time to prepare the large construction projects necessary to reach the planned growth. In order to complete the national housing construction programmes in these years, almost any municipality could get approval for its building plans, provided it could start immediately.

After 1973, however, circumstances changed considerably. A new way of fixing rent prices for subsidized housing, imposed by the national government, made institutional investors less eager to invest in projects of subsidized housing. Many contributors to pension funds, for instance, became

TABLE 6

HOUSING CONSTRUCTION IN THE NETHERLANDS 1965–82

Year		1965	1970	1975	1980	1982
1. Social housing		43	39	33	36	53
2. Subsidized:	rent	15	22	19	9	18
	others	10	22	26	30	21
3. Non-subsidized:	rent	9	2	1	2	1
	others	23	15	21	24	7
Total	percentage	100	100	100	100	100
	absolute	115,027	117,284	120,774	113,756	123,310

Source: Central Bureau of Statistics, The Netherlands

afraid of not getting their money back in time. As a consequence of the economic problems in the years after the oil crisis, there was also a decline in demand for owner-occupied, subsidized housing. The number of new houses available annually went down. In the late 1970s, in particular, the construction of non-subsidized housing diminished considerably (Table 6). Construction projects initiated by the government gained in relative importance. Many of these were realized in the growth municipalities. Suburbanization outside these planned growth municipalities became less important. This trend was intensified because, finally, spatial planning interests on a regional and national level began to outweigh housing interests on a local level. Next to the spatial planning policy, already in existence for a long time, the instruments to implement this policy gradually became more suitable. A new problem is now posed, however, by the still existing rule that people have a right to adequate housing not only in the municipality where they work, with which they have so-called 'economic ties', but also in the municipality where they were born and or grew up, with which they have so-called 'social ties'. In a quantitative sense, because of the above-average natural increase, 'suburbanization' will continue here. But, more important, in view of the socio-economic characteristics of the autochthonous population, it will prove to be extremely difficult to guarantee its right to adequate housing under the existing financing system for housing construction or at a reasonable price for society.

Processes leading to population growth

The processes leading to population growth in suburban areas can be quite different. It is important to gain at least some idea of these processes, because different processes require different planning approaches and different control measures.

Three perspectives are central in this matter. *First,* the scale or dimension in an absolute, as well as in a relative, sense. *Second,* the distance between the areas of population growth and the existing cities. It is important here, whether the population growth takes place on the edge of the cities or in a more dispersed way, throughout the (formerly) rural area. And *third,* the social content of the process, that is the kind of people involved, especially with regard to age/life-cycle and socio-economic status.

In instances where we can observe a more or less planned population increase in the so-called growth municipalities or small towns and other regional centres in the rural area, it is the scale of the process in an absolute sense which is especially important. This was expressed in the Second Report on Spatial Planning in the Netherlands (1966), by the term '40,000 + -municipalities', meaning that these municipalities should grow by (at least) 40,000 inhabitants before the year 2000. In such instances *planned suburbanization* occurs, or even urbanization if the number of job opportunities also increases. The municipalities in which planned suburbanization occurs (for example, Nieuwegein and Zoetermeer) generally have, or acquire, a clearly urban character. In the housing projects, apartment buildings, or at least multi-family housing, has a considerable share. Here, we observe not only the in-migration of households but also the arrival of firms. Part of these municipalities is already characterized by employment which is quite extensive in both absolute and relative terms. Among the people moving into these municipalities we find many who want to take advantage of the big city but do not want to live there or could not (yet) get an appropriate dwelling in the city. These people do not really want to live in a house somewhere in the countryside though they do enjoy the slightly more spacious residential areas in these planned suburbs. The great majority of them belong to the middle or even lower classes. Lower-class people are especially numerous where the houses were built in co-operation with one of the large cities, as was done when the cities were unable to meet their annual housing construction requirements in their own territory.

For all other municipalities, it is primarily the relative scale of the population growth which is important. When this growth is lower than the natural increase, as in cases where an out-migration surplus exists, or when the population growth is below the national average, one cannot speak of suburbanization but rather of *rurbanization*. The term rurbanization applies, then, to the phenomenon of *autochthonous* people continuing to live in their home village although they find their job elsewhere, usually in the cities. Through this process the socio-psychological (or mental), the socio-economic, as well as the morphological (or physical) urbanization of the village is furthered. But these *rurban stayers* make a positive contribution to the preservation of the village society, as they are taking part in its social life.

Ruralization takes place when the population in a rural area experiences an above-average increase not as a result of urban—rural migration but as a result of an above-average natural growth, combined with the tendency among the autochthonous people not to leave the village. This implies the development of autochthonous, migration-replacing, commuting. But, in general, this also implies the development of employment opportunities within the area itself, usually in the form of semi-agricultural activities or activities such as transport and the construction of houses, roads or waterworks.

Real suburbanization occurs only in those municipalities which are not involved in the process of planned suburbanization and in which the population increase is faster than the natural growth and the national average, implying an in-migration surplus. Two types of real suburbanization can be distinguished: *genuine* and *dispersed* suburbanization. *Genuine suburbanization* occurs in municipalities within a short distance of a large city. These municipalities have generally been drawn further into the sphere of urbanization. They are strongly orientated toward the city, particularly with regard to employment. In addition to residential suburbanization, they also experience industrial and commercial suburbanization. Generally, the housing standards and housing prices in these municipalities are rather high; something which makes for a selection of preponderantly upper-middle-class and higher-class households, often in a more advanced stage of the life-cycle. Those municipalities which are situated relatively farther away from the large cities are, however, less intensively and less directly orientated toward just one city. In the Green Heart these municipalities are orientated more toward the Urban Ring as a whole, or at least a large segment of it. Firms in these municipalities are more specialized in local or regional services or in transport. The growth of these municipalities is less directly connected with in-migration from large cities. In part they have a role as concentration points within a rural area. Their economic activities, too, are more closely tied up with the traditional activities of the region. In these instances, we can speak of *dispersed suburbanization*. Here, we find more people who are autochthonous to the rural area at large. Because of the relatively low infrastructural costs, housing in these municipalities is slightly cheaper and this influences the selection of urban households moving in from the cities. Lower-middle-class and young people at the beginning of their careers dominate.

The problem with this diversity of processes is, however, that they intermingle and overlap. Municipalities are influenced in their development by several of these processes in different degrees and combinations and in different periods of time. Thus, in municipalities in which, at a first glance, only rurbanization or ruralization seems to occur, we can observe that autochthonous people sell their houses to urban householders. Here a kind of *exchange migration* takes place. Although numerically the village society is not weakened, socially it *is*, for most of the urban householders who want to live in these villages in the countryside very rarely participate in social event there. To designate this process, the term *'hidden suburbanization'* has come into use (Lewan 1969; van Ginkel 1976; Veldman 1978).

Another complication can be expected to occur in the 1990s when the children of households that suburbanized in the late 1960s and early 1970s will begin to establish their own households. At this time, a kind of *second generation* suburbanization is likely to occur.

Suburban movers and rurban stayers

Because of the complexity of processes going on in peri-urban areas, our research dealing with population growth in the Green Heart has distinguished between *suburban movers* and *rurban stayers*. The first are allochthonous, most of them coming from some city in the Urban Ring, whereas the latter are autochthonous and thus born somewhere in the Green Heart. To give an indication of the relative importance of these two groups in the development of Green Heart municipalities, as well as of their main characteristics, we can make use of the data assembled by the Geographical Institute of the University of Utrecht in a government-contracted research programme (Ottens 1976, 1979, van Ginkel 1976, 1979). This research project included interviews with the inhabitants of dwellings completed since January 1, 1960, in all 124 municipalities of the Green Heart. Altogether almost 15,000 heads of households were interviewed. According to the results of this investigation, almost half of all the heads of households living in these new dwellings had already lived in the Green Heart before 1960; that is, before suburbanization became quantitatively important (Table 7). Two-thirds of them already lived in the same municipality as during the inquiry, and one-third came from another municipality within the Green Heart. Slightly more than half of all heads of households interviewed came after January 1, 1960 from the Urban Ring or from elsewhere in the Netherlands. This last group very often went to the Green Heart in connection with a change of workplace to the Urban Ring, and therefore is comparable to the group coming from the Urban Ring itself. In the Rim Area, which is closer to the Urban Ring, a smaller share of the heads of households came from the Green Heart and a larger share from the outside,

TABLE 7

RURBAN STAYERS AND SUBURBAN MOVERS IN THE GREEN HEART
IN DWELLINGS COMPLETED SINCE JANUARY 1, 1960

Area	Rurban stayers born in:		Suburban movers originating from:		
	the same municipality	another municipality	Urban Ring total	one of the four largest cities	Rest of the Netherlands
Green Heart	32	16	40	24	11
of which in					
Rim Area	30	13	45	27	11
Core Area	35	19	34	20	11

Source: Survey, Geographical Institute Utrecht

whereas in the Core Area of the Green Heart—and quite in concurrence with the distance-decay hypothesis—the opposite is true (Table 7).

The share of allochthonous suburban movers in the population of the dwellings constructed since the beginning of the 1960s, was highest in some of the municipalities in the south-west; being close to the Hague as well as Rotterdam and Leiden. Another concentration area was found in the northeast, adjoining Amsterdam, Utrecht and Hilversum. The pressure placed on this area's housing market by suburban movers from Amsterdam was so strong that the suburban zone of Utrecht was pushed to the south. The share of autochthonous rurban stayers among the heads of households interviewed was the highest in some employment centres (agricultural centres with related industries in the Bulb Area, Boskoop, Ter Aar, Leerdam), and in some relatively isolated, only slowly growing, small municipalities in Lopikerwaard, Krimpenerwaard, Alblasserwaard and Vijf-heerenlanden (that is, mainly in the Rivers Area).

Important differences in the socio-economic characteristics of suburban movers and rurban stayers were noticeable. When the occupations of the heads of households are categorized roughly into three groups, according to 'higher', 'middle' and 'lower' occupations, the share of the higher occupations among the rurban stayers is only half the share of these occupations among the suburban movers. Conversely, the share of lower occupations amongst the rurban stayers is more than double that among the suburban movers (Table 8).

The share of people working in construction activities (houses, roads, waterworks) is, among rurban stayers, about double that among suburban movers. Occupations in transport and communication are also proportionally higher among rurban stayers than among suburban

TABLE 8

OCCUPATIONS AND ECONOMIC ACTIVITIES OF SUBURBAN MOVERS
AND RURBAN STAYERS IN THE GREEN HEART,
IN DWELLINGS COMPLETED SINCE JANUARY 1, 1960

	Suburban movers	Rurban stayers
1. Occupations:		
'Higher'	48	23
'Middle'	29	23
'Lower'	28	38
2. Economic Activities:		
Manufacturing	25	27
Construction	7	12
Bank/Commerce	12	11
Transport/Communications	7	9
Other Services	38	19

Source: Survey, Geographical Institute Utrecht

movers. In commerce, banking and insurance both groups are almost equally occupied. But the share of those working in other services among suburban movers is about double that among rurban stayers. The percentage of those having no occupation among the rurban stayers is almost four times as high as among the suburban movers.

From these data it can be concluded that the rurban stayers, in comparison with the suburban movers, belong to the lower income groups, work more often in construction activities, transport and communication, or have already retired. A positive statistical relation also exists between rurban stayers and heads of households living in their first dwelling, having younger children (less than ten years of age), commuting to employment centres within the Green Heart itself, commuting without any fixed working place (construction activities, transport and communication) and living in a rented house.

In contrast to the complex characteristics of rurban stayers, suburban movers display positive statistical relationships with: daily commuting to fixed working places on the Urban Ring; people working in other services, having had another dwelling in an apartment flat before coming from the Urban Ring; living in a privately owned house; having at least one car; commuting by car; and households with older children (15 years and over).

Patterns of population growth

In the population growth of autochthonous and allochthonous origin in the Green Heart over the period studied, some clear stages can be distinguished on the basis of the amount of growth, and according to municipalities that were primarily involved.

Although autochthonous population growth in the Green Heart was still considerable, the *differences* in population growth during the 1960s and 1970s were primarily caused by allochthonous growth. The out-migration from the nine large cities on the Urban Ring to the Green Heart was decisive in this respect. This migration was, to a large degree, provoked by the houses constructed. Among others, this can be concluded from the high correlation of 0.93 between the total amount of houses constructed in the country and the net out-migration of the four largest cities from 1960 to 1977. In the first half of the 1960s, 13,700 persons migrated from these large cities to the Green Heart each year; 10,000 came from the four largest cities. In the second half of the 1960s, the comparable figure was 21,200 per annum (four largest cities: 16,000). In 1970–73: 28,500 persons (22,100); in 1974–77: 31,700 persons (21,500). But, in 1978–81, this figure decreased again to a total of 22,200 persons moving from all the large cities on the Urban Ring each year, of which 17,400 came from the four largest. These data indicate that suburbanization in the Green Heart continued to grow until the mid-1970s but that in the late 1970s the situation changed, first of all in the four largest cities. The main reason was declining housing construction: in 1973 more than 155,000 new dwellings were built, in 1979 less than 90,000. Since then housing construction stabilized on a yearly total of 110,000 to 120,000. But these houses were realized in the designated growth municipalities to a much higher degree.

As a result of the amount and location of the houses built in the period, we can distinguish four stages in the development of suburbanization in the Green Heart on the basis of the spatial patterns of population growth in the years 1960–76 (Figure 14). In a first stage of *'beginning suburbanization'*, population growth in many of the Green Heart municipalities was still below the national average. A very slow growth, and even population decrease, was particularly common in the small municipalities in the central and southern part of the Green Heart (Rivers Area), but also in the lakes areas in the north-east and north-west. At the same time, however, a relatively fast growth was observed in a few municipalities: to the west of Utrecht, south of Amsterdam (Uithoorn and Mijdrecht also became industrialized), along the Oude Rijn river, Zoetermeer (a new town for the Hague), Moordrecht and Waddinxveen (two adjoining municipalities building houses for Gouda in the 1960s).

In 1966–70, a second stage of *'dispersing suburbanization'* developed. There was an especially large increase in the number of municipalities in the highest growth class (more than four times the national average); most conspicuously in the south-west where the suburbanization fields of the Hague, Rotterdam and Leiden overlap. Many municipalities in the more isolated parts (Krimpenerwaard, Lopikerwaard, Alblasserwaard) still lagged behind.

In a third period (1971–73), the stage of *'dispersed suburbanization'*, the number of municipalities in the highest growth class reached a peak. Even in the more isolated parts of the Green Heart, most of the municipalities had a growth rate well above the national average. But at the same time, we see that quite a few municipalities at the edge of the large cities were even characterized by a population decrease. When housing construction in these municipalities went down or even stopped, the population decreased, partly because young adults left their parental homes.

In the fourth stage (1974–76) of *'concentrating suburbanization'* high growth rates become more rare and at the same time many municipalities are characterized by a population decrease. High growth rates became concentrated in a few *new towns* (Zoetermeer, Nieuwegein), *regional centres* (for example, Alphen aan den Rijn, Gouda), *small towns* (for example, IJsselstein, Vianen) and *suburbs* on the edge of the large cities.

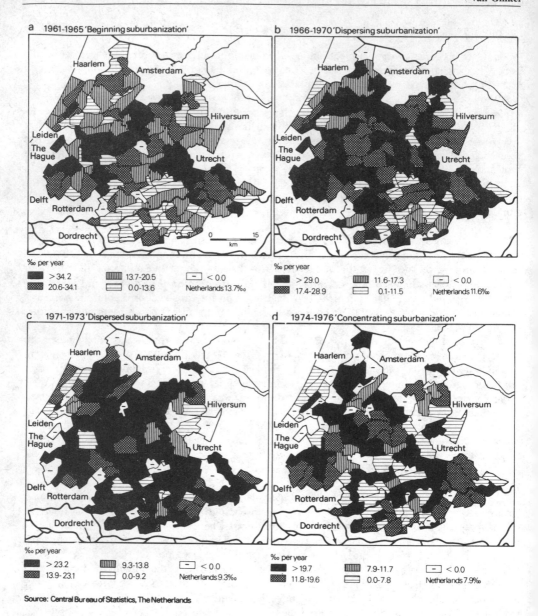

a   1961-1965 'Beginning suburbanization'

b   1966-1970 'Dispersing suburbanization'

‰ per year

> 34.2   13.7-20.5   < 0.0
20.6-34.1   0.0-13.6   Netherlands 13.7‰

‰ per year

> 29.0   11.6-17.3   < 0.0
17.4-28.9   0.1-11.5   Netherlands 11.6‰

c   1971-1973 'Dispersed suburbanization'

d   1974-1976 'Concentrating suburbanization'

‰ per year

> 23.2   9.3-13.8   < 0.0
13.9-23.1   0.0-9.2   Netherlands 9.3‰

‰ per year

> 19.7   7.9-11.7   < 0.0
11.8-19.6   0.0-7.8   Netherlands 7.9‰

Source: Central Bureau of Statistics, The Netherlands

FIGURE 14 *Population growth in the municipalities*

Conclusion

During the peak period of suburbanization in the Green Heart (1960–76) there have been a variety of relationships between the population growth in the area and the settlement pattern. In the beginning, population growth was particularly strong in municipalities close to the Urban Ring. But, gradually, municipalities at a greater distance became involved in the process and, especially in the 1970s, population growth focussed more and more on the towns and other regional centres in the area. The planned growth municipalities, after all, developed favourably. Looking back over the whole period, one is amazed to see that the variety of population growth processes that have been occurring has accentuated the existing settlement pattern more than it has changed it. A comparison of the rank-size distribution of municipalities in the Green Heart in 1960 and 1980 teaches us that the distribution as such did not change much. All municipalities grew over the whole period, as did the difference between the smallest and largest municipalities, though not very spectacularly. The major changes were brought about by the fast growth of some planned 'new towns'. Suburban growth has diminished over the last few years and at the same time has become concentrated in areas of extensive housing construction activity in the more accessible parts of the Green Heart. But even during the peak period of suburbanization in the Green Heart, almost half of all the houses completed were built in only 14 of the 124 municipalities in this area.

In the 1980s, suburbanization in the Green Heart will no longer be a hot issue on the Netherlands' spatial planning scene. But new problems are already coming into sight. Problems of liveability threaten to pose themselves in several of the relatively isolated small municipalities and settlements. Until now the attention of the authorities and the planners was directed mainly at the growth municipalities, to create an attractive atmosphere there. The smallest municipalities and settlements did not get much attention, except for the question of how to prevent them from growing. But, as the efforts to control their growth seem very effective, the population now has a right to an equally effective policy to maintain and possibly improve their living conditions.

Bibliography

BORCHERT, J. G.—GINKEL, J. A. VAN (1979) *Die Randstad Holland in der niederlandischen Raumordnung,* (Kiel: Verlag Ferdinand Hirt).

GIBBS, J. P. (1963) "The Evolution of Population Concentration", *Economic Geography* 39, no. 2: 119–129.

GINKEL, J. A. VAN (1976) *Bewoners van het Groene Hart: een nadere verkenning* (Inhabitants of the Green Heart: a Further Exploration), (Onderzoek Middengebied Randstad, rapport no. 38. Geografisch Instituut Utrecht).

GINKEL, J. A. VAN (1979) *Suburbanisatie en Recente Woonmilieus* (Suburbanisation and Recent Living Environments). Vol. I and II, (Utrechtse Geografische Studies 15 and 16, Utrecht).

GOTTMANN, J. (1961) *Megalopolis, the Urbanized Northeastern Seaboard of the United States,* (Cambridge, Mass.: M.I.T. Press, 3rd ed. 1966).

KLAASSEN, L. H. (1979) *Urban Developments in Western Europe* (Paper for the 50th Anniversary Congress on Dynamics of Urban Development), (Rotterdam: Netherlands Economic Institute).

LEWAN, N. (1969) "Hidden Urbanization in Sweden", *Tijdschrift voor Economische en Sociale Geografie* 60, no. 3: 193–197.

OTTENS, H. F. L. (1976) *Het Groene Hart binnen de Randstad: Een beeld van de suburbanisatie in West-Nederland* (The Green Heart in the Randstad: An Image of the Suburbanization of West Netherlands), (Assen: Van Gorcum).

OTTENS, H. F. . (1979) "Spatial Development in the Green Heart of the Randstad: Policies versus Theoretical and Empirical Evidence", *Tijdschrift voor Economische en Sociale Geografie* 70, no. 3: 130–143.

VELDMAN, J. (1978) "Een sociaal proces door ruimtelijke vorm: verborgen suburbanisatie in landelijke gebieden" (Social Process by Spatial Form: Hidden Suburbanization in Rural Areas), *Geografisch Tijdschrift Nieuwe Reeks* 12, no. 3: 326–334.

THE CHANGING RURAL SERVICE PROVISION IN A PERI-URBAN AREA

PETR F. DOSTÁL AND JAN D. MARKUSSE

KEY-WORDS: *agrarianism; Alkmaar* region; *commuting; depopulation; hierarchy* of services; *peri-urbanization; population,* qualitative ~ change, quantitative ~ change, differentiation in ~ growth, selective ~ development; *repopulation; rural* service provision; *socio-econonomic composition,* blue collar ~, heterogeneous ~, white collar ~.

Introduction

Despite a great number of geographical studies on selective depopulation and repopulation (the latter usually being suburbanization) in rural areas, there are still many questions to be answered concerning both these phenomena and their socio-economic causes and welfare geographical effects, that is, effects on the locally-bounded life chances of rural populations. Some of these effects relate to the maintenance of an adequate level of rural service provision. Further, despite enormous stimulants to geographical research in hierarchical relationships between settlements within rural areas which Christaller's dissertation of 1933 has brought about, we still lack insights into the relationships between, on the one hand, the changing demographic and socio-economic composition of settlements and, on the other hand, the changing composition of the hierarchy of service provision in the rural areas. We will devote this study to these relationships.

The significance of these relationships has been emphasized in some recent studies. Moseley (1979) stressed the tendency of rural service outlets to become fewer, larger and more widely spaced in relation to the problems of economic costs, geographical concentration/deconcentration and differential accessibility. Gilder (1979) emphasized the lack of systematic evidence of economic scale tendencies within the networks of *small* rural settlements. He arrived at the conclusion that within the range of small settlement sizes, demographic factors, accessibility and socio-economic composition of such settlements are of considerably greater importance in explaining the *changes* in rural service provision than the size of settlement. Consequently, he inclined to consider the search for 'optimal' settlement sizes at such small scales as being a fruitless exercise (Gilder 1979). In a study of rural settlement policies and plants Woodruffe (1976) recognized the shortage of specific insights into the relationships between these phenomena. However, the lack of information and insights does not match the relatively long tradition of popular distribution policies which constitute a traditional component of the rural settlement policies in many countries with different institutional contexts (see, for instance, for Great Britain Cloke (1979) or Slepicka (1981) for Czechoslovakia). On the one hand, planners tackle policy issues of providing services and labour opportunities within scattered depopulating settlement networks. On the other hand, planners are confronted with the social and physical pressure and accompanying problems of suburbanization in rural areas surrounding large urban agglomerations and cities. These problems relate to the allocation of both positive and negative spillover effects of both urbanization and suburbanization processes. Recent studies have made clear that population distribution policies have been introduced in all types of rural areas, both depopulating and expanding (Cloke 1983). Accordingly, there is a very clear need to gain a profound insight into the relationships between population development and its welfare geographical implications. However, we do not pretend to be able to close the above-mentioned information gaps. Our more modest aim is to analyse certain quantitative and qualitative changes in the population composition within a network of small settlements; assess the effects of such changes on the expansion, stagnation or decline of the rural service provision within the network, in a specific Dutch local area. In the last 50 years in the Netherlands both depopulation and repopulation and associated policy problems have arisen within the socio-economic and spatio-physical context of the so-called peri-urban areas. Peri-urban areas are defined stressing two general phenomena. Firstly, the position of such areas is within the reach of both the daily labour-markets and the extent of housing markets of the larger urban agglomerations and cities. Secondly, the increasing influences of various socio-economic and physical phenomena originating in larger urban agglomerations and cities on such rural areas are emphasized (see Veldman 1982, Cloke 1979). According to this conceptualization of the peri-urbanization process of rural areas, the basic assumption is made that the development of rural service provision can generally benefit from the involvement of such rural areas into the urban market relationships via increasing the influences of (sub)urban phenomena: "The continually growing number of inhabitants offers a sound carrying capacity to the public and private services to maintain themselves at least" (Veldman 1982, 13; see also PPD-NH 1976, 126–146; Derde Nota Ruimtelijke Ordening, Deel 3a 1977, 35). As regards the explanation of *changes* in the rural service provision within the peri-urban areas, the following two causal relationships are generally assumed:

(1) repopulation (i.e. usually suburbanization) provides an additional (quantitative) local demand for rural services and, consequently, it supports or even enlarges the rural service provision;

(2) the (sub)urban population changes the socio-economic (qualitative) composition of small rural settlements radically and, consequently, it creates an additional demand for new (i.e. urban-like) services.

These two assumptions will be analysed in this contribution and they will also be the main hypotheses which will be tested using statistical information concerning all settlement units within the rural area surrounding the Dutch regional and local centre of Alkmaar.

In the last 50 years the settlements within the rural area of Alkmaar have shown both depopulation and repopulation tendencies (Alderhout 1975). Moreover, this rural area has been involved increasingly in the urban relationships of the large metropolitan regions of the Randstad. Accordingly, this rural area has been selected as a suitable study area because it provides the opportunity to study the above-mentioned relationships during the period of peri-urbanization with accompanying radical demographic and socio-economic changes.

In the next section the process of peri-urbanization of the study area will be indicated in general terms. After that the main objective will be to analyse the consequences of the changes in the quantitative growth and in the socio-economic composition of the settlements' population within the area for their changing positions within the hierarchy of rural service provision during the period 1972–1982. In the concluding section a few remarks will be made concerning the recent rural settlement policies of the Dutch authorities.

The changing position of the area

The rural area of Alkmaar forms part of the main metropolitan region of the Randstad (Figure 15). The delineation of the rural study area of Alkmaar is based upon the outcome of the nation-wide investigations carried out by Buursink (1971) and the RPD (1974). The town of Alkmaar has been classified in these investigations of the hierarchical relationships between larger settlements as one of 21 or 22 main primary regional centres of the country. However, the rural area selected for this study is much smaller than the large primary central region of Alkmaar. There are about 105 such tertiary areas in the Netherlands.

The area covered is about 380 square kilometres and included 15 municipalities in 1982. It contained, including Alkmaar, 103,534 inhabitants in 1947. By 1982, this number had doubled to

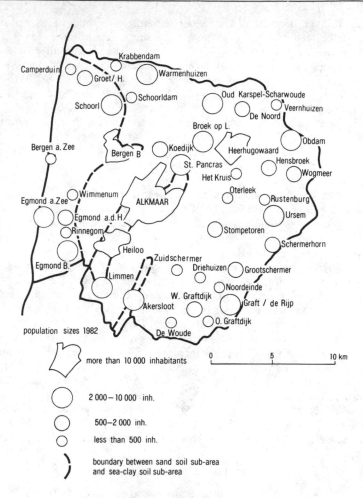

FIGURE 15 *The local area of Alkmaar*

208,239 inhabitants. Compared with both the national and provincial population increases during the same period (the Netherlands: 48.4%; the province of Noord-Holland: 30.3%) the area experienced a considerable demographic expansion. The population growth has been significantly influenced by the net migration component. In-migration into the area from Amsterdam and other centres of the Randstad determined the growth pattern during the post-war period to a great degree (PPD-NH 1976, pp. 19–22, van Weesep 1981, pp. 151–157). About one-third of newly-built houses accommodated the suburbanization flows from the Randstad centres.

According to differences in the soils which influenced the settlement development within the study area, the territory can be divided into two sub-areas. Municipalities Bergen, Egmond. Schoorl, Heiloo and some parts of municipalities Limmen, Akersloot and St. Pancras form a sub-area of sandy soils (Figure 15). The rest of the area, involving 11 municipalities, covers a larger area of sea-clay soils. The sandy soils sub-area has been preferred as an attractive residential environment above the sub-area of sea-clay soils. Moreover, the construction of houses and other buildings has been considerably cheaper on the firm sandy soils than on the soft sea-clay soils. Only higher prices of land for building purposes could 'equalize' the sandy soils sub-area with that of the sea-clay soils in this respect.

Using inter-municipal commuting data from the last three Dutch censuses, the increasing socio-economic integration (i.e. peri-urbanization) of the local area of Alkmaar into the metropolitan labour-market relationships of the Randstad can be described in general terms. Table 9 shows the main tendencies in the in tensity of commuting, the changes of the integration of the local labour-market of Alkmaar and the labour-market orientation of the area's population towards the main employment concentrations of the northern Randstad. Given the above-mentioned differences in the physical-geographical conditions for settlement development, the changes in commuting relating to the two sub-areas are indicated separately. Firstly, the intensity of inter-municipal commuting increased considerably during the period 1947–1971. The economically active population of the sea-clay sub-area became involved in extra-municipal commuting relationships after a certain time-lag. The intensity of the extra-municipal labour-market relations, however, reached very similar levels. Secondly, commuting towards the regional and local centre, Alkmaar, decreased significantly. After World War II, the sandy soils sub-area was a suburban area of Alkmaar in this respect. However, the integration of the local labour-market has been decreasing

TABLE 9

INTERNAL AND EXTERNAL COMMUTING OF ALKMAAR RURAL AREA 1947–1971

	Year	Sand soils sub-area	Sea-clay soils sub-area	Total area
% of commuters in the economically	1947	16.9	11.5	13.7
active population	1960	36.3	25.8	30.3
(excl. Alkmaar)	1971	37.9	35.2	36.3
Commuting to Alkmaar in	1947	60.7	37.0	48.6
% of the number of commuters	1960	43.9	35.2	39.7
	1971	34.2	30.8	32.3
Commuting from the local area	1947	15.4	20.2	18.5
to main employment concentrations	1960	30.4	41.2	36.9
of northern Randstad*	1971	40.9	51.3	47.7
in % of the number of commuters				

* Amsterdam, Zaanstreek, IJmond and Haarlem.

during the entire post-war period. In 1971, only about 30% of commuters from the total local labour-market had employment within the municipality of Alkmaar. In accordance with these changes, commuting from the area increased considerably, and about two-thirds of the commuting labour of the sea-clay sub-area must find employment outside its local residential area. Thirdly, commuting towards the large concentrations of employment in the northern Randstad has been increasing during the entire post-war period.

These general tendencies illustrate the increasing involvement of the population of the labour-market area of Alkmaar into the metropolitan relations of the northern Randstad. In 1971, almost half of the commuting population participated daily in the labour-market of that large urbanized area.

The changing population expansion
and socio-economic composition of settlements

The main dimensions of the explanatory variables will be specified in this section. Firstly, the population size and growth will be described. Secondly, the existing types of socio-economic composition of the settlements will be specified. In the last but one chapter these dimensions and their significant differences will be used to interpret statistically the expansion, stagnation and decline of the services of individual settlements within the changing hierarchy of rural service provision during the period 1972–1982.

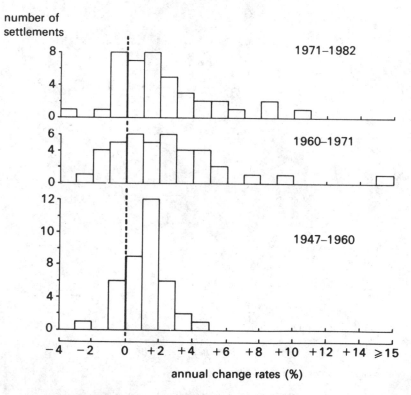

FIGURE 16 *Annual population change rates 1947–1982 (N = 41)*

Figure 16 shows the annual population change rates for three post-war periods.[1] During the •
period 1947–1960, the settlement network stagnated. This stagnation occurred despite the
beginning of the peri-urbanization within the area. During 1960–1971, however, a certain
differentiation in expansion started. On the one hand, Heerhugowaard grew 38.9% and 13 other
settlements grew more than 2% annually. On the other hand, ten settlements were still suffering
depopulation despite the intensive peri-urbanization of the entire area during that period. Only
three of them are located within the sandy soils sub-area. During the most recent period this
differentiation in population expansion within the settlement network remained: ten settlements are
depopulating while 16 settlements are expanding faster than 2% annually. The population
expansion during 1971–1982 was concentrated within the northern part of the study area (Figure
17). This is an area which was involved in the peri-urbanization process after a certain time-lag, i.e.
during the second half of the 1960s and during the 1970s. Moreover, the expansion is concentrated
in the larger settlements in this sub-area. This pattern suggests a correlation between population size
and population expansion during the period 1971–82. Such correlation is modest, however; the

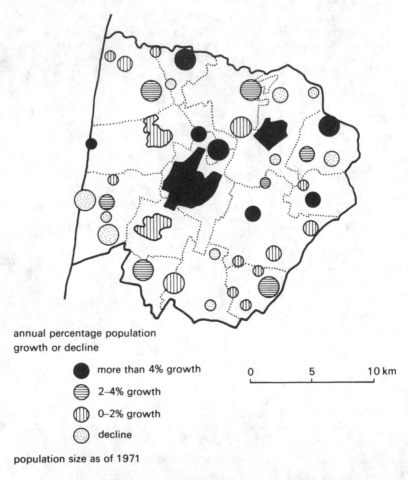

annual percentage population
growth or decline

⬤ more than 4% growth

⊜ 2–4% growth

▥ 0–2% growth

⊙ decline

population size as of 1971

FIGURE 17 *Population development of the settlements 1971–1982*

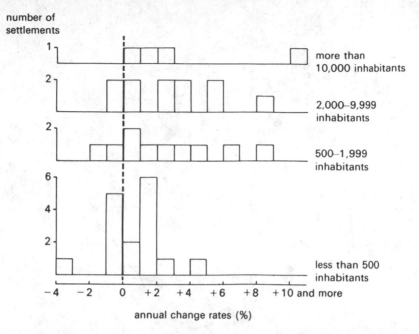

number of settlements

more than
10,000 inhabitants

2,000–9,999
inhabitants

500–1,999
inhabitants

less than 500
inhabitants

−4 −2 0 +2 +4 +6 +8 +10 and more

annual change rates (%)

FIGURE 18 *Annual population change rates 1971–1982 and population size 1971*

logarithm of the population size of 1971 can explain statistically only 17.8% of the variation of the population growth rates during the period 1971–1982 ($r = 0.422$). However, further information concerning the relationship between population size and population expansion during the last period can be derived from Figure 18. It shows a considerable variation in growth rates within each size class. Growth rates both below and above an annual increase of two percent are present in each size class. Accordingly, the conclusion must be drawn that the above-mentioned differentiation in population change rates and its relationship to population size shows a considerable complexity, and subsequently the two variables can be used as two different, explanatory, *quantitative* conditions influencing the changing rural service provision.

An additional *qualitative* differentiation within the entire settlement network can be derived from the information concerning the main dimensions of socio-economic composition of the 41 settlements. Such qualitative dimensions can be derived from a multi-variate analysis. Using the general data from the last two Dutch censuses, 1960 and 1971, at the level of the census tracts, five variables were selected as indicators of the socio-economic differences between the settlements.[2] The five variables describe the main socio-economic changes and they can be used as general indicators of the process of socio-economic urbanization (or suburbanization) of the populations of the 41 settlement units (see for the rationale of this approach Dostál 1974). The basic idea is that the *agrarianism* of the settlements is changing in three general directions: towards a *white-collar* composition, towards a *blue-collar* composition or towards a *heterogeneous* composition. The last one implies the most urban-like socio-economic composition of the populations of the settlements. To specify the main dimensions of socio-economic composition for both years a principle component analysis has been applied. The socio-economic (sub)urbanization appears to be a two-dimensional phenomenon. For both 1960 and 1971, the first two components account for more than 75% of the total variation of the five indicators. The component loadings are consistent with the

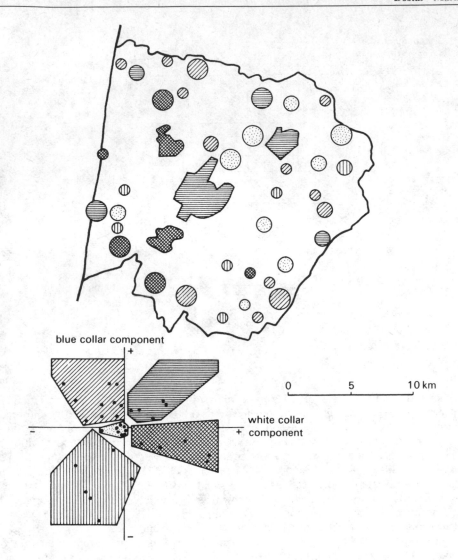

FIGURE 19 *Types of socio-economic composition 1971*

idea of a *decreasing* agrarianism of the settlements' populations. After a varimax rotation procedure, the white-collar and the blue-collar indicators load significantly on their respective dimensions. Accordingly, the two dimensions can be used as an index of white-collar (sub)urbanization and an index of blue-collar (sub)urbanization. Using these two indices, five types of settlements can be distinguished. Figure 19 shows the composition of the settlement network in respect to these socio-economic types.

A group of six settlements score significantly on the positive side of both components. The populations of these settlements have a heterogeneous composition and they represent the most urban-like settlements within the entire network. The largest settlements of the network, Alkmaar and Heerhugowaard, are the leading members of this group. On the positive side of the white-collar dimension four settlements score highly: Bergen-Binnen, Heiloo, Bergen aan Zee and Schoorl. To this group of high-status settlements tend also to belong Egmond-Binnen, Limmen and Driehuizen. A third group consists of 13 settlements in which the blue-collar population is over-represented. Nine settlements can be characterized as transitive. They score near the average position on both components. In respect to these units no clear segregational tendency or any other change can be distinguished during the period 1960–1971. Within the entire settlement network only six units maintained a socio-economic composition in which agrarianism prevails. These settlements have considerable negative scores on both components. Moreover, all these settlements showed a transition towards a more extreme agrarianism during 1960–1971. The map reveals an unequal distribution of the types among the two sub-areas. The white-collar settlements predominate within the sea-clay sub-area. The transitive settlements are also concentrated within this sub-area. Members of the heterogeneous settlement group and the agrarian settlements are more equally spread over the study area.

The changing hierarchy of rural service provision

In this section attention is devoted to the way in which the rural service provision within the settlement network in 1972 and in 1982 was split into hierarchical levels. Further, some basic dimensions of the changing service provision during the period 1971–1982 are identified. The results of the investigation will be used in the next section in which the above-specified quantitative and qualitative differentiations within the settlement network will function as explanatory conditions of the changing service provision.

There are many ways in which service provision can be described (see Beavon 1977, for a critical assessment). In our analysis we have chosen 53 services which functioned within the local area in 1972 and 1982. We do not pretend to offer a complete inventory of all existing services within the research area. We can assume, however, that the 53 services selected do include the most important services which play an indispensable role in the differentiation of the locally-bounded welfare situations within the entire network[3]. The selection includes commercial as well as public and semi-public services in both services and goods provision. Traditionally, in establishing a hierarchy of services, the researcher has to choose between varieties and attributes of the services and goods provision. In this study we have chosen the attribute approach. Our choice is based on the simple fact that in small settlements the presence of at least one outlet of a service or goods provision is more important and probable than the occurrence of more outles of the same functional type. When the last food shop is closed in a settlement unit, the welfare geographical implications of such an event are considerably more important than a reduction of the choice between different outlets of the same type within the same settlement unit.

These choices made it possible to define an input matrix of 40 settlement units by 53 services. Alkmaar has been excluded from the analysis since it clearly dominates the entire network and because it possessed all 53 services selected in both 1972 and 1982. The subsequent analysis, then, is based on two intercorrelation matrices of order 53 by 53 or 40 by 40, independently derived for each

TABLE 10

COMPOSITION OF FIVE HIERARCHICAL LEVELS OF SERVICES PROVISION 1972–1982

Level	Services composition 1972	Composition changes 1972–1982
Fifth level	record shop day-care centre advanced trade school advanced secondary school poultry shop veterinarian plumbing shop leather wares chemist art and antiques shop sporting goods toy shop secondary school baby articles optician obstetrician	gift shop notary book shop public bathhouse/swimming trade school pet shop camera shop
Fourth level	liquor store gift shop library notary book shop central heating maintenance public bathhouse/swimming trade school pet shop community centre camera shop tobacco shop kitchen utensils shop shoe shop cars and accessories jewelry and clock shop drug store dentist	day-care centre plumbing shop art and antiques shop toy shop hardware and hobby shop town hall fish shop kruisvereniging*
Third level	hardware and hobbyshop furniture shop town hall general physician hairdresser fish shop bicycle (repair) shop police office flower and plant shop electrical appliances shop clothing and textile shop bank office kruisvereniging*	cars and accessories paint, glass etc. shop
Second level	elementary school kindergarten post office café/restaurant paint, glass etc. shop	bank office food shop
First level	food shop	

TABLE 11

HIERARCHICAL POSITIONS OF THE SETTLEMENTS 1972–1982

Level	Hierarchical position 1972	Changes in position 1972–1982
Fifth level	Bergen-Binnen Heerhugowaard Heiloo Oudkarspel/Scharwoude	
Fourth level	Akersloot Broek op Langedijk Egmond aan Zee Graft/de Rijp Limmen Obdam Sint Pancras Schoorl Warmenhuizen	Ursem
Third level	Egmond-Binnen Egmond aan de Hoef West Graftdijk Groet/Hargen Groot Schermer Hensbroek Koedijk Oterleek Schermerhorn Stompetoren Ursem Zuid Schermer	Bergen aan Zee
Second level	Bergen aan Zee Driehuizen Krabbendam Het Kruis De Noord Schoorldam De Woude	Oost Graftdijk
First level	Camperduin Oost Graftdijk Rinnegom Rustenburg Veernhuizen Wogmeer	Schoorldam
Zero level	Noordeinde Wimmenum	Camperduin Rinnegom Veernhuizen Wogmeer

* kruisverenigings are associations which are providing professional assistance and necessary equipment for ill and disabled people nursed at home; they also organize medical checks of babies and children.

year of the study. The correlations were measured using binary proportional correlation coefficient introduced by Hamann (see Tinkler 1971)[4]. To establish service levels we employed the principle component procedure. From a visual representation of the relative positions of the 53 services on the first two components five clusters can be recognized, quite similar in both 1972 and 1982. The clusters indicate the composition of five hierarchical levels of service provision[5]. Table 10 gives both the composition of the hierarchial levels in 1972 and the changes which occurred during the period 1972–1982.

A first level of service provision is the presence of a single food shop in 1972. This very elementary level can be distinguished clearly from the next level which consists of five services. Three of them can be classified as (semi-)public services: primary school, nursery school and post office. A third level consits of 13 types of services. A fourth level is represented by a larger number—18 services. The highest level consists of 17 services. Some dramatic changes can be recognized for the period between 1972 and 1982:

(i) the elementary level of food provision vanished during 1972–1982; this important change points to the 'dying hamlets' problem and it may have important welfare geographical implications within the settlement network;

(ii) the noteworthy tendency of the overall pattern is the centralization of service provision; 13 services are centralizing and only six services shifted to lower levels;

(iii) the relative gains at levels 4 and 5 are another relevant tendency of the overall pattern;

(iv) in 1982, the lowest existing level of service provision consisted of six elementary services; the three (semi-)public elementary services could retain their position and might be thought of as a necessary base for a future strengthening at this level.

The application of the principal component analysis to the intercorrelation matrices of the 40 settlements produced five clusters of settlements corresponding with the five hierarchical service provision levels (Table 11)[6]. A fifth level consisted of the largest settlements of the entire area. A fourth level consisted of nine settlements. A larger group of 12 settlements represented a third level within the network. A second level consisted of seven settlements. An elementary level within the hierarchy consisted of six settlements in 1972. At that point in time only two settlements (Noordeinde and Wimmenum) had no single service.

During the period 1972–1982, the most dramatic changes took place at the two lowest levels. Four settlements lost their last service outlet and belong now to the group of so-called 'dying hamlets'. The elementary level from 1972 is represented by only two settlement units in 1982. Consequently, the elementary level of rural service provision in 1982 consisted of six settlements which were able to maintain five elementary services and attract a basic (commercial) bank service. The three (semi-)public services seem to have an important *stabilizing* impact on the maintenance of an *elementary* service and goods provision in the study area.

The changing service provision
and the population and socio-economic composition

The above-specified dimensions of the rural service provision within the entire settlement network and the resulting positions of individual settlement units both in 1972 and 1982 will be related in this section to the demographic expansion differences and the types of socio-economic differentiation described above.

A strong relationship between the size of settlements and the number of services is an essential feature of every settlement network. In our study area a considerable correlation occurred in 1972 between the number of services and the logarithm of population size 1971: $r = 0.939$.

To be able to test the hypothesis of a causal relationship between the expansion, stagnation or decline of the service provision and the *quantitative* repopulation and depopulation phenomena, however, a correlation must be estimated between the increase or decrease of the number of services

change in the
number of services

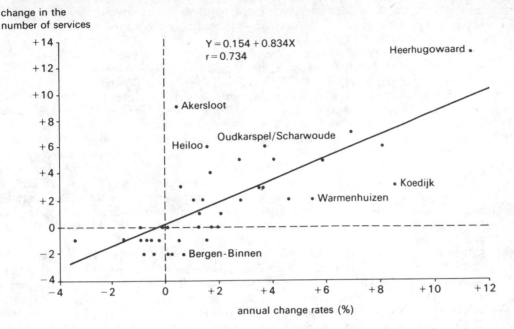

FIGURE 20 *Annual population change rates 1971–1982 and changes in the provision of services 1972–1982*

during 1972–1982. The correlation is considerable: $r = 0.734$. This outcome implies that more than 50% of the variation in the changes of service provision can be explained statistically by the regression on the population growth variation within the settlement network ($r^2 = 0.539$). However, a scatter diagram of the changing service provision during the 1970s reveals some important thresholds of and deviations from this relationship (Figure 20).

Firstly, an annual growth rate of 4% seems to imply an average expansion of the service provision by approximately three new services. Secondly, an annual growth of 2% seems to be an important threshold which distinguishes between stagnation and decline of the service provision within the network. Thirdly, some clear positive deviations can be registered. Despite a very moderate population expansion of 0.5% annually, Akersloot was able to expand its provision with nine new services. To a lesser degree, the same tendency applies to three of the four largest settlements, Heiloo, Oudkarspel/Scharwoude and Heerhugowaard. The fastest-expanding settlement, Heerhugowaard, obtained 13 new types of service which is a greater gain than one could expect according to the average regression line of the two phenomena within the entire settlement network. Fourthly, some negative deviations must be mentioned. The settlement unit Koedijk, near Alkmaar, expanded 8% annually but it could expand its services by only three new functions. Further, the annual expansion of more than 5% of the central settlement of Warmenhuizen municipality created a service expansion of only two new functions instead of the five or six which could be expected. Fifthly, the five settlements with a declining service provision accompanied by a moderate population growth attract the attention. Four of them are located in the north-west of the study area (Camperduin, Krabbendam, Groet and Bergen-Binnen). The membership of one of the largest settlements of the entire network, the white-collar settlement of Bergen-Binnen, is surprising. Sixthly, in eight settlements the depopulation was accompanied by a decline in service provision.

With the exception of Egmond aan Zee, these depopulating and declining settlements posses positions at the lowest levels of service provision—three at the zero level, one at the first level, two at the second level and one at the third level.

This outcome suggests a relationship between the number of services in 1972 and the changes of this number during 1972–1982. However, the correlation is quite moderate ($r = 0.497$). The interaction of this relationship with the depopulation/repopulation 1971–1982 is interesting. The latter variable, in combination with the number of services in 1972, can explain statistically 58% of the changes in the service provision ($R^2 = 0.579$). There is a moderate correlation between the population growth 1971–1982 and the number of services in 1972 ($r = 0.428$). When one assumes that the number of services in all 40 settlements was identical, the population growth still appears to be an important predictor of the expansion, stagnation and decline of the service provision (partial correlation coefficient ($r^2_{12.3} = 0.442$). The conclusion must be drawn that the size of the settlements, both in respect to the number of inhabitants and the number of services, cannot be considered to be an important predictor of the *changes* in the service provision within the entire settlement network during the 1970s. We therefore devote the attention to the *qualitative* differences within the network, that is to the above-defined five types of socio-economic composition of the settlements (Table 12).

In the group of the most urban-like, heterogeneous, settlements only two showed an expansion of the service provision (Heerhugowaard and Oudkarspel/Scharwoude). Egmond aan Zee, Groet and Schermerhorn experienced a decline. These settlements were also stagnating or depopulating during 1971–1982. In the group of white-collar settlements only one settlement (Bergen-Binnen) experienced a decline. The other members of this high-status group experienced an expansion or maintenance of their service provision. A one-sided higher-status composition of the population

TABLE 12

CHANGE IN THE SERVICE PROVISION 1971–1982
BY SOCIO-ECONOMIC TYPES OF SETTLEMENTS 1971

Service provision	Socio-economic types				
	Hetero- genous	White collar	Blue collar	Transi- tional	Agrarian
Expanding	2	5	6	8	0
Stagnant	0	1	2	0	3
Declining	3	1	5	1	3

seems to be a favourable condition as regards the expansion or maintenance of the local welfare situation.

In the category of blue-collar settlements one discerns a different pattern. The majority of these settlements experienced a decline or stagnation of their service and goods provision. Consequently, a one-sided blue-collar population composition does not seem to support an adequate service provision. The transitional settlement units were able to expand local service provision. These settlements became involved in peri-urbanization in the 1970s and they could offer, to a considerable degree, sufficient housing accomodation to a usually white-collar population from the northern Randstad. Finally, the most unfavourable condition for the expansion of services seems to be a one-sided agrarian composition of the population.

From these statistical examinations it appears that both the *quantitative* dimensions of the population change and the *qualitative* differentiation in the socio-economic types are important conditions influencing the changes in rural service and goods provision. As regards these two explanatory conditions the important question is to what extent these conditions can be used as two

TABLE 13

MEAN ANNUAL POPULATION CHANGE RATES 1971–1982 BY SOCIO-ECONOMIC
TYPES OF SETTLEMENTS 1971

Mean annual population change rates (%)	Socio-economic types				
	Hetero-genous	White collar	Blue collar	Transi-tional	Agrarian
≥ 4	1	1	3	3	0
2 – 3.99	1	2	1	2	1
0 – 1.99	2	3	6	3	1
Negative	1	1	3	1	4

separate, additive, explanatory variables. In Table 13 the relationships between the population expansion 1971–1982 and the five socio-economic types are summarized. Only in the category of agrarian settlements can a clear negative association be established. In the other four categories the differentiation of the population growth is considerable.

Conclusions

The main aim of this contribution was to assess the basic explanatory quantitative and qualitative population conditions of the changing rural service and goods provision. Firstly, the population expansion appeared to be an important quantitative condition for the expansion or maintenance of the provision of services and goods. Moreover, an annual expansion of 2% seemed to be a significant threshold. Settlement units which are not able to realize such a moderate population growth tend clearly to lose their services. Secondly, the size differentiation of the settlement network seemend to be no clear explanatory condition as regards the *changes* in the rural service provision. The same applied to the number of services which the settlement units possess. Thirdly, the *qualitative* socio-economic differentiation within the settlement network can be used as an important *additive* explanatory condition. A one-sided white-collar population seems to be a favourable condition for the expansion and maintenance of the rural service and goods provision. A one-sided blue-collar composition of the population does not offer favourable circumstances in this respect. Settlements with a mainly agrarian population can clearly be associated with the decline and stagnation of service and goods provision.

The level of rural service provision is also an important basic component of the local welfare situation within the so-called peri-urban areas. Depopulation also occurs within such areas, and so-called (key-)settlement policies are implemented. In the area considered, some *selective* population developments are planned in the recent sub-regional development plan (Streekplan voor Noord Kennemerland 1982). Only two critical remarks will be made. Firstly, according to this sub-regional plan, only very moderate population growth and housing construction are allowed in the sandy soils sub-area and in the south-eastern part of the sea-clay soils area. In accordance with the results of this study it seems to be probable that the maintenance of services in the preferred residential sandy soils area will be difficult, given the above discussed annual population expansion threshold of 2% which appears to be a critical condition of the maintenance of service provision. The same applies for the many small settlements in the south-east of the study area which already have low service provision levels. Secondly, the further concentration of expansion of commercial services in the·Alkmaar— Heerhugowaard agglomeration proposed by the plan will strengthen the overall pattern of concentration of service and goods provision within the entire area of the settlement network considered, and consequently an increasing inequality between locally-bounded welfare situations can be expected.

In this study the emphasis has been put on how the local welfare position of individual sttlement units has changed with time. This emphasis made it necessary to provide a considerable amount of empirical information. Such detailed factual information, however, is indispensable for a critical assessment of the probable welfare geographical implications of (key-)settlement policies even within the peri-urban areas of the large metropolitan regions.

Notes

[1] For the study of local settlement networks within the Dutch municipalities, some basic demographic and socio-economic data can be derived from the censuses of 1947, 1960 and 1971 (see CBS 1964 for a description). Keeping in mind the territorial distribution of the population, the CBS divided all territorial groupings of houses which form, more or less, clusters, from houses which are more widely scattered in the rural space. More than 10,000 census tracts were delineated within the national territory. On the basis of this primarily topographical distinction, a sub-division of the municipalities into separate settlements and areas of widely scattered houses (usually farms) can be made. In some cases we agglomerated the census tracts of the CBS to obtain larger settlements forming contiguous built-up areal units. Because the last Dutch census was held on February 28, 1971, we could use for 1982 population data only those which were kindly supplied by the Physical Planning Office of the province of Noord-Holland.

[2] These variables are the share of employed persons with secondary and higher education (1) and agriculturally-employed persons (2) in the total labour force and the share of higher employees (3), high income workers (4), and low income workers (5) in the total number of heads of households. These general *intra*-municipal data can be obtained only from the results of the last two Dutch censuses (1960 and 1971). We acknowledge the help and assistance of George Herber and Henk Kooreman (both from the Institute of Human Geography, University of Amsterdam) during the statistical manipulations of the data.

[3] Information concerning the geographical location of the 53 services in both 1972 and 1982 has been obtained from the so-called Golden Guides (Gouden Gids Alkmaar 1971/2, Amsterdam, 122 pp.; Gouden Gids Alkmaar 1982/3, Amstelveen, 215 pp.). Golden Guides are published by a commercial organisation in co-operation with the Dutch TTCo. They are a form of telephone directory of all commercial, public and semi-public establishments within an area which is centred on a major town or city. This information source covers about 98% of all establishments which function within an area. Under Dutch conditions one can assume that all establishments we wish to consider possess a telephone connection.

[4] Hamann's correlation coefficient can be presented as $H = \dfrac{r - r'}{N}$ where r = number of coincident pairs, r' = number of non-coincident pairs, and N = number of settlements or services respectively (see also Sokal and Sneath 1964, 132–134). One can say that this correlation coefficient takes all zeros in 2 by 2 matrices seriously.

[5] By way of definition, the first component represents the differences between the highest and the lowest levels in the hierarchy. The second component represents settlements or services which possess no clear negative or positive correlations with the settlement units or services which are represented by the first component, that is the dimension of the lowest and the highest levels. These first two components account for 70.3% of the total variance in 1972 and for 69.4% in 1982. No varimax rotations were needed.

[6] The first two components of the 40 by 40 matrices for both 1972 and 1982 represent, by way of definition of the empirical input data, identical accounts of the total variance (see Note 5).

Bibliography

ALDERHOUT, J. (1975) *De regio Alkmaar. Een toetsing van enkele concepten van de theorie der centrale plaatsen* (The Alkmaar Region. A Test of Some Concepts of Central Place Theory), (M. A. Study, Institute of Human Geography, University of Amsterdam).

BEAVON, K. S. O. (1977) *Central Place Theory: a Reinterpretation,* (New York: Longman).

BUURSINK, J. (1971) *Centraliteit en hiërarchie* (Centrality and Hierarchy), (Assen: Van Gorcum).

CHRISTALLER, W. (1933) *Central Places in Southern Germany,* (London: Englewood Cliffs, 1966).

CLOKE, P. (1979) *Key-Settlements in Rural Areas,* (London: Methuen).

CLOKE, P. (1983) *An Introduction to Rural Settlement Planning,* (London: Methuen).

NOTA LANDELIJKE GEBIEDEN ·(1977) (Report on Rural Areas), ('s-Gravenhage: Staatsuitgeverij).

DOSTÁL, P. F. (1974) *A Multivariate Analysis and Regionalisation of the Socio-Economic Suburbanization and Its Spatial Form,* (Groningen: Sociaal-Geografische Reeks. Publikatie no. 6).

GILDER, I. M. (1979) "Rural Planning Policies: an Economic Appraisal", *Progress in Planning* 11, no. 3: 213–271.

MOSELEY, M. (1979) *Accessibility—the Rural Challenge,* (London: Methuen).

PROVINCIAL PLANNING AGENCY NOORD-HOLLAND (1976) *Studienota kleine kernen* (Research Note on Small Settlements), (Haarlem).

NATIONAL PLANNING AGENCY (1974) *Hiërarchie van kernen in Nederland* (Settlement Hierarchy in the Netherlands), (Den Haag).

SLEPICKA, A. (1981) *Venkov a/nebo mesto* (Countryside or Town?), (Prague: Svoboda).

SOKAL, R. R.—SNEATH, P. H. A. (1963) *Principles of Numerical Taxonomy,* (San Francisco: Freeman and Co.).

STREEKPLAN VOOR NOORD-KENNEMERLAND (1982) (Regional Plan for North Kennemerland).

TINKLER, K. T. (1971) "A Coefficient of Association for Binary Data", *Area* 3, no. 1: 31–35.

VELDMAN, J. (1982) "Proposal for a Theoretical Base for Human Geography of Rural Areas". In: *The Changing Countryside* (eds.: Clark, G.—Groenendijk, J.—Thissen, F.), (Norwich: Geobooks).

WEESEP, J. VAN (1981) "De ontwikkeling van een stedelijk komplex op regionale schaal" (The Development of an Urban Complex at Regional Level). In: *Zicht op de Nederlandse stad* (ed.: Deurloo, M. C.), (Bussum: Unieboek).

WOODRUFFE, B. J. (1976) *Rural Settlement Policies and Plans,* (Oxford: University Press).

THE FORMATION OF NEW, CLUSTERED, RURAL SETTLEMENTS IN HUNGARY

BÁLINT CSATÁRI AND GYÖRGY ENYEDI

KEY-WORDS: 'agricultural towns'; auxiliary farming activities; basic services; central villages; collectivization of agriculture; Danube–Tisza Interfluve; dispersed farmsteads; dual organization of Hungarian agriculture; household plots of the cooperative members; large-scale farms; new forms of rural settlements; 'new villages'; rural communities, ~ functions, ~ market towns, ~ population, ~ settlement pattern, ~ society; settlement-development policy; tanya.

The problem

There is a growing interest everywhere in Europe in the new phenomena emerging in the rural settlement pattern. After long decades of rural depopulation and decline, we are witnessing a new dynamism in some of the rural areas. This new dynamism is connected to a certain re-evaluation of rural settlements from the point of view of residence, of recreation and in some area, of food production (Enyedi 1984). Regional policies in European countries were aimed at regional balance, thus special attention was paid to the less developed rural areas. International co-operation for rural development was propagated within the European Community (Sant 1974, Kuklinski–Lambooy 1983).

Rural research has focussed on the growth or the decline of the rural population, on the changes in rural functions, and on the transformation of rural society. Relatively little attention has been paid to the new forms of rural settlements which, for different reasons, have emerged in the European rural scene. There are two main factors in the formation of new rural settlements:
—modern agriculture has had its impact on rural settlements; and
—since the majority of the rural population has non-agricultural professions, the connections between utilized surfaces (land) and the rural settlements have weakened.

The importance and the forms of the new rural settlements differ from country to country. In France, urban dwellers move out to the rural edge of the peri-urban zone and form mixed, rural-urban (rurbaine in French term) settlements (Berger et al. 1980, Bauer–Roux 1976). In Switzerland, land consolidation has resulted in new dispersed settlements (Chiffelle 1968). In Eastern Europe, the collectivization of agriculture has dramatically changed land/residence ties, and there has been a general move towards a radical reconstruction of the rural settlement network—although this has been carried out but by exception (von Känel 1980, Vaitekunas 1980).

In Hungary, as early as the end of the 1940s, at the beginning of the first wave of collectivization, the government planned to cluster the population of the dispersed farmsteads (tanyas) into newly built villages. The idea failed, since out-migrants from the tanya zones left agriculture and moved to larger industrial-urban centres. In the early 1960s, when collectivization was finished, urbanists again schemed to rebuild rural settlement networks into 'agricultural towns' (Borsos 1975). This idea never got official support.

Actually, the number of rural communities did not change a lot in the last two decades. There was a slight decline in their number, but it was caused mainly by reorganization of public administration (i.e. merger of small hamlets), and, by and large, it was independent of large-scale farming.

At the same time, there were important changes in the *tanya* zone (mostly in the Danube–Tisza Interfluve) and in the sparsely populated areas of western Hungary, *within* the administrative boundaries of rural communities. Large-scale farms spontaneously started to form their own special settlements where traditional rural settlement pattern did not fit modern farming. These changes were not planned, and, for a long time, they were not in line with the official settlement policy (seeking to create *agrovilles*). Two new settlement forms were recognized quite early by settlement geographers. Edit Lettrich stated that in Bács-Kiskun county alone, there were 52 newly clustering rural settlements within the *tanya* zone by the end of the 1960s (Lettrich 1968). Klára Körmendi wrote later (Körmendi 1976), that "we can list among the small villages the new settlements connected to large farm centers, located mostly in the Alföld (the Great Hungarian Plain). We have no idea about their exact number, but there are certainly several hundreds". In his book on *tanya* problems, Pál Romány also noticed the clustering process in the *tanya* zones (Romány 1973).

Two decades after the collectivization, we still know nothing accurate about these new settlements. We are merely summarizing the results of a case study of Bács-Kiskun county, carried out between 1982–84 by the Centre for Regional Studies of the Hungarian Academy of Sciences which gave the first set of reliable information about the new settlements. The research was sponsored by the County Council which intended to incorporate new rural settlements into the county's long term settlement-development policy.

We formulated our main questions as follows:

(a) Under what circumstances were the new rural settlements created? Are they temporary settlements, or can we forecast their permanent existence? Can we state that these small settlements with 2–300 inhabitants are of viable size?

(b) What kind of people live in these settlements (concerning their age, sex, profession and education)? Where do they come from, where do they work?

(c) How are the inhabitants satisfied with their settlement? How are the infrastructure and basic services developed?

After analysing the data of the new rural settlements of the county, we selected 13 new villages, where 473 households (with 1,669 people) were interviewed, and questionnaires were filled out. The sampling represented 10 percent of the total population of the new villages in the county. Monographs were written on each of the 13 settlements which dealt with their history, economic conditions etc. and evaluated the answers given to the questionnaires.

New villages in Bács-Kiskun county

It is extremely difficult to derivate even the simplest population data of the new villages from the census data. The new clustered rural settlements are located within the administrative boundaries of towns (former rural market towns) or large rural communities. There is no official delineation of these settlements. The Hungarian population census distinguishes the population of the 'inner settlement' and that of the 'outer settlement'. The latter comprises mostly of dispersed farmsteads, agricultural workers' settlements of the former big estates or the present state farms. A special feature of farmsteads was their close connection to the central clustered settlement (where public administration was located). Usually, farmsteads of outer settlement zones were owned by dwellers of the inner zone, so farmer families alternated 'inner' and 'outer' residence, following the rhythm of agricultural work (Enyedi 1976). Young people (the owner's adult children), tenants, agricultural workers or poor farmers represented the permanent population of the *tanya*s.

Tanya population was very important a few decades ago. In 1930, one fifth of the country's total population (one third of the Alföld population), amounting to 1,900,000 people lived in detached farmsteads. This ratio dropped to 8.3% in 1970, and to some 4% in 1980. The *tanya* population almost disappeared from east of the Tisza; but it is still important in the Danube–Tisza Interfluve (Becsei 1983).

Bács-Kiskun county has had the highest 'outer settlement' population ratio in this century. In 1930, half of the county's population lived in detached farmsteads: this ratio dropped to 42% by 1949 and to 18% by 1980. There was a growing trend of population decline of the *tanya*s in the county: 15% between 1949 and 1959; 22% between 1960 and 1969 and 38% between 1970–79. Earlier, the out-migrants usually left the county and moved to Budapest or to some other industrialized area. In the 1970s, most of the people who left the *tanya* moved a small distance within the county, very often to one of the new villages. These new villages have three types of origin:

—expansion of earlier estate centres or basic service centres established in the *tanya* zone in the 1940s and 1950s;

—new residential areas developed by large-scale state or cooperative farms;

—clustering of earlier detached farmsteads by accelerated construction between farm homes.

We identified 125 clustered rural settlements within the administrative territory of other communities, with an estimated 12–15,000 population. Of these there were 39 settlements which had a net population growth during 1970–79. Four of these settlements have more than 1,000 inhabitants, but, we repeat, they have not the slightest administrative independence—public administration still did not notice the existence of these rapidly growing settlements.[1]

In the following chapters we shall discuss some of the characteristics of the 'new settlements' based on the detailed analysis of the 13 settlements we have sampled.

Population of the new settlements

It is generally supposed that small rural settlements, especially in the *tanya* zone have had a serious population loss and consequently, their population is aged and dying out. Mass media spread this idea by way of heart-breaking reports on lonely old people in remote areas, on abandoned, half ruined farm houses. Actually, population of the new clustered settlements is strikingly young (Figure 21): 27% are children (0–14 years); 41% are young adults (15–39 years); 24% are middle aged (40–59 years) and old people (over 60 years) represent only 8% (the national rural average is near 20%). Due to the high ratio of young adults, the natural population increase is significant, more so, since there is a natural population decrease in the country generally, especially in traditional rural areas.[2]

When and from where did these people come to the 'new villages'? 92% of the families moved in after 1960. There was a strong wave of migration between 1970 and 1974, when the first subdivisions were carried out by local and the county councils. In the 1960s, they moved mostly to the expanding former estate centres; in the next decade the newly established cooperative farm residential areas got priority, then, in the 1980s there are some signs of suburbanization, mostly around the county seat, Kecskemét, and this also draws people to the 'new villages'. Three quarters of the families lived in a detached farm-house before their move. 12% of the dwellers came from a town (42% in the case of Katonatelep), mostly young couples seeking cheaper or better housing.

The employment rate is very high among the 'new village' population. 68% of the women in the active age work. Two-thirds of the men are employed in agriculture, but mostly in the so-called auxiliary (industrial, service, transport etc.) activities of the agribusiness, only a minority does 'real' farming. Agricultural employment is less prevalent among women: 38% of them is employed in the tertiary sector, 14% in the secondary sector (Figure 22). Heads of households, employed in cooperative farms have had easier access to the new subdivisions carried out by the farms themselves, their wives had less opportunity—or less desire—to be employed on the farms. Since the tertiary sector is poorly developed in the new villages, many women commute in order to engage in tertiary occupations. So, we can find more agricultural workers and fewer commuters among the men than among the women. The commuting distances are small. More than half of the commuters

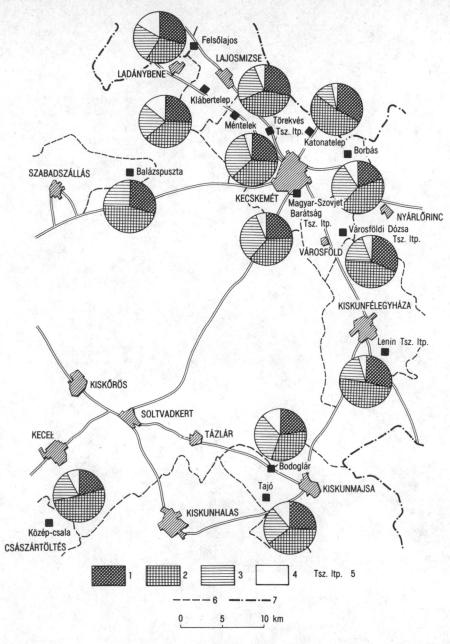

FIGURE 21 *The age composition of population in new villages 1983 (survey results)*

1 = 0–14
2 = 15–39
3 = 40–59
4 = 60–x years old

5 = new residential areas of cooperative farms
6 = boundaries of towns and villages comprising new rural settlements
7 = county border

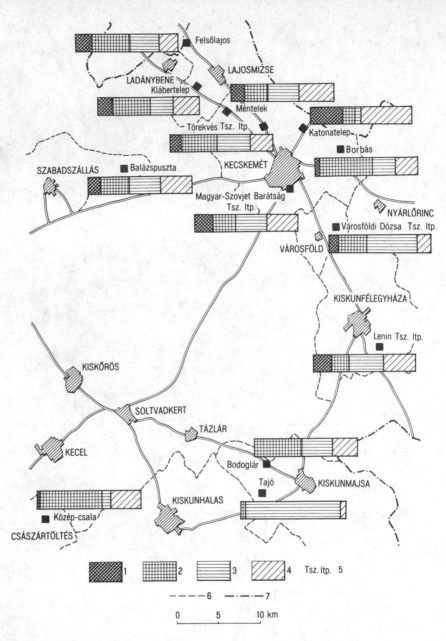

FIGURE 22 *The occupational structure of the active population in new villages 1983 (survey results)*

1 = employed in the industrial sector
2 = employed in farming
3 = employed in non-farming (auxiliary) activities within the agricultural sector

4 = employed in the tertiary sector
5 = new residential areas of cooperative farms
6 = boundaries of towns and villages comprising new rural settlements
7 = county border

reach their workplace within ten minutes, and only 9% travels more than 30 minutes (to get there or back). The closeness of the workplace (one quarter of the active people can *walk* to their workplace) is an important advantage of the new villages.

The educational level of the population is slightly higher than the rural average of the county.

We can conclude that the new villages have a young, economically active, and well-educated population, which suggests their viability.

Housing conditions and basic services

The infrastructural supply of the new villages is characterized by high-level housing and low-level basic services.

Producers' cooperatives have iniated the subdivisions near the farm centres to assure young and skilled manpower. Large-scale farms also had an interest in abolishing the old detached farms which presented a hindrance to large-scale cultivation. The construction fields formed by the subdivision (on the collectively-owned land) are large enough for some household farming activity, mostly for livestock raising. Applicants for the parcels have to be members of the cooperative; they have to build their home within a limited time (2–3 years); and they have to sign a contract with the coop to remain a member for several years (up to 10). In return, applicants get the land (which becomes their private property) at very low, symbolic prices, and they also get many other kinds of help with the construction (for example, free transportation of building material). Other homes are built by the construction units of the cooperatives.[3]

Construction slowed down, generally speaking, after the mid 1970s (except for the suburban type settlements around Kecskemét). The merger of cooperatives which climaxed in the early 1970s, disturbed the formation of these settlements, too. (Farm centres were relocated in some cases.) There are still empty fields in the subdivisions. Three-quarters of the homes were built by the present owners; one-tenth was bought from the first ower, and the remaining part was built by the cooperatives and offered at very low rent as a 'service residence' for young professionals (for example, agricultural engineers, veterinarians) who were hesitant to settle on the farm permanently.

Housing conditions are favourable compared to the national or county averages. First of all, these homes are larger than those in the cities or in rural communities. In Bács-Kiskun county, the average size of the housing units built in 1982 was 74 m²; in the rural communities of the county it was 86 m², and in the 'new villages' it was 97 m². In every case, the 'new villages' had larger homes than their central settlement. In most cases—except for the few homes built before 1960 by state farms—the homes are well equipped: all of them have electricity and running water, half of them (71% of those built after 1980) have central heating. Thus, owners have invested heavily in construction which expresses their intention to settle down definitively, or at least for a long time, in the new villages.

Nevertheless, the future of these villages is still uncertain. Large-scale farms have their manpower for a generation, but what will happen to the next generation? There are signs of a declining interest in settling in the new villages. The stability of the new settlements depends partly upon their geographical location (namely, their distance from cities) and their service level. In the first years, new settlers are satisfield with the much better residential amenities; then they become more keen to claim public services. At the moment, the new villages still have a very low level of basic services.

Only 9% of the interviewed persons stated that the retail trade services were satisfactory. Low consumer density makes the location of commerce inefficient in most cases. Mobile shops are rare. Improved accessibility to shops located in the central villages or in the nearby cities can offer a solution. Because of the low level of individual motorization and the relatively high cost of using cars, mass transportation has to assure this accessibility; thus, again, low consumer density is a problem.

The basic public services are also poorly developed. In some cases, cooperative farms try to run public services (kindergartens, consulting rooms) for their members. One of the basic problems is that these settlements have no form of self-government: they have no associations, in most cases not even a place for public meetings. (Schools and churches, the traditional rural community centres, are usually non-existent.) They are residential areas, not yet real settlements. Although settlement development taxes are collected both from producers' cooperatives and from house owners, they are usually spent on the central villages. We have to add that till now[4], the local councils have had very limited local resources, and rural public services are inadequate in the central villages, too.

Lifestyle in the new villages

Despite the low-level basic services, most of the inhabitants are satisfied with their settlement. These villages are the world of hard work yielding a relatively good income. Although most of the dwellers have no traditional farming occupation, they have a peasant (or, according to some of the sociologists, post-peasant) way of life, where work has the highest priority.

As many as 81% of the interviewed families (over 90% around Kecskemét) are satisfied with their settlement. 68% of families suppose that their village is the 'right size'; one-tenth of the families (those who moved from a distant farmstead to the small clustered villages) feel the small village crowded; and 14% want to see further growth (the remaining families have no opinion).

The time-budget of the average family in the new settlements—as we can conclude from the interviews—is characterized by continuous work. The workday starts at 5 a.m. with feeding the household animals. Then wife and husband go to work, and return back home around 2–3 p.m. (work time is 10 hours in agriculture during the main season). In the afternoon, they work on their household plot (*all* the families have an auxiliary farm) till dinner (7 p.m.). (Women share their afternoon between the household and the fields.) In the summer-time, especially when there is urgent work in the vineyards, they continue to work till 10 p.m. Children also participate in the work, but to a lesser extent than in the traditional peasant families. During the summer, they have no time even to watch TV.

They usually continue to work during the weekend, too. This work includes house cleaning, tending the flowers in the front-yard, etc. Sunday afternoon is the real free time when they often receive guests or are invited by friends and relatives. Only the single young adults living in the new villages near Kecskemét said that they frequently go to the city on the week-ends for entertainment. Summer holidays are usually spent at homme, working.

This 'workaholic' way of life is what contributes largely to the family income—and to the abundant food supply of the country. According to our estimates, 30 to 40% of the family income comes from auxiliary farming activity. In addition, there is important self-consumption in certain products (fruits, vegetables, eggs). We estimate that two-thirds of the vegetable production is consumed by the producers' families.[5] The good possibilities for auxiliary farming are an important attraction of the new villages.

There are three areas of auxiliary farming. First, the piece of land around the homes where the animals are kept (and fed on purchased fodder) and where truck farming is significant. Next, the household plots of the cooperative members (1–2 acres) which are intensively cultivated. The non-agricultural families conduct their farming activities usually in rented vineyards and orchards.

Although we cannot define the family incomes precisely, we can conclude that (a) the highest total income is reached by agricultural families; next come the families where the head of the family has an industrial job; tertiary families are in third place; while families with a retired head have the lowest income; (b) incomes are more equalized among families in settlements run by large-scale farms where auxiliary farming activities are well organized and are accessible to all.

Conclusions

(i) We can clearly distinguish 4 types among our 13 sample settlements, types which are presumably valid for all the new villages. The types differ in respect of all important characteristics, and express various degrees of urbanization: from the traditional agricultural settlement to the suburban one.

Katonatelep belongs to the *first type*. It is becoming a suburb of Kecskemét: its new settlers are those moving out of the city: the ratio of the non-agricultural population and the educational level of the population is the highest of the 4 types, the standard of housing is the best.

The *second type* is the new residential area built by a large-scale farm. It is in this case that the name of 'new village' is the most justified. A young agricultural population dominates these settlements where auxiliary farming is the most developed. These high income settlements are typical among cooperative farm settlements. In the case of the state farm residential units, where the homes are rented by state farm workers, the population is less stable and less affluent. Most of them consider their residence there as a transitory stage in their move to the city.

Small settlements belong to the *third type* (3 settlements); these settlements were built earlier (in some cases before 1960), but were renewed in the 1970s due to their close location to larger, clustered settlements.

Finally, the remaining 5 settlements belong to the *fourth type:* these have less favourable transport connections and are not backed by large-scale farms. In some respect they are stagnating; perhaps their existence will be transitory.

(ii) The importance of these new villages justifies their inclusion in the settlement development policy. It would be necessary to separate the dynamic, more populated new villages from the transitory ones, and to guarantee their normal development. The most important thing is to remove the impediments to the formation of independent rural communities, or to give them the possibility of a certain self-government, of expressing their interests within the administrative rural communities.

What type of future can we forecast for these settlements? Can we suppose that the dual organization of Hungarian agriculture will last for a long time?

Some of the new villages will follow a suburban type of development. Prospects for the 'real' new villages (type 2) will depend on the social development of Hungarian agriculture. What this will be is a highly debated issue among Hungarian social scientists.

The classical Marxist theory supposed that large-scale collective farming will be the only adequate form of agriculture in a socialist society. But classical Marxist theory also supposed that socialism will be a post-capitalist social form, established first in the most advanced western countries (where there was a tendency in the middle of the 19th century for capitalist rented estates to dominate). When finally socialist society was established first in the less developed eastern periphery of Europe where only the big landed estates had the traditions of market production—the small peasant farms having had a self-sufficient character—socialist agriculture, too, was based on this tradition. Large-scale (state or cooperative) farms fed the urban markets, and household plots fed the agricultural families. It was supposed that as large-scale farms would develop and the separation of rural and urban markets would end, the household plots would lose their function. For this reason, the household plots were liquidated in the most advanced Eastern European socialist countries, in the GDR, and in Czechoslovakia. In Hungary where household plots and generally auxiliary farms contribute largely to the market production, the government accepts their importance in a pragmatic way—but it does not discuss their future.

We think that the dual organization of Hungarian agriculture is normal for East-Central Europe, and has a century-old tradition. The capitalist modernization of agriculture, from Prussia through Poland to Hungary and to Romania, also had this special form, where large-scale farms (big landed estates) produced first of all for the market, supplying it primarily with grains and industrial crops.

On the other hand, a great number of strongly self-sufficient peasant farms also sold the bulk of their labour-intensive crops and animal products on the market. This dual organization (developed under special historical and economic conditions) was disturbed twice in the last decades. First in 1945 when land reform liquidated the big landed estates, an absolutely necessary step politically, but one which had negative effects for market production. Compulsory delivery was introduced to assure the urban population's food supply. Then in the 1950s, during collectivization which liquidated small-scale, labour-intensive production, and resulted in a food shortage. As far as we can see, the development of Hungarian agriculture since the 1960s has re-established the dual form of Eastern European agriculture under the new social conditions; the differences in the marginal costs of the different agricultural products have again made large-scale farms grain and industrial-crop producers, while small-scale (auxiliary) farms produce the bulk of the labour-intensive crops and animal products, from wine and berries to honey and eggs.

(iii) We can conclude that the population size of a given settlement is not definitive for its viability. There are dynamic, high-level rural settlements of 2–300 inhabitants in the Danube–Tisza Interfluve, while settlements of this size are rapidly depopulating in northern Hungary or in south-western Hungary. Small population size is a disadvantage for the location of certain types of services, but the basic reasons for the decline of the small settlements in the north and the south-west are their deteriorating economic functions, their bad accessibility to urban centres, and the long demographic erosion of local societies, heavily disturbed by forced resettlement in the 1940s.

Notes

[1] Actually, the already existing rural communities will not be abolished till a total depopulation takes place; but the establishment of a *new* community has to face a great number of pre-conditions which are difficult to meet. This is still a remnant of the earlier, over-centralized settlement policy.

[2] The number of births given by young women is still above average in traditionally rural area.

[3] Rural construction—including that of public buildings—is generally carried out by the construction units of cooperative farms and by private contractors since state building enterprises only operate in the cities.

[4] A new settlement fund redistribution system is introduced on January 1, 1986 in which the financial independence of the local councils will be much strengthened.

[5] We have only estimates concerning auxiliary farming. We have tried to get close to the truth by indirect questions, but the farmers had a tendency to underestimate their household production and income, since they were not always able to clearly distinguish an interviewing research assistant from a junior tax office clerk.

Bibliography

BAUER, G.—ROUX, J. M. (1976) *La rurbanisation ou la ville éparpillée* (Paris: Seuil).

BECSEI, J. (1983) *Békéscsaba, Békés, Gyula és tanyavilágának településmorfológiája* (Settlement Morphology of the Towns of Békéscsaba, Békés and Gyula and their *Tanya* Zones), (Budapest: Akadémiai Kiadó).

BELUSZKY, P. (1973) "A tanyarendszer időszerű problémái—a tanyafelszámolódás folyamata" (The Problems of the *Tanya* Network Today—the Progress of the Liquidation of Detached Farmsteads), *Földrajzi Közlemények* no. 1: 19–39.

BERGER, M. et al. (1980) "Rurbanisation et analyse des espaces ruraux périurbains", *Espace Géographique* no. 4: 303–313.

CSATÁRI, B. (1983) "A tanyaátalakulás néhány vonása a Duna–Tisza Közén" (Some Features of *Tanya* Transformation in the Danube–Tisza Interfluve). In: *Társadalmi-gazdasági változások és településstruktúránk fejlődése,* (eds.: Tóth, J.—Dövényi, Z.), (Békéscsaba: Békés megyei Tanács).

CHIFFELLE, F. (1968) *Le Bas Pays neuchâtelois,* (Neuchâtel: Ed. de la Baconnière).

CLOKE, P. J. (1979) *Key-Settlements in Rural Areas,* (London: Methuen).

CLOUT, H. D. (1972) *Rural Geography,* (London: Methuen).

ENYEDI, GY. (ed.) (1976) *Rural Transformation in Hungary,* (Studies in Geography in Hungary 13, Budapest: Akadémiai Kiadó).

ENYEDI, GY. (1982) "Part-Time Farming in Hungary", *GeoJournal* 6, no. 4: 323–326.

ENYEDI, GY. (1983) *Formation of New Villages in Hungary,* (Paper presented for the 12th European Congress of Rural Sociology, Budapest: Mimeo).

ENYEDI, GY. (1984) *Az urbanizációs ciklus és a magyar településhálózat átalakulása* (Urbanization Cycle and the Transformation of the Hungarian Settlement Network), (Budapest: Akadémiai Kiadó).

ERDEI, F. (1975) *Magyar tanyák* (Hungarian *Tanya*s), (Facsimile Edition, Budapest: Akadémiai Kiadó).

KÄNEL, A. VON (1981) "Zur Entwicklung von Siedlungssystemen in Agrargebiet der DDR", *Beitrage zur Geographie* 30: 183–193.

KULCSÁR, V. (ed.) (1976) *A változó falu* (The Changing Village), (Budapest: Gondolat Könyvkiadó).

LETTRICH, E. (1968) *Kecskemét és tanyavilága* (Kecskemét and its *Tanya* Zone), (Budapest: Akadémiai Kiadó).

MATHIEU, N.—BONTRON, J. C. (1973) "Les transformations de l'espace rural: problèmes et méthode", *Etudes Rurales* no. 49/50: 137–159.

PÖLÖSKEI, F.—SZABAD, GY. (eds.) (1980) *A magyar tanyarendszer múltja* (The Past of Hungarian *Tanya* Network), (Budapest: Akadémiai Kiadó).

ROMÁNY, P. (1973) *A tanyarendszer ma* (The *Tanya* System Today), (Budapest: Kossuth Könyvkiadó).

SANT, M. (ed.) (1974) Regional Policy and Panning for Europe, (Farnborough: Saxon House).

TÓTH, J. (1977) *Az urbanizáció népességfölrajzi vonatkozásai a Dél-Alföldön* (Population Geographical Aspects of Urbanization in the South-Alföld), (Budapest: Akadémiai Kiadó).

VAITEKUNAS, V. (1980) "Ликвидация хуторской системы сельского расселения в Литовской CCP" (Liquidation of the Dispersed Farm Settlement System in the Lithuanian SSR), *Geografia* 16: 98–107.

VÁGVÖLGYI, A. (ed.) (1982) *A falu a mai magyar társadalomban* (The Village in Hungarian Society Today), (Budapest: Akadémiai Kiadó).

RURAL DEVELOPMENT ISSUES
IN PERIPHERAL AREAS

Case Study of the Mid-Békés Settlement Ensemble

JÓZSEF TÓTH

KEY-WORDS: *accessibility; Alföld* (Great Hungarian Plain); *attraction* zone; *Békéscsaba—Gyula—Békés; central* functions, ~ position; *development* strategy; *division* of functions; *functional* relationships; *hierarchical* level; *outer* zone; *peripheral* position; *regional* development policy, ~ differences, ~ planning; *relative* concentration of population; *settlement* ensemble, ~ network development plan.

The development of productive forces involves distinct regional differentiation particularly in periods of accelerated progress or when circumstances call for preferences for certain economic sectors and, consequently, for certain regions. A consequence of this largely spontaneous process is the production and reproduction of peripheral areas which represent outdated standards and structure. Regional planning and regional development policy have a decisive role to play in the study of these problems, in the outlining of opportunities for spatial levelling up and in how to procure the necessary requirements for this process. Geographical research can be of considerable help in fulfilling this function.

Presented in the following are the problems of regional development in a given area as well as the results of three years' complex geographical research aimed at solving these problems. Because of its centres, this region is on the one hand a dynamic focus of a macro-region in a peripheral position and, on the other hand, by the attached rural areas, an expressed periphery with special opportunities. The region in question is the Mid-Békés settlement ensemble in the south-east of Hungary.

Position and some characteristic features
of the Mid-Békés settlement ensemble

The Mid-Békés settlement ensemble is situated in the Alföld, the Great Hungarian Plain, a portion of a larger area which, as a whole, is characterized by relative backwardness. Owing to the peculiar history of Hungary, it was also considered one of the backward areas in earlier times. The situation did not change substantially even after the Second World War (Enyedi 1970) since in the first 20 years, the most effective elements in the existing national spatial structure were developed, having been motivated primarily by the objectives of rapid reconstruction and socialist industrialization. The Alföld, being in an unfavourable position, contributed to this process only with the labour released by agriculture during the organization of large-scale socialist farming. Within the Alföld, however, even in this period and especially since the launching of its planned development in the late 1960s there were some areas where the trend and nature of development was similar to the national ones and the dynamism reached or occasionally exceeded the national average (Sárfalvi 1971, Zoltán 1980).

The same process that took place between the Alföld and other regions occurred on a smaller scale within the Great Hungarian Plain itself. Some areas of the Alföld began to develop rapidly at an early date while others remained backward and caught up with delay. The changed economic geographical position of the Alföld, the alteration of the significance of transit routes and the international transport lines also contributed to the fact that certain areas became sites of a more efficient development of the productive forces.

The particular features of Hungarian history and the consequences of the change in economic geographical position resulted in a specific spatial structure in the Alföld. In the relatively loose texture, the spontaneous development progressed along the main traffic routes or the populous central settlements. Accordingly, the Budapest—Cegléd—Szolnok—Debrecen—Nyíregyháza—Záhony line and the Kecskemét—Szeged line were the first areas of dynamic development. Later, the same phenomenon could be observed along the southern stretches of the Danube, along the Tisza river between Szolnok and Szeged, in some centres of the Nyírség and also in the Mid-Békés region (Tóth 1980).

The post-war socio-economic development of the Alföld is still to be evaluated in a comprehensive way covering almost each element and considering also regional differences. Only some aspects of this problem are treated here. The global task of regional development in the Alföld is to raise the level of development of the productive forces in the macro-region to the levels in other parts of the country. To this end it must be realized that *the area is far from being homogeneous;* today, several relatively developed areas can also be delimited in the Alföld by the level of development of the productive forces (Enyedi 1976, Krajkó—Mészáros 1979). This lack of uniformity demands *differentiation* in the way and means of development. Considering the close interrelationship of regional development and the development of settlement network involves that the settlement network also has to be developed in various ways. This is not reflected in the settlement network development plan: neither in the treatment of the settlement network of the Alföld or other regions concerning their specific features and development planning accordingly, nor in the differentiation between the various areas of the Alföld. The lack of differentiation has adverse effects through the merging of problems or through the inability to solve the problems due to the uniform approach; it may lead to the conservation of the existing structure in many cases.

Conforming to a major requirement of the national plan for settlement network development, settlements of the same hierarchical level are located *in approximately equal distances* from each other over the area of the Alföld as well. This is so in spite of the remarkable differences within the Alföld as far as sellement size, structure and the population ratio between the inner area and the outskirts are concerned. In numerous instances this situation generates a *confrontation of interests* concerning the establishment of hierarchical levels and their rightfulness in the plan for settlement network development—especially because, explicitly or implicitly, the levels of hierarchy involve development funds. The nature of the settlement network in some parts of the Alföld makes it possible to promote a settlement into a higher hierarchical group than it would be justified from the real prominence of the given settlement as regards its central functions and its relative level of urbanization within its immediate neighbourhood only because of its central position or other factors. This is unfortunate for the development strategy or the related interests because it prefers the formation of a settlement hierarchical system which, unlike in other regions of the country, is not found in the Alföld. This will *inevitably* cause conflicts with the specific settlement structure of the Alföld.

The perspective settlement network, reflecting regional homogeneity, is in contrast to actual *regional inhomogeneity*. This refers not only to settlement network but to the level of the productive forces and the economic structure manifested in it. If regional development policy acknowledges some central places or areas in the Alföld and attempts to level up the whole area through effective development, the settlements and their network in these areas *have to be treated in a different manner* from the settlements in other areas as a direct consequence of the close interaction between regional and settlement development. In the settlement network development plan the *agglomeration trends*—due to urbanization—have to be taken into consideration also in the Alföld even if they are *only in their early stages.* They have been acknowledged administratively in the vicinity of Szeged which is in the most advanced stage of progress but similar trends are also observed around Szolnok and Debrecen and, in a special form, in the Mid-Békés urban region. The process of urbanization covering the entire country, which accelerated after the Second World War and particularly in the last decades, has intensified and diversified the inter-central relationships of settlements. Accordingly, ensembles of settlements in cooperation and mutual interdependence have appeared in the nation's settlement network and spatial structure. They can be grouped into three *grades* by the development stage of urbanization and the intensity and diversity of regional relationships (Figure 23). The first, with the most intensive interrelationships, comprises the *'agglomerations and agglomerated areas':* the Budapest agglomeration and the settlements along the NE—SW urban-industrial axis. *'Settlement ensembles'* represent a lower level of agglomeration, they also involve less developed and less urbanized parts of the country. Among them is the Mid-Békés settlement ensemble which has a significant role to play. Even today, besides the increased attention that settlement ensembles deserve all over the country, attention must be paid to the so-called *'settlement groups'* which are the most widespread in the Alföld. Their further development, the increased urbanization of constituent settlements and the intensified relationships between them have to be confronted with the problems of a necessary coordinated development in the near future.

Examining the highest levels of hierarchy, the Hungarian urban network is arranged in a *double concentric circle* around Budapest, the national centre (Figure 24). Between the constituents of these rings, aligned along radial lines of force starting from Budapest, there are alternative relationships in numerous places and so-called 'centres of absence' in some places. Among these centres of absence are the Tata basin, the settlement ensemble of Tatabánya, Tata and Oroszlány in the inner

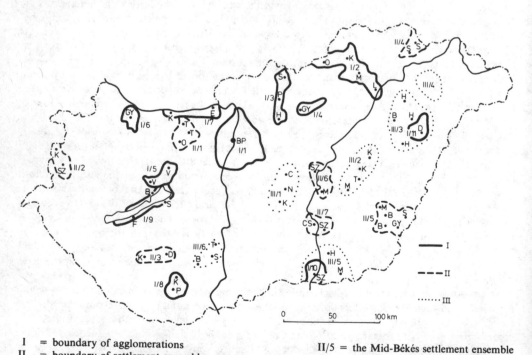

I	= boundary of agglomerations	II/5	= the Mid-Békés settlement ensemble
II	= boundary of settlement ensembles	III	= boundary of settlement groups

FIGURE 23 *Agglomerations, settlement ensembles and settlement groups in Hungary*

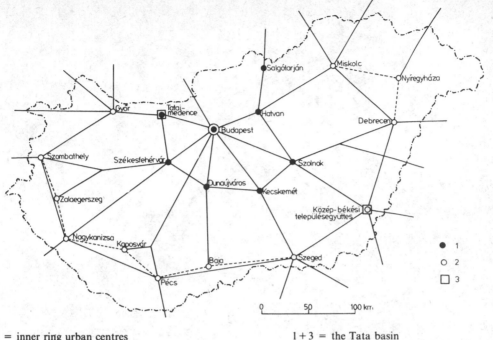

1 = inner ring urban centres
2 = outer ring urban centres
3 = settlement ensembles

1 + 3 = the Tata basin
2 + 3 = the Mid-Békés settlement ensemble

FIGURE 24 *The radial-circular structure of the Hungarian urban network*

ring between Budapest and Győr, and the Mid-Békés settlement ensemble between Debrecen and Szeged in the outer ring of settlements. This radial-circular arrangement is an essential feature of the Hungarian settlement network on which the development plan for settlement network has to be founded and which must be taken into account in long-term planning.

The Mid-Békés area, more advanced than its surroundings (Beluszky 1981), does not have a single urban centre like Szeged, Szolnok, Kecskemét, Debrecen or Nyíregyháza in other parts of the Alföld but it consists of three towns: Békéscsaba, Gyula and Békés. There is a certain division of functions between these three towns, they are in close functional relationships; the intensity of inter-central connections is higher here than in any other parts of the Alföld. The three legally recognized towns are accompanied in the geographical sense by two towns, Mezőberény and Sarkad, as well as by several smaller settlements in the area lying between.

The realization of national interests in this region presents some particular features because as a focus for development, the region is an urban one. The fundamental concept of a multidisciplinary study carried out in this area was that the development here could be accelerated through *coordination* supported by objective development and its realization. The accelerated development is useful not only for the area but also for the entire Alföld and a significant element in the formation of a *healthy spatial structure* for the whole of Hungary.

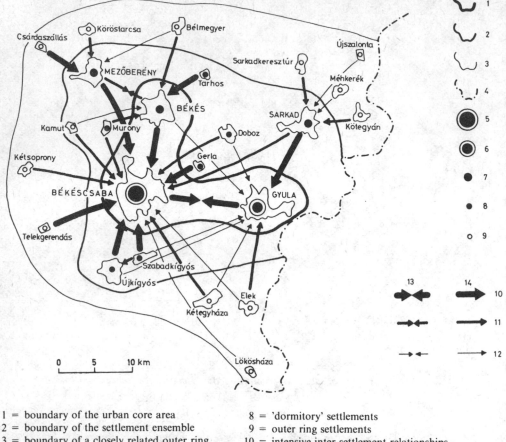

1 = boundary of the urban core area
2 = boundary of the settlement ensemble
3 = boundary of a closely related outer ring
4 = national border
5 = the major urban centre
6 = co-centre
7 = satellite centres

8 = 'dormitory' settlements
9 = outer ring settlements
10 = intensive inter-settlement relationships
11 = inter-settlement relationships of medium intensity
12 = loose inter-settlement relationships
13 = balanced inter-settlement relationships
14 = dominant inter-settlement relationships

FIGURE 25 *Functional relationships of the Mid-Békés settlement ensemble 1981*

The internal structure of the Mid-Békés settlement ensemble and the development problems in its peripheral areas

The results of the multidisciplinary research—aimed at the analysis of the functional and structural features, and the development opportunities of the Mid-Békés settlement network supported by central and county bodies—were published in five volumes with more than 2,000 pages (Tóth et al. 1981). Only some of the results and opportunities for development can be reviewed here.

The total area of the 24 settlements belonging to the Mid-Békés settlement ensemble is 1,758 km^2 in which there were 195,000 people in 1980 (Figure 25). Out of this, 124,000 people lived in Békéscsaba, Gyula and Békés. The remaining 21 communities had 71,000 inhabitants. These 21 settlements were divided into two zones of intensity as to what grade of attraction to towns do they represent as well as what is their peripheral position. In general, the following statements can be made:
—the life of these settlements is bound to the members of the settlement ensemble of legal urban status;
—the affinity for ever intensifies;
—the affinity is being transformed into a mutual interrelationship;
—two zones of intensity can be differentiated according to the degree of affinity;
—differentiation grows both for the degree of affinity and the level and rate of functional development;
—although affinity can be specified towards one of the towns out of the three, it can also be detected towards the others with varying intensity;
—development potential is greatest in settlements of multiple intensive relationships;
—Mezőberény and Sarkad have their own independent central functions within the group of settlements, therefore, they are in special positions;
—in spite of improvements in recent years, the regional system of administration does not reflect actual attraction zones;
—there are characteristic and differentiated changes in settlement-morphology of the towns and in its outskirts, too (Tóth 1976, Becsei 1983);
—the relationship of the area's settlements with the towns and between themselves necessitates comprehensive regional planning even on their present level;
—the unique character of the Mid-Békés settlement ensemble in the country provides opportunities for studying the special path of progress for the atrracted settlements without urban status.

Nine settlements belong to the *inner attraction zone.* They are in close and diverse relationships with the urban centres of the settlement ensemble. This is the scene of relative concentration of population: occupational structure reflects a higher urban level than the average of communities; population density (80 per km^2) is relatively high. The nine settlements of the zone are of three types:

(1) Mezőberény and Sarkad are considered as towns in settlement geography with relatively developed and differentiated socio-economic structures, independent attraction of some settlements, urban morphology and infrastructure in their centres (Tóth 1980, Szabó 1982);

(2) Gerla, Újkígyós, Szabadkígyós and Murony are residential settlements most intensively linked to the urban members of the settlement ensemble with large-scale commuting, subsidiary intensive agrarian production and rapidly changing outlook;

(3) Doboz, Tarhos, Kamut are settlements connected to the urban centres primarily through recreation, cultural and agricultural functions and, secondly, through their commuters, with slower changes in morphology.

The *outer zone,* previously attached to the urban members of the settlement ensemble, comprises 12 settlements. Their socio-economic structure is more traditional and their population density (45 per km^2) is lower than that of the communities in the inner zone. Three types can be differentiated:

(1) Kétegyháza and Elek are relatively populous settlements with higher-than-average level of infrastructure, good accessibility, many commuters and high-level agriculture;

(2) Telekgerendás, Kétsoprony, Köröstarcsa, and Csárdaszállás are settlements of various size with outstanding level of agriculture and average infrastructure which show intensive affinity to one of the urban centres of the settlement ensemble and loose bonds with the others;

(3) Lökösháza, Kötegyán, Méhkerék and Újszalonta are communities of the settlement ensemble along the border, the first two of which stand out from the periphery due to their transport facilities while the position of Méhkerék and Újszalonta is backward in several respects (Tóth–Csatári 1983).

Some elements of the strategy to be followed

All the essential features listed above have to be considered in the development strategy. The relationship of the settlements with each other and with the three towns even at their present level necessitates (and will even more so in the future) comprehensive regional planning and development. This, however, should not mean uniform treatment since the size, structure and dynamics are different for the particular settlements.

Depending on which of the three theoretically-possible types of regional development (concentrated, deconcentrated and micro-regional) gains prominence in the coming decades, the population number of settlements projected for the year 2000 shows variations. We believe that it is the *development of micro-regions* that would supply these settlements with the greatest energy for development. The difference between the two zones would increase regardless of which variant will be realized; a relative (perhaps even absolute) growth of population can be forecasted in the inner zone.

In-migration to towns has continued in the area. Its proportion will be similar to those of recent years: Békéscsaba (60%), Gyula (30%) and Békés (10%). A survey of non-local residents claiming dwelling in the three towns shows that 50 per cent of them intend to move to Békéscsaba. 70 per cent of those who wish to move to Gyula and 80 per cent in the case of Békés live in the non-urban settlements of the settlement ensemble. This indicates that migration will continue, although perhaps at a slower rate, because of the development variant to be performed in the future. Only a much more rapid development of intrastucture in the area could lead to a change on a larger scale.

The development of infrastructure is a key problem in the development of the whole area. The development of transport networks (establishing missing links and modernizing existing ones, organizing water transport, raising the level of telecommunication to that of at least Eastern European standards, wider supply etc.) would highly promote the functioning of the settlements of the area as an integral system.

In the elaboration of the development strategy, special attention must be paid to Mezőberény and Sarkad. These settlements are towns because of their functions; they have their own attraction zones and differentiated inner structures. In order to give better supply to other settlements, to widen the system of relationships in the settlement ensemble and to form a denser texture, their functions have also to be strengthened with the relocation of certain urban functions there.

In the transformation of the settlement ensemble into a loosely built-up area of comfortable surroundings but, nevertheless, of a possibly urbanized character, the recreation functions of non-urban settlements have a major role to play. It is necessary to merge the interests of agriculture, artifacts and leisure functions as soon as possible.

In planning—which has just started and which is backed by county bodies and the ministry, too—and later in development, differentiation has to be made between the two significantly distinct zones of settlements in the area and within them, according to the size and functions, the socio-economic structure of settlements and the intensity of their affinity to towns. This differentiation has to be carried out in a way that the local population can take an initiating and creative role in the integration of the varied elements into a settlement ensemble. We hope that the future practice of national settlement development gives a favourable opportunity for this in the discussed area.

Bibliography

BECSEI, J. (1983) *Békéscsaba, Békés és Gyula és tanyavilágának településmorfológiája* (Settlement Morphology of the Towns of Békéscsaba, Békés and Gyula and their *Tanya* Zones), (Budapest: Akadémiai Kiadó).

BELUSZKY, P. (1981) "Két hátrányos helyzetű terület az Alföldön: a Közép-Tisza-vidék és a Berettyó—Kőrös-vidék" (Two Underprivileged Regions in the Alföld), *Alföldi Tanulmányok* 5, (Békéscsaba): 131–160.

ENYEDI, GY. (1970) "Az Alföld gazdasági földrajzi problémái" (Economic Geographical Problems of the Alföld), *Földrajzi Közlemények* 18, no. 3: 177–196.

ENYEDI, GY. (ed.) (1976) *Rural Transformation in Hungary* (Studies in Geography in Hungary 13, Budapest: Akadémia Kiadó).

KRAJKÓ, GY.—MÉSZÁROS, R. (1979) 'Effects of Industrialization on the Economic and Social Changes in Village Areas on the South Hungarian Plain", *Acta Geographica* 19, (Szeged: Acta Universitatis Szegediensis): 3–33.

SÁRFALVI, B. (ed.) (1971) *The Changing Face of the Great Hungarian Plain*, (Studies in Geography in Hungary 9, Budapest: Akadémiai Kiadó).

SZABÓ, S. (1982) "Sarkad városiasodási szintje és fejlődési lehetőségei a közép-békési településegyüttesben" (The Level of Urbanization and the Development Prospects of the Community of Sarkad within the Mid-Békés Settlement Ensemble), *Békési Élet* 17, no. 1: 60–78.

TÓTH, J. (ed.) (1976) *Békéscsaba földrajza* (The Geography of the Town of Békéscsaba), (Békéscsaba).

TÓTH, J. (1980) "A területfejlesztés eredményei és feladatai az Alföldön" (Results and Objectives of Spatial Development in the Alföld), *Alföldi Tanulmányok* 4, (Békéscsaba): 147–161.

TÓTH, J. (ed.) (1980) *Mezőberény, a helyét kereső kisváros* (Mezőberény, a Small Town in Search of Itself), (Békéscsaba: Békés megyei Tanács—Mezőberény Nagyközségi Tanács).

TÓTH, J. et al. (eds.) (1981) *A közép-békési centrumok koordinált fejlesztését megalapozó kutatások (1978–1980) részletes eredményei* (Detailed Results of Studies (1978–1980) for the Coordinated Development of Mid-Békés Urban Centres). Vol. 1–5. (Békéscsaba).

TÓTH, J.—CSATÁRI, B. (1983) "Az Alföld határmenti területeinek fejlesztési problémái" (Development Problems of Border Regions in the Alföld), *Területi Kutatások* 6: 78–92.

ZOLTÁN, Z. (1980) *A változó Alföld* (The Changing Alföld), (Budapest: Tankönyvkiadó).

ACCESS AND THE SETTLEMENT PATTERN
IN PERIPHERAL RURAL AREAS

PAULUS HUIGEN

KEY-WORDS: *access; access-simulation-programme; accessibility; activity* programme; *bundle; constraints,* authority ~, capability ~, coupling ~; *mobile* shops; *path; physical* time-space structure; *primary* school; *prism; public* transport; *settlement* hierarchy; *shops; Southwest* Friesland; *time* demand, ~ supply; *time-space* approach.

Introduction

This paper will deal with the problems of the development of the settlement pattern in peripheral rural areas. These problems will be approached on a regional scale. Of the large number of subjects that might be considered to be part of these problems, the subject 'access' will take a central position. Access and accessibility are perhaps the key issues within the problematic nature of the settlement pattern in peripheral rural areas. For, being a general phenomenon in urban areas as well as in rural areas, it is at its most extreme in the latter. It is not without reason that Moseley (1979) gave his well-known book on access (and accessibility) the subtitle: 'The rural challenge'. The first section of this paper is an attempt to outline an approach to the access problem in relation to the settlement pattern in peripheral rural areas. By developing an access-simulation-programme (ASP)*, a method was found of measuring and standardizing 'access'. This ASP simulates the carrying out of activity programmes of individuals. A description of the objective, plan and operation of this programme has been included in the second chapter. The third chapter has a report of the application of the ASP. This deals with an evaluation in terms of access to a spatial contraction of employment and services. This spatial contraction may be regarded as the possible outcome of a stringent key-village policy. An exercise took place in Southwest Friesland, a peripheral rural area in the north of the Netherlands. The last section contains some concluding remarks on the subject of this paper.

The access problem in peripheral rural areas

Being situated virtually outside an urban regional housing-market and labour-market, peripheral rural areas are characterized by an almost continuous appearance of area-bound activities. The land of these areas is used predominantly for arable farming (Symes 1981). The direct consequence of this situation is a habitation pattern notable for its large number of small and relatively small villages. Due to a lack of sufficient demand, services have been organized on a regional scale. Economic activity offering employment outside agriculture and its related industries is scarce by its very nature and, in general, concentrated in large settlements. Consequently, inhabitants of peripheral rural areas are, in general, forced to cover large distances to be able to reach service locations and non-agricultural employment. Regarded in terms of time-space, there is a budget problem in peripheral

* The author is deeply indebted to Mr. P. J. Haringhuizen who has programmed the Access Simulation Programme.

rural areas between time-supply and time-demand. The daily time-supply of a population amounts to 24 hours multiplied by the population. The time-demand consists of the interaction between the population and the activity-system including all activities of the population (Parkes and Thrift 1980, p. 257). On the one hand, the budget problem consists of the distribution of an individual's time over activities and, on the other hand, of the distribution of activities over individuals (Hägerstrand 1972). Solving this budget problem is hindered in peripheral rural areas by the nature of their physical-spatial structure. When distributing activities over individuals the concept accessibility emerges. Activities require of their participants a certain time-use. The low number of inhabitants in peripheral rural areas, together with the fact that participation in activities is burdened by the use of a comparatively large part of the time-supply needed for covering distances, causes the placing of activities in time-space (moment and location) in such a way that the minimum of volume required for the development of activity will be reached. Accessibility, a characteristic of an activity localized in time and space and indicating the difficulty or ease with which this activity can be reached from the surrounding (potential) service area, is to be as large as possible.

In distributing time of individuals over activities—the other part of the budget problem—an important role is played by the concept access. Access is a characteristic of people and indicates the possibility to participate in activities. It could be described as the mobility of an individual enabling him to take part in every desired activity within the scope of his time and money budget. The quality of the access consists of the number of choices an individual can make to participate in various activities and in alternative activities of the same kind.

Maintaining the quality of life is often stated as an important objective of spatial planning and policy for peripheral rural areas. Within the framework outlined above, this objective can be stated as enabling all inhabitants of peripheral rural areas to take part in an activity supply of great variety. This should be seen against the background of the current economic depression and processes such as enlargement of scale and specialization. The economic depression entails in many cases a lower disposable income which will cause more difficulties for people to cover the necessary distances in order to take part in activities. Processes such as scale enlargement and specialization lead to a rise of thresholds for establishment, which will induce more and more services to vanish from peripheral rural areas. Cuts in government spending have the same influence on socio-cultural services. Within this context it seems important for the policy concerning peripheral rural areas to localize activities in time and space in such a manner that inhabitants can take part in them.

The Access Simulation Programme (ASP)

Much research has been aimed at making the concepts access and accessibility operational. Literature on this subject produces three important matters:
—problems of access and accesibility are concerned with possible behaviour and not with manifested behaviour (Hägerstrand 1974);
—research on the subject is done usually on a too-high aggregated level (Moseley 1977, 1979; Breheny 1978; Wachs and Kumagai 1973; de Boer 1977; Lenntorp 1976, 1980);
—the time-dimension is to be considered explicitly (Hägerstrand 1972; Lenntorp 1976, 1980).

Making the concept of access and accessibility operational, we keep to the general idea of the access and accessibility problem as was outlined by Moseley (1977, 1979): people—link—activity.

Measuring access is tantamount to answering the following questions:
—Can individuals take part in certain activities by using the transport available to them within the time available to them?
—How much choice do individuals have participating in activities?
These questions are to be answered by confronting the following elements of Moseley's model with each other:

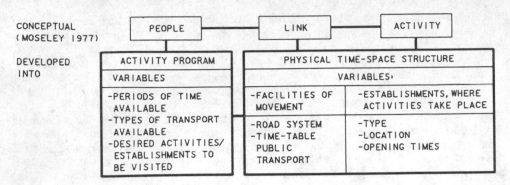

FIGURE 26 *Our approach to the access problem*

—time-space characteristics of individuals (residence, time-budget, means of transport available, etc.)
—time-space characteristics of facilities of movement (road-system, public transport timetable)
—time-space characteristics of activities in which participation is to be made (type, location, opening times).

The objective of the ASP is to simulate possible participation in activities so as to correspond with reality as much as possible. The results of the programme give an insight into the number of choices that can be made when participation is possible and provide a number of indicators concerning the ease (or difficulty) involved. We see the ability to take part as the ability to spend a certain period of time at the place (establishment) and for the period that this activity can take place (opening times). By a confrontation of activity programmes (a series of visits to be paid) with the physical time-space structure of a research area, the bottlenecks of the participation in activities can be studied. Our approach to the access problem is presented in Figure 26.

Several concepts derived from the time-space approach from Lund (for a review of this approach see Carlstein et al. 1978) underly the ASP. The 'path' concept is the most important of these: an individual (as well as an object) follows a path in time-space. This path is the sequence of positions taken by an individual in time-space. An individual is at a certain place at every point of time during his life. The concept 'prism' links up closely with the concept 'path'. A 'prism' is the accessible part of time-space. It contains all those positions in time-space in which the possibility to be part of an individual path is larger than zero. The projection of a prism on the earth's surface indicates which locations can be reached by an individual. The volume of the prism depends on the means of transport and time-interval available. These limits of the prism are the result of 'capability constraints'. These are constraints arising from the fact that people spend a large amount of their available time taking part in activities that enable them to survive (eating, sleeping) (Burns 1979). The maximum speed within the transport system, depending on the stage of technology, also belongs to these 'capability constraints'. The number of possible paths within the prism limited by capability constraints is even more limited by the action of 'authority constraints' and 'coupling constraints'. 'Authority constraints' determine who will have access to a specific position in time-space in consequence of the existing legislation, general regulations, balancing of power, etc. (for instance, a cinema show for adults). 'Coupling constraints' indicate that, if a given activity is to take place, there has to be a coming together in time-space by the participants (and objects) that are required for the activity. Both synchorization (coming together in space) and synchronization (coming together in time) are essential; in other words, a 'bundle'' must be made in time-space. Since individuals are coupled to given positions in time-space by means of 'coupling constraints' in the form of obligatory activities (labour, schooling), other spatial positions are not accessible at the same time. The situation in time-space of these obligatory activites (location and point of time) determines, together with the means of transport available within the prism limited by capability constraints, the accessible positions in time-space.

These concepts are being made operational in the ASP. The number of possible paths is generated in an existing physical time-space structure and, hence, the influence of those constraints present is pointed out.

As the ASP does not use probabilities it might be called deterministic. The programme is primarily of a descriptive nature. That is not to say that the application of the programme could not serve purposes of explanation. If an activity programme cannot be carried out, non-participation in the activities included in the activity programme is to be explained from the interplay of the constraints that are built into the physical time-space structure and into the activity programmes.

As for starting points and plan, the ASP follows the PESASP model developed by Lenntorp (1976). Differences between PESASP and the ASP are to be found especially in the way of making activity programmes and physical time-space structure operational.

ASP-PLAN

The overall plan of the ASP has been included in Figure 27. The input consists of one or more activity programmes and the physical time-space structure of the research area. In the first operation of the programme their consistency is checked and the number of theoretical paths

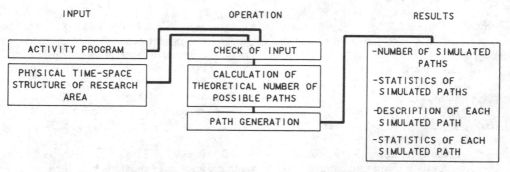

FIGURE 27 *The overall plan of the ASP*

possible is calculated on the basis of the input, and then the path generation—the actual simulation programme—starts. The number of simulated paths and some of their statistics make up the programme's results.

ACTIVITY PROGRAMMES

A schematic outline of an activity programme is given in Figure 28. At its centre is the payment of several visits. In this, participation in an activity is made operational. The Lund terminology speaks of a series of bundles to be made in time-space. In the ASP, there is a possibility to limit a visit in time and space. A visit limited in space means that the location of the establishment to be visited has been stated. If required, a visit can be limited in space in the sense that it should be paid to the nearest (measured by the road) establishment of the stated type. Another possible limitation that can be

ELEMENT	VARIABLES	
	OBLIGATORY	OPTIONAL
ACTIVITY PROGRAMME	-DAY OF THE WEEK	-RESIDENTIAL ZONE -NAME
START	-TIME OF STARTING -FIRST LOCATION	

VISIT	-TYPE OF ESTABLISHMENT
	  TO BE VISITED
	-DURATION OF VISIT
		-TIME OF ARRIVAL
		-LOCATION
		-NEAREST
		-MORE THAN ONE VISIT
		  TO THE SAME ESTABLISHMENT
		  AS THE ONE ALREADY VISITED
		-MEANS OF TRANSPORT
		  TO BE USED
		-SEQUENCE OF VISITS

END	-TIME OF ENDING -LAST LOCATION	
MEANS OF TRANSPORT		-TYPE -AVAILIBILITY INTERVAL

FIGURE 28 *The schematic outline of an activity programme*

chosen concerns that situation when several visits are to be paid to the same establishment. A visit limited in time means that the time of arrival of a visit has been stated. It is also possible to limit the number of possible sequences of several visits in time by stating a sequence of precedences in time. As a last limitation for a visit to be paid can be mentioned the obligatory use of a means of transport for the movements required.

In the elements 'start' and 'end' of an activity programme it is made operational that, during his life, an individual always takes a position in time-space. When the activity programme involves a daily path, the first location will be almost invariably the same as the last location, that is the individual's residence. Start and end form in Lund terms the points of beginning and ending in time of the (daily) prism in time-space.

The element 'type of transport' can indicate at which point in time which means of transport is available for the carrying out of the activity programme. The programme starts from the notion that movement on foot and by public transport is always possible. Bicycle, moped and motor-car can be stated as available means of transport. The options relating to the simulation of the ways in which individuals can move are different from the PESASP model developed by Lenntorp.

PHYSICAL TIME-SPACE STRUCTURE

The physical time-space structure of a research area consists of two elements: the facilities of movement in the area, and the establishments where activities can take place. The establishments form the structure's components, and the facilities of movement form the relationships between the establishments. Both elements are made operational in such a way that their positions in time-space are fixed. This operation is presented in Figure 29. The facilities of movement are made operational in a road-system and a public transport system. Being always accessible, the road-system presents a network of passages in time-space. The length of such a passage is equal to the distance between the distinct physical zones. In the ASP a distance matrix is made containing all distances between the distinct zones and the distances within these zones. Multiplication by the average speed of the means

ELEMENT	MAKING OPERATIONAL	VARIABLES
FACILITIES OF MOVEMENT	ROAD SYSTEM	-DISTANCES (INTERZONAL AND INTRAZONAL) -AVERAGE SPEED OF EACH MEANS OF TRANSPORT -PARKING TIME OF EACH ZONE
	PUBLIC TRANSPORT SYSTEM	-ROUTES -DEPARTURES
ACTIVITY	ESTABLISHMENTS WHERE ACTIVITIES TAKE PLACE	-TYPE -LOCATION (ZONE) -OPERATING-TIMES FOR EACH DAY

FIGURE 29 *The operationalization of the physical time-space structure elements*

of transport produces the travel-time. In simulating movements by motor-car, this travel-time can be increased by a certain period of time passed by parking in a specific zone. Further movements within this zone are made on foot.

Contrary to the road-system, the public transport system is not accessible in time-space at any moment. It takes the form of lines in time-space. Consequently, these lines are the paths of public transport vehicles. A movement by public transport implies that a 'bundle' is to be made in which the passenger and the public transport vehicle are the components. Grounded on route-descriptions (the sequence of zones which the route passes, and the travel-time between these zones) and on the departure-times of the public transport time-table, travel-times and waiting-times of a movement by public transport are calculated.

The establishments are fixed in time-space by their location and opening-times. For each type of establishment the zone in question and the opening-hours per day in the week are to be stated.

PATH GENERATION

The path generation consists of the payment of the visits included in the activity programme within the given physical time-space structure. The search area for the number of possible establishments which can be visited is limited as follows. Visits for which the time of arrival or departure is stated in an activity programme can be regarded as fixed in time. In every activity programme there are at least two 'fixed' visits—usually the start and end of an activity programme. The search area, in which the relevant establishments to be visited are located, has the form of an ellipse. The foci of this ellipse are the location of the first fixed visit (B1) and the location of the subsequent fixed visit (B2). The size of this ellipse can be determined by calculating the available time-interval for movements, that is the given point in time at B2, minus the given point in time at B1, minus the duration of the visit to be paid for which the relevant establishments are searched. Only those establishments are eligible to which it applied that the sum of the duration of movement from the establishment to the locations of fixed visits (B1, B2) is smaller than or equal to the time available for travelling (Lenntorp 1976).

In the programme the waiting-time, which might arise in the path-generation, is minimized, and the time of staying at private residence is maximized. This means, among other things, that, on leaving private residence, whether the departure might be postponed, will be tested each time. If, in a path, waiting-time arises and the means of transport is other than public transport, the possibility of a visit to private residence is considered. This visit is simulated when the possible time of staying at private residence is more than the sum of the durations of the travel to and from private residence plus a minimum of time of staying at private residence. Thus, the idea is made operational that, when individuals dispose of time to spend freely, they will usually go home because the attraction of the private residence is generally very high.

OUTPUT

The ASP output can be the starting-point for many further analyses. Both a description of each path found and a number of statistics of each path found can be attained as a result. For example, for each separate path, it is possible to calculate the length of the path in time-space, the area of the path, the total time of staying in private residence, the total waiting-time, the total travel-time, the distance covered, the number of zones visited and the number of establishments that can be visited. A total table is made for each zone, which mentions the number of paths found for each means of transport and the distribution of travel-time, waiting-time and distance covered, by mean, standard deviation, minimum and maximum. Besides attaining these results, it is possible to follow the simulation through its various stages and in doing so an insight can be gained, whenever the simulation fails, into the reasons for this failure. In short, we can say that the ASP provides the number of possibilities to carry out an activity programme and a number of indicators of the difficulty (or ease) involved therein.

Application of the access simulation model

By means of the ASP an exercise was carried out with the purpose of examining the consequences of a spatial contraction of services (schools, shops, workplaces, post offices). This contraction could be seen as the possible result of a realized key-village policy.

AREA OF APPLICATION

The exercise took place in Southwest Friesland, a region in the north of the Netherlands. According to research on identifying rural areas in the Netherlands by Hauer and Veldman (1980), the region of Southwest Friesland can be said to be peripheral rural. In 1981, this region had 109,290 inhabitants living in 124 settlements. The hierarchy of these settlements, as was drafted by the

TABLE 14

POPULATION NUMBER OF SOUTHWEST FRIESLAND IN 1981 ACCORDING
TO THE SETTLEMENT HIERARCHY

Settlement hierarchy	Population number		Number of settlements
	abs.	%	
Towns	50,883	46.56	4
Key villages of first order	11,714	10.72	4
Key villages of second order	3,521	3.22	2
Independent villages	13,588	12.43	11
Partly independent villages	7,957	7.28	11
Dependent villages	18,977	17.36	68
Rural area	2,650	2.43	24
Total	109,290	100.00	124

Source: Streekplan Friesland 1982

Provincial Planning Agency Friesland (Streekplan Friesland 1982), presents a picture as was sketched in the first section of this paper. Characteristic of the regions's habitation pattern is a large number of small and relatively small settlements, inhabited by a relatively small part of the total population (Table 14).

Apart from the 124 settlements of the research area, 11 external zones have been included in the application of the ASP. These external zones form a belt around the research area. In this way the research area is considered in relation to its surroundings and not as an isolated area. This is of particular importance in Southwest Friesland because some larger settlements are situated adjacent to the research area.

PLAN OF APPLICATION

The exercise consists of simulating the carrying out of two activity programmes in two different settings. One setting contains the number and spread of establishments to be visited in the activity programmes of Southwest Friesland in 1981. For the second setting a spatial contraction of services was constructed. So the second setting contains the number and spread of relevant establishments after spatial contraction. By comparing the results of the simulation of the carrying out of the activity programmes in these two settings we hope to gain some insight into the possible consequences of a possible spatial contraction of services on the access situation of the population in a peripheral rural area.

The following have been used as indicators for the access situation of a settlement: the number of choices for each means of transport to carry out an activity programme as well as the area of the minimum path per means of transport. The path area is calculated as follows: when an activity in the path is a stationary activity, the duration of that activity will be multiplied by the distance to the private residence. In case of a movement, the duration is to be multiplied by the covered distance, and the sum total is divided by two. The sum of these sub-areas accounts for the path area. It is the area of the path covered in time-space with regard to the private residence. A characteristic of this measure is that as the staying in private residence takes longer, the path area will be smaller. The minimum path is defined as the path having the smallest area. In this minimum path the time of staying in private residence is at its maximum and the distance from the private residence is at its minimum. The area of the minimum path indicates the ease (difficulty) involved in the carrying out of an activity programme as near as possible to the private residence.

INPUT

The basis data of this exercise are the road transport and public transport system and the average speed of the means of transport. The road system has been made operational in a distance matrix listing the shortest distances—measured by road—between the settlements concerned. Along with these inter-zonal distances intra-zonal distances have been calculated on the basis of the built-up areas. The public transport system was reconstructed from the data of the time-tables. The average speed for private means of transport, calculated on the basis of a time-space survey held in five settlements in Southwest Friesland in 1980 is: for bicycles about 13 kilometres per hour; for cars about 43 km/hour; and for pedestrians 5 km/hour.

Two activity programmes have been used in the exercise: a 'primary school' activity programme and a 'work' activity programme. Both activity programmes are based on data from a time-space survey carried out in 1982 in five settlements in Southwest Friesland (Huigen 1984).

The 'primary school' activity programme is as follows:

start: departure from private residence possible from 13.05;

visit to: 1. nearest primary school for five minutes to bring the child to school; time of arrival is 13.25 (school starts at 13.30);

2. private residence for at least 15 minutes; arrival in private residence not after 13.50;

3. nearest primary school for five minutes to take the child from school to private residence;

4. private residence for at least 15 minutes; arrival in private residence not after 15.55;

5. post office for ten minutes;

6. shops offering daily goods for 20 minutes;

7. shop centre offering a wide assortment of goods for 20 minutes;

end: arrival in private residence not after 17.35.

This activity programme gives a maximum travel time of 20 minutes from private residence to the nearest primary school and back. To reduce the number of permutations it has been stated that the visits nos. 5, 6 and 7 could not take place before visit no. 2. The accomplishment of the activity programme has been simulated in three phases, namely: firstly, walking and public transport, secondly, the bicycle, and thirdly, the motor-car as means of transport.

The 'work' activity programme is as follows:

start: departure from private residence possible from 7.00 a.m.;

visit to: 1. workplace for 240 minutes; arrival at work on 8.15 a.m.;

           2. same workplace as above for another 240 minutes; arrival at work on 13.00;

           3. shop for daily goods for ten minutes;

end: arrival at private residence not after 18.00.

This activity programme gives a travel-time of more than an hour to go to work. There is a lunch-break of 45 minutes. The simulation of the accomplishment of this activity programme was done in three phases: firstly, the bicycle as means of transport; secondly, the motor-car; and thirdly, public transport for the movement from and to work, and walking for the movement from and to the shop for daily goods.

For the first simulation series, the establishment of the relevant services of Southwest Friesland in 1981 has been filed. The file comprises the location and opening hours of schools for primary education (children aged from six to 12), shops for daily goods, post offices, shop centres offering a wide assortment of goods and employment centres (Table 15). To determine the location of these

TABLE 15

SERVICES USED IN THE EXERCISES

Number of settlements with at least one establishment

	1981	After constructed spatial contraction
Primary school	82	63
Shop for daily goods	99	79
Shop centre	31	19
Post offices	45	38
Employment centre	31	19

latter two services the settlement-hierarchy, as perceived by the Provincial Planning Agency Friesland (Streekplan Friesland 1982), has been used. All settlements that were classified as independent villages or higher in the settlement-hierarchy were listed as employment centres and shop centres offering a wide assortment of goods. Mobile shops for daily goods have been added to the file as the establishments with the most restricted opening hours.

In order to determine the changes that may occur in the access situation when a spatial contraction of the establishments in question occurs, a second file of establishments has been made. In doing so we observed the rule that services are to be concentrated in the settlements that take a higher position in the settlement-hierarchy. This can be regarded as one of the rules of a key-village policy. This rule was practised by discontinuing services at some locations. Shops for daily goods, localized in settlements that have been classified as rural areas or dependent villages in the service-scale, have been removed from the file. The number of mobile shops present, all offering daily goods, have remained and in some cases expanded. When, in a settlement classified as a dependent village, there were one or more shops for daily goods, but no mobile shop, a mobile shop has been added, while the shops for daily goods have been removed. Post offices localized in the settlements classified as rural areas or dependent villages have been presumed to have vanished. Shop centres offering a wide assortment of goods, and centres of employment have been concentrated in the settlements on the level of key-villages or higher. As for primary schools, all schools with two teachers at most were removed from the file. When a settlement had more than one school with two teachers at most it has been seen to that at least one school remained. Table 15 contains the results of this formulated spatial contraction.

RESULTS

The results of the exercise are shown in Table 16 and Figure 30. Before we go into the effects of the constructed spatial contraction we will describe some results of the simulation series carried out in the 1981 setting. The results, as was expected, show the existence of the well-known, almost trivial, variety of means of transport used. Those persons having the disposal of a car have by far the most possibilities to carry out the activity programmes. Also the minimum path areas are relatively small, indicating that the accomplishment of the activity programmes is relatively easy. For those

TABLE 16

SOME RESULTS OF THE EXERCISE
'primary school' activity programme

		Settlements without possibilities	Mean number of possibilities	Mean of the minimum path areas*
Walking	1981	100	2.4	81
after contraction		112	.9	90
Bicycle	1981	42	9.1	37
after contraction		73	3.7	61
Motor-car	1981	24	30.5	21
after contraction		44	20.8	37
Walking and public transport	1981	105	1.3	85
after contraction		117	.3	95

'work' activity programme

		Settlements without possibilities	Mean number of possibilities	Mean of the minimum path areas*
Bicycle	1981	–	10.5	13
after contraction		3	37.4	20
Motor-car	1981	–	50.0	7
after contraction		–	37.4	11
Public transport	1981	42	1.7	43.
after contraction		59	.9	57

* This measure ranks from 0 to 100. 0 indicates that all of the time is spent at home. 100 indicates that all the time in the activity programme is spent on travel, so that no visits can be made.

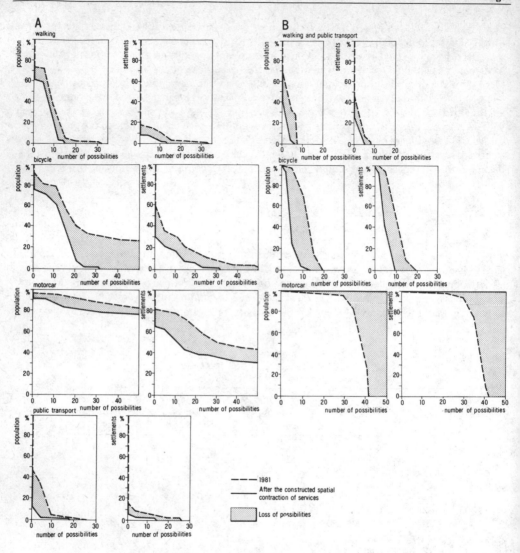

FIGURE 30 *The number of possibilities to accomplish two activity programmes before and after a constructed spatial contraction of services*

individuals with a bicycle there seems to be a reasonable number of possibilities to carry out the activity programmes, although it is impossible for the inhabitants of 42 settlements (total population 8,500) to accomplish the 'primary school' programme by bicycle. The actual problems seem to arise for those persons to whom neither car nor bicycle is available and who are to accomplish the activity programmes by public transport or walking or both. This category of individuals, however, will be the minority, as appeared from a time-space survey held in this area. In this context we must consider that the car-ownership in rural areas is higher than the national average.

It is also evident that the public transport cannot play an important role in the accomplishment of the 'primary school' programme as it appeared to be impossible to accomplish this activity programme from 105 settlements (85 per cent) by the combination of walking and public transport. On the other hand, public transport seems to offer a reasonable number of possibilities to accomplish the 'work' activity programme. Here it turns out to be impossible to pay the stated visits by public transport from 42 (34 per cent) of the settlements. For the public transport it is the synchronization aspect, the co-ordination of the time of departure of the vehicles at the time that people want to use them, that makes public transport rather inefficient in terms of access in the peripheral rural areas. Access is not a matter of the quality of the possible movement but of co-ordinating the individual's possibilities, the characteristics of the possible movements and the space-time characteristics of the establishments to be visited. An explanation for the minor role of public transport in terms of access in rural areas can be found in the trade-offs between the three, always conflicting, goals of an exploitation scheme of public transport in rural areas, namely (1) offering a service of high quality (high frequency, comfortable), (2) complete social (for all kind of people) and spatial (for all settlements) coverage and (3) low costs (Moseley 1979).

When the results of the 'primary school' simulations are compared with the results of the 'work' simulations it becomes evident that the accomplishment of the 'primary school' activity programme gives more trouble. The number of settlements without any possibilities to carry out the activity programme, the mean number of possibilities and the mean of the minimum path areas all indicate this. Due to the distribution (low density) and the number (small) of establishments of services in peripheral rural areas, the accomplishment of relatively complex multipurpose trips is often impossible.

When we consider the number of settlements and the population size in relation to the number of possibilities to carry out the activity programmes (Figure 30) we see emerging one of the choices which a policy for peripheral rural areas will have to decide on. For example, in 1981, it is impossible to accomplish the 'primary school' activity programme with walking as a means of transport from 80 per cent (100) of the settlements in Southwest Friesland. This is a rather high number. If we look to the population size we see that (only) 26 per cent (28,535) of the population of Southwest Friesland live in these settlements. This raises the fundamental question of weighing the efficiency of the settlement pattern against equity.

Table 16 and Figure 30 also show some of the effects of the formulated spatial contraction of services on the access situation in Southwest Friesland. As could be expected, the access situation in general has become less favourable after the spatial contraction. When we ascertain this fact we should use great care because, although the number and proportion of settlements without any possibilities to accomplish the activity programmes has risen considerably, this affects only a minor part of the population (Figure 30).

The effect is greatest for individuals who want to accomplish the 'primary school' programme by bicycle or by public transport in combination with walking. In 1981, this activity programme could not be carried out by bicycle in 42 settlements (8,467 inhabitants). After service contraction this is true for 73 settlements (22,615 inhabitants). For public transport, it was impossible to accomplish the 'primary school' programme from 105 settlements (56,754 inhabitants) in 1981. After the service contraction 94,050 inhabitants living in 117 settlements could not accomplish this activity programme. Compared with the other simulations, the 'primary school'—public transport simulation shows another picture on the topic of percentage of settlements versus percentage of population. The percentage of population living in settlements without any possibilities to carry out the 'primary school' programme by public transport and walking indicates a less favourable access situation than the percentage of settlements. Even for inhabitants of relatively large settlements there seem to be problems in using the public transport for the accomplishment of the 'primary school' activity programme.

By way of a rough conclusion, we may say that the impact of the formulated spatial contraction of services is relatively large:

—for the accomplishment of the 'primary school' activity programme. This suggests that problems can be expected in visiting several establishments offering daily goods and services if planning does not involve the co-ordination of the time-space characteristics of these services in time and space;

—for those individuals having motor-car at their disposal. Evidence from the already mentioned time-space survey points out that these individuals are to be found mainly among women with young children, the retired, housewives, men without jobs and students (mainly attending secondary education); and

—for settlements that have been classified lower than key-villages. For the inhabitants of the settlements classified as independent villages, especially the fall in the number of choices to carry out the activity programmes and the enlargement of the areas of the paths look quite dramatic. However, this can be explained largely by the way in which the contraction of services was practised.

Concluding remarks

The last part of this paper contains some concluding remarks. The first remark concerns the forming of a theory on the problems of rural areas. This paper has made a plea for the time-dimension to be considered explicitly and it seems that an application of the time-space approach in rural areas may yield fine results.

A second remark concerns the measurement of access. The ASP introduced here is in the development stage. The measurement of access by means of simulating the accomplishment of activity programmes appears to be a method which is theoretically sound and practically applicable. However, we must make mention of the problematic nature of the aggregation levels in measuring access. As the level of aggregation becomes lower, the measurement of access will be more in accordance with reality but a general picture of the access situation will be more difficult to determine. Further study on the complexity of the access situation—the relations between the results of different access measurements on a low level of aggregation—seems desirable.

The last concluding remarks deal with the settlement pattern in peripheral rural areas. Our exercise demonstrates that, after a spatial contraction of services, those persons having no car at their disposal may be expected to run into difficulties. In view of the current economic recession, future public transport policies are not likely to improve the access situation in peripheral rural areas. The question arises of who will be the inhabitants of those settlements that are not designated as key-villages. Will these become: "the countryside where only the most affluent could afford the necessary personal mobility to exist on urban based facilities, however expensive"? (Cloke 1983, p. 26).

Authorities and regional planners should contemplate carefully whether investing in improvements in the access situation of many small settlements with a rather low population total will be justified. The main question is whether the many small settlements should and can be maintained as independent spatial entities. These questions can be answered satisfactorily only if all spatial activities (living, working, using services) are involved in stating the problem. It is desirable to come to an integral policy and planning for peripheral rural areas which takes into account all activities in time and space.

Bibliography

BOER, E. DE (1977) "Bereikbaarheidsbeleid" (Policies for Accessibility). In: *Colloquium ver-voersplanologisch speurwerk* 1977 (eds.: Jansen, G. R. M. et al): 799–819.

BREHENY, M. J. (1978) "The Measurement of Spatial Opportunity in Strategic Planning", *Regional Studies* 2, no. 4: 463–479.

BURNS, L. D. (1979) *Transportation, Temporal and Spatial Components of Accessibility,* (Lexington, Mass.: D. C. Heath and Co.)

CARLSTEIN, T.—PARKES, D.—THRIFT, N. (eds.) (1978) *Timing Space and Spacing Time* Vol. 1, 2, 3, (London: Edward Arnold).

CLOKE, P. J. (1983) *An Introduction to Rural Settlement Planning,* (London: Methuen).

HÄGERSTRAND, T. (1972) *Tatörtsgrupper som regions am hällen* (Groups of Settlements as Regional Centres), (Stockholm: Allmann forlagert): 141–173.

HÄGERSTRAND, T. (1974) "The Impact of Transport on the Quality of Life". In: *Fifth International Symposium on the Theory and Practice in Transport Economics,* (Athens 22–23 October 1973, Transport in the 1980–1990 Decade, Vol. 1, Introductory Reports).

HAUER, J.—VELDMAN, J. (1980) *Kenmerken van landelijke gebieden op COROP-niveau* (Characteristics of Rural Areas on the COROP-Level), (Utrecht: Geografisch Instituut).

HUIGEN, P. (1984) "Access in Remote Rural Areas". In: *The Changing Countryside* (eds.: Clark, G.—Groenendijk, J.—Thissen, F.), (Norwich: Geobooks): 87–98.

LENNTORP, B. (1976) *Paths in Space-Time Environments. A Time Geographic Study of Movement Possibilities of Individuals,* (Lund: Department of Geography).

LENNTORP, B. (1980) *On Behaviour, Accessibility and Production* (Rapporter och notiser 58, Lund: Department of Geography).

MAYNTZ, R. (1967) "Modellkonstruktion: Ansatz, Typen und Zweck". In: *Formalisierte Modelle in der Soziologie,* (Soziologische Texte, Band 39, Niewied am Rhein und Berlin): 11–31.

MOSELEY, M. J.—HARMAN, R. G.—COLES, O. B.—SPENCER, M. B. (1977) *Rural Transport and Accessibility.* Vol. 1, 2, (Norwich: University of East Anglia).

MOSELEY, M. J. (1979) *Accessibility: the Rural Challenge,* (London: Methuen).

PARKES, D. N.—THRIFT, N. J. (1980) *Times, Spaces and Places, a Chronogeographic Perspective,* (Chichester: John Wiley and Sons).

STREEKPLAN FRIESLAND (1982) (Regional Plan Friesland), (Leeuwarden: Provinciale Staten van Friesland).

SYMES. D. G. (1981) *Settlement and Infrastructural Development (a Discussion Paper),* (Paper for the XI Congress for European Rural Sociology, Helsinki, August 9th–15th 1981).

WACHS, M.—KUMAGAL, T. G. (1973) "Physical Accessibility as a Local Indicator", *Socio-Economic Planning* 7, no. 5: 437–456.

PERIPHERAL SETTLEMENTS IN HUNGARY

The Example of Baranya County

ZOLTÁN KÁRPÁTI

KEY-WORDS: *centre*—periphery relations; *community* power and autonomy; *'first'* economy; *first generation* industrial worker; *key*-settlement; *labour*-market; *local* authority, ~ identity, ~ initiatives; *periphery*, geographical ~, rural ~, social ~, urban ~; *'second'* economy; *second generation* industrial worker; *small* village; *social* erosion, ~ inequalities, ~ marginality, ~ structure.

It is a task of future inquiries to elaborate the notion of 'periphery' in the East-Central European region. Though Wallerstein's (1974, 1976) analysis of the world economic system gives impetus to such investigations, centre—periphery relations on the national level have not yet been surveyed in their socio-economic complexity. Much has likewise been done on regional inequalities, but these projects have been focussing primarily on the geographic, demographic and economic dynamics, paying less attention to the sociological consequences. In our view, 'social periphery' is to be examined in its historical perspective: geographic, economic and social components are of equal significance to the establishment of peripheries over time. Sociologically seen, periphery can hardly be separated from social marginality; one has to take into account the changes in social structure, in the social composition and power structure of the communities, and in the forms of social reproduction in general. Family strategies and individual aspirations also deserve more attention.

In East-European societies, the socio-spatial distance comprises a series of factors: the function the settlement plays in national and regional production, the local development of the economy, like people's access to the labour-market both in the 'first' and in the 'second' economy; the settlement's chances in the allocation of state subsidies for communal development, as well as people's willingness and ability to supply and maintain basic amenities (road, water, communications, etc.) from private resources; the variety of local communal institutions, like health-care, schools, and generally, access to those goods and facilities which entail a higher level of urbanization; the efficiency of the settlement's land-use and housing policy, better housing conditions, etc.

It is obvious that deeply rooted spatial and social inequalities cannot be eliminated by short-term economic and developmental programmes. In the last decade, the Hungarian government has taken significant steps to encourage local initiatives, which, undoubtedly, widened the possibilities for development in the peripheral settlement units. Yet, the continued maldistribution of the central economic and development funds still delays the establishment of community power and autonomy. The efforts of the local authorities are also restricted by the fact that as a result of a tremendous population turnover in the peripheral zones, community feeling and the sense of local identity have gradually weakened.

In this paper we are focussing on the situation of small villages in Hungary by taking illustrations from a region (Baranya county) including a geographical periphery and an urban agglomeration which is also peripheral in many respects.

The economic policy worked out by the administration in the early 1950s was intended to abolish a lag of centuries within the shortest possible time. With the programme of very rapid industrialization, the economic management of the country endeavoured to achieve a fundamental change: to transform the agro-industrial structure into a primarily industrial one. For this reason, agricultural investments were limited to 13% of the total investments. At the same time, the proportion of the infrastructural investments—which in the developed capitalist countries was as high as 60%—was only approximately one-third of the total investments. Because of the shortage of capital and the difficulties of restoration after the war damages, and also as a result of the prevailing concept of industrial development: 'socialism is nothing but industrialization'; industrial investments were concentrated in the already existing urban-industrial centres, which had been the traditional seats of the extracting and primary manufacturing industries. As a consequence, villages and large agricultural areas found themselves in a relatively even more handicapped position.

The principle of industrialization which had formed the basis of extensive economic growth has remained a fundamental goal of economic policy even after the change to the stage of intensive development. This fact has had a number of consequences for settlement development and life style. First among these consequences are the problems connected with the development of the infrastructure. Despite the realizations and modifications, *the proportion of the national income devoted to infrastructural-communal investments has to these days remained an unjustifiably small part of total investments in terms of the level of economic development.* This is partly due to the fact that economic policy treats the question of infrastructural and communal development as 'non-productive' investments: such investments are made only where the settlement of a skilled workforce is an indispensable condition of industrial production. In the agricultural regions, the turn of the 1960s, the switch to the intensive stage, only opened the way for infrastructural-communal investments requiring little capital. This, however, brought no fundamental change in the direction of the accumulation of handicaps, or in the territorial distribution of power relations in the sphere of production. It is important to emphasize here once again *that the location of industry had to be built on the historically developed, extremely disproportionate settlement structure* and on the vast, existing differences in infrastructural levels.

The wave of rural industrialization, the decentralizing industrial policy of the 1960s, which aimed at freeing Budapest from its excessive burden and keeping surplus village labour at home, led to the creation of jobs on a mass scale in the countryside. Rural industrialization, however, was carried out in a manner full of contradictions (Barta—Enyedi 1981).

The location of the village workshops was basically financed by the centrally located city firms, whose aim was to save as much as they could by using the old machinery, employing cheap labour and sharing the infrastructure already on the spot. As a result, with some exceptions, rural industry has always lagged behind city industry in terms of technological level.

Since the production and reproduction of the workforce itself has come to be regarded as a 'non-productive' sector, another, no less important source of tensions has been the rigid separation of the habitation and production functions of the settlements, an attitude supported also by the dualism, and frequent conflict, of sectoral—organizational and local—territorial interests. The village industries are more or less under the control of national or county organs which have little interest in the communal development of villages. The profit realized in the value produced does not appear in the settlement which accomodates the production enterprises, but in the centre which redistributes it according to the stage they carry out in the production process. It is the locating industries that divide the production process in terms of territory, and adjust the different stages to the hierarchy of settlement in accordance with the training and composition of the local labour force and the capital-intensive nature of the investment. The finished product always appears in the town, and there it receives its elegant form of exchange value. The more developed the settlement, the more important its role in the production process, the more significant the industry that would settle there. At the same time, this is also the basis of its more dynamic further development, since the state development subvention is a factor of the accumulated capital value. For this reason the extension of the legal sphere of authority of the local council and the increase in their independence according to the new measures of 1971 can only be formal, since their financial independence extends only as far as the utilization of the village development fund.

Of the effects which industrialization has had on village society, the mass spread of *commuting* is of great significance. As a result of commuting, a characteristic new social stratum has developed: the two-centred workers, who have travelled the various roads from peasant to worker, and as a result have created a specific life style. Commuters are overwhelmingly those peasant-workers who work in an urban industry, but live in the nearby villages, doing part-time farming after eight hours of work in the town. At the same time, this stratum which constantly seeks a better position on the labour-market both in the primary and in the second economy, is geographically very mobile. This migration, however, has a selective character: *those with higher qualifications orient themselves towards the higher class of settlement,* a necessary consequence of the hierarchical structuring of industry described above. Thus the social structure of the settlement system is also transformed, but this process hits the lowest class of settlement groups the worst, thereby relatively accelerating the rate at which handicaps accumulate.

Tiny and small settlements, especially 'non-economic' sized villages, definitely belong to the lowest class of settlements. Their extremely peripheral situation stems primarily from the coincidence of geographical distance (many are located at the country borders, far from any urban centre) and the lack or poor accessibility of provisions. Their social structure is distorted; the population is aged or socially marginal, and they suffer from the lack of political and economic autonomy. Our sociological survey in Baranya county (south-western Hungary)[1] indicates that this coincidence is nothing but an accumulation over time of disadvantageous social processes.

Since World War II, a rapid population decrease has taken place in Baranya's small villages. This was partly due to the evacuation of the German inhabitants who were replaced by poorer agricultural labourers and agrarian proletariat volunteering and asking for land whose farming traditions and skills were insufficient to maintain the former standards of cultivation and market-oriented activity. Since the 'new-comers' found it difficult to fit in, the resettlement campaign led to further migrations, which contributed to the relatively fast deterioration of houses and farm buildings. This process was only accelerated by the change to large-scale agricultural methods. The landscape and natural potentials (the marked surface divisions and eroded hills) proved to be extremely unfavourable for the development of mechanized large-scale farming built on the extensive production of grain. Thus, failing to provide a living, this modernization led to the out-migration of the core (native Hungarian) inhabitants experienced in traditional farming. As a consequence, the *social erosion* continued: the falling price of land and housing gave way to the inflow of gipsy and other marginal population. For budgetary and planning reasons, the state regarded—by now 'justly'—non-economic the further maintenance of local institutions (commerce, education, health, etc.) and moved these to the higher classes of settlement. Simultaneously, it also changed the public administrative status of these villages, making them sub-villages of low-level centres.

The central town district of the county (Pécs and its urban region) emerges like an island from the sea of neighbouring settlements, including the county's slowly developing small towns (Mohács, Szigetvár, Siklós). In this settlement structure, based on the opposing poles of tiny village and—by Hungarian standards—great city, the target of migration is almost exclusively Pécs. This, however, leads to the relatively bad housing conditions in the city, in spite of the fact that almost 90% of the county's development fund has regularly been invested in the city's housing, health care and education. The strong syphoning power of the urban centre prevails in different ways as well: the county seat absorbs not only population and money but also institutions from its near environment, creating a development vacuum in the shadow of the 'great metropolis'. The villages around Pécs are less urbanized than some of the recently developed key-settlements in the outer zone, far enough away to avoid direct symphoning effects, and to develop more autonomy both economic, and in communal policy making. The villages in the urban agglomeration have incomplete or outdated infrastructures, most of them suffering permanently from water and air pollution. Since energy comes directly from the centre, there are frequent water shortages and black-outs. Sometimes they function as transitory residences on people's way to the city, so socially they are almost as unstable as the geographic periphery. The inhabitants of these quasi-communities are greatly dependent on the city's labour-market (at least in the 'first' economy); their everyday activities (work, shopping, leisure) are bound to the urban centre.

Though in these villages the level of urbanization is low—they are nothing but the rural extensions of the urban periphery, though strictly separated from the urban world by administrative borderlines—we cannot say that the villagers are just surviving on the fringe of the society. While the people in the remote tiny villages are in a marginal social situation, those in urban agglomeration enjoy the benefits of their environment without being the victims of urban constraints. Instead of the privileged status of an urbanite, they have chosen a more profitable semi-peasant life. Under the present economic conditions in Hungary, people strive to be sober and rational: they sacrifice urban life and culture in order to acquire properties (land and home) at more reasonable prices and in order to benefit from the second economy (household farming).

As a consequence of this attitude, migration to the city has gradually slowed down. Though the city is still attractive, the great variety of additional income sources keep people in the rural areas, and even attract some of those urbanites who have no chance to improve their position in the city's housing market. The wide range of 'second economy' activities and the promise of cheaper housing seem to compensate for the low-level infrastructure and the lack of basic amenities in rural areas. (Table 17 provides an insight into the differences in housing conditions of town and village workers.) This compensation gains even greater importance in the peripheral villages where—

TABLE 17

HOUSING CONDITIONS OF TOWN AND VILLAGE WORKERS
IN THE PÉCS AGGLOMERATION

The percentage of:	The size of flat or house square meters/person	
	12 m² or less	24 m² or more
First-generation *rural* industrial workers (N = 250)	15.5	31.8
Second-generation *rural* industrial workers (N = 250)	23.6	27.6
First-generation *urban* industrial workers (N = 250)	32.6	15.6
Second-generation *urban* industrial workers (N = 250)	41.6	11.8

Source: Survey results

mutatis mutandis—wages are lower than the average, and multiplied secondary income sources are necessary both to stabilize the household economy, and to pay for the high cost of migration for those willing to move upward in the hierarchy of settlements. The need for the second economy grows as we move down along the urbanization 'slope', from the urban centre toward rural peripheries (peripheries caused by the maldistribution of the development fund). As it is shown in Table 18, even urban industrial workers are doing part-time farming.

It needs no elaboration that a peasant origin and inherited agricultural skills play a considerable role in part-time farming. Urban industrial workers of peasant origin are more successful than their second-generation peers in the villages of the urban region. The rather low technological level, the

TABLE 18

PART-TIME FARMING AND HOUSEHOLD PLOTS IN THE PÉCS AGGLOMERATION

	Proportion of part-time farmers (%)	Average size of land per household (in acres)
Second-generation *urban* industrial workers (N = 250)	13.8	0.34
First-generation *urban* industrial workers (N = 250)	29.3	0.48
Second-generation *rural* industrial workers (N = 250)	58.0	0.78
First-generation *rural* industrial workers (N = 250)	64.4	0.96

Source: Survey results

legally or voluntarily restricted size of the arable land, are insufficient for accumulation and further investment in agriculture, and the most the worker-peasant can achieve is housing reconstruction, or building a new family house. The more people are willing to enlarge and intensify their agricultural enterprise, the more they have to withdraw from the urban region, and the less time and opportunity they have to share the benefits of urban civilization. Urbanization and economy seem to have contradictory effects on the average labourer household. Amenities are plentiful in the urban centre, but a lack of additional income sources delays the rise from social marginality in the case of people still coping with serious housing and income difficulties. In the villages of an urban region, housing conditions and additional income possibilities may improve, but the lack of infrastructure, communal services and institutions encumber everyday life.[2]

The results of our survey indicate that the concept of 'social periphery' must be evaluated in the context of several factors: a peripheral situation clearly appears where geographic (and also redistributional) distance parallels social marginality, that is, in small village areas along administrative (country- and county-) borders. In the urban region, the centre—periphery relationship is more complicated: an interplay of counteracting effects comes into being. Still, there is significant inequality between town and village, and urban agglomeration is to be considered peripheral in the process of urbanization. On the other hand, the closeness to the centre enhances the accessibility of urban civilization, while the rural environment may offer more chances for the material improvement of living conditions. Both town and village have their own advantages and disadvantages, and it has become more or less a matter of economic necessity and personal decision which alternative to chose. The real losers in this process are those rural labourers who live on the geographic fringe, too poor and too far from the centre to be able to overcome the historically rooted social, economic and spatial gaps; or those urban labourers who live in the centre, but have no chance, no traditional capability or inclination to become involved in the 'second economy'.

Notes

[1] The survey was carried out between 1977 and 1981, under the aegis of the Hungarian Academy of Sciences. We chose 1,000 industrial working class families in the city of Pécs and in the villages of its agglomeration. The main results of the survey were published in several articles and reports. See for example: Zs. Hantó–Z. Kárpáti: *Ipari munkások életmódja a pécsi agglomerációban* (The Life Styles of Industrial Workers in the Pécs Agglomeration), Transdanubian Research Institute, HAS 1981,

Pécs, 181 p.); Z. Kárpáti: *Az urbanizációs folyamat társadalmi és gazdasági meghatározói. Munkások munka- és lakáspiaci magatartása a pécsi agglomerációban.* (Social and Economic Determinants in the Urbanization Process. Workers' Attitudes on the Labour and Housing Market in the Agglomeration of the City of Pécs), Dissertation for the Candidate of Science degree, Institute of Sociology, HAS, Budapest, 1984, 219 p.

² In speaking of 'additional income sources' we mean primarily agricultural activities. There are also other forms of the 'second economy', for example semi-private enterprises in industry and service, moonlighting, 'black-jobs', etc. To a limited extent, urban labourers can also participate in these. On the other hand, living in a village does not necessarily mean being involved in part-time farming.

Bibliography

ANDORKA, R. (1979) *A magyar községek társadalmának átalakulása* (The Social Transformation of the Hungarian Villages), (Budapest: Magvető Kiadó).

BARTA, GY.—ENYEDI, GY. (1981) *Iparosodás és a falu átalakulása* (Industrialization and the Transformation of the Village), (Budapest: Közgazdasági és Jogi Könyvkiadó).

BOGÁR, L. (1983) *A fejlődés ára* (The Price of Development), (Budapest: Közgazdasági és Jogi Könyvkiadó).

BEREND, T. I. (1979) *A szocialista gazdaság fejlődése Magyarországon, 1945–1975* (The Development of the Socialist Economy in Hungary 1945–1975), (Budapest: Kossuth Könyvkiadó).

ENYEDI, GY. (1980) *Falvaink sorsa* (The Prospects of Our Villages), (Budapest: Magvető Kiadó).

ERDEI, F. (1974) *Magyar falu* (The Hungarian Village), (Budapest: Akadémiai Kiadó).

FERGE, ZS. (1963) *Társadalmunk rétegződése* (The Stratification of Our Society), (Budapest: Kossuth Könyvkiadó).

FERGE, ZS. (1979) *A Society in the Making. Hungarian Social and Societal Policy 1945–1975* (Harmondsworth: Penguin Books).

HANTÓ, ZS.—KÁRPÁTI, Z. (1978) "The Development of Settlement Structure in the Hungarian Village". In: *Hungarian Society and Marxist Sociology in the Nineteen-seventies*, (eds.: Huszár, T.—Kulcsár, K.—Szalai, S.), (Budapest: Corvina Kiadó).

HANTÓ, ZS. —KÁRPÁTI, Z. (1982) "Településrendszer és életmódfeltételek egy aprófalvas régióban" (Settlement System and Living Conditions in a Region of Small Villages). In: *A falu a mai magyar társadalomban* (The Village in the Hungarian Society Today), (ed.: Vágvölgyi, A.), (Budapest: Akadémiai Kiadó).

HEGEDŰS, M. (1973) *Gazdasági fejlődés és urbanizáció* (Economic Development and Urbanization), (Budapest: Akadémiai Kiadó).

KÁRPÁTI, Z. (1972) *Regional Handicaps and Urbanization of Living Conditions,* (Budapest: Institute of Sociology, Hungarian Academy of Sciences).

GÁBOR, R.—GALASI, P. (1981) *A második gazdaság* (The Second Economy), (Budapest: Közgazdasági és Jogi Könyvkiadó).

KONRÁD, GY.—SZELÉNYI, I. (1971) "A késleltetett városfejlődés társadalmi konfliktusai" (The Social Conflicts of the Delayed Urbanization), *Valóság* 14, no. 12: 19–35.

KULCSÁR, K. (1982) *A mai magyar társadalom* (The Contemporary Hungarian Society), (Budapest: Kossuth Könyvkiadó).

RUPP, K. (1973) "Társadalmi mobilitás és településszerkezet" (Social Mobility and Settlement Structure), *Szociológia*, no. 1: 29–43.

SZALAI, J. (1981) "Hiány és társadalmi szelekció" (Shortage and Social Selection), *Valóság* 24, no. 8: 23–36.

VÁGI, G. (1982) *Versengés a fejlesztési forrásokért* (Competition for Development Resources), (Budapest: Közgazdasági és Jogi Könyvkiadó).

THEORY AND PRACTICE
IN RURAL SETTLEMENT PLANNING

An Example of the Province of Friesland

DINNY DE BAKKER AND ANDRIES PIERSMA

KEY-WORDS: *central place theory* assumptions, ~ application, ~ hierarchy; *concentration* of population, ~ of services, ~ tendencies, policy of ~; *country* towns; *Dorpenplan* (Village Plan); *economies* of scale; *Friesland*, Provincial Government of ~, Provincial Planning Agency ~, Southwest ~; *gemeente* (municipality); *IJsselmeerpolders; image* of man; *key-village; liveability; municipality* (gemeente); *nuclei* of industrialization; *peripheral* rural areas; *services*, daily ~, non-daily ~; *settlement* planning, ~ category, key-~ policy; *suburbanization; threshold* concept; *Village* Plan (Dorpenplan), dependent ~, independent ~.

Introduction

This paper deals with the consequences of rural settlement developments in peripheral rural areas in the Netherlands. Emphasis is laid on the relevance of geographical theory for spatial planning of the settlement pattern in the past and the effects of planning policy for the development of settlement patterns. The scale on which the analysis takes place is a regional one. Attention will be devoted to changes in the planning policy for the province of Friesland. The effects of this policy will be examined with empirical evidence from the south-western part of this province.

Spatial planning of the settlement pattern in the peripheral rural areas of the Netherlands has a very short history. Two interrelated problems which emerged after the Second World War gave rise to government action is this field. The economic disparity in relation to the more urbanized part of the country was the first major problem. The rapid decrease of employment in agriculture was not composated by an increase of employment in industry. This imbalance caused a net migration loss with the western part of the Netherlands, which was undesirable for two reasons. In the first place it helped to maintain the difference in prosperity and well-being between the peripheral and the urbanized areas. In the second place it created pressure on the overcrowded western part of the country. These problems were countered by a policy of dispersal of economic activities to the peripheral rural areas. This policy of dispersal created the planning problem of how to spread government investments over the peripheral rural areas.

The second problem is concerned with the service structure. Rising population thresholds for the establishment of services for daily needs and rising expectations of the public with respect to the service level created the planning problem of where to maintain existing services and where to locate new ones.

Both of these problems were countered from an economic, rational, point of view. The slogan with respect to the spread of government investments was national dispersal of industrialization by regional concentration (Hoofdcommissie 1951). New housing, infrastructure, industrial estates, public amenities and schooling facilities were concentrated in centres selected for their growth potential or labour surplus or both, the so-called nuclei of industrialization. Cost minimization for potential new industry and an understanding of the effects of agglomeration were the foundation of this policy.

Concentration of housing, services and employment was also seen as the panacea for the second problem. The key-villages in which this concentration would take place were, however, considerably smaller than the nuclei of industrialization. A second difference with the nuclei of industrialization policy was the application of central place theory ideas in the preparation of key-village plans. In the first half of the 1960s, the idea was common that the settlement pattern in peripheral rural areas was denser than necessary for the provision of the rural population. Experience in the settlement planning in the IJsselmeerpolders supported this idea. An outstanding example of rural settlement planning according to central place theory is the Village Plan (Dorpenplan) in the province of Friesland. In this paper the application of this theory for rural settlement planning in Friesland will be evaluated.

Application of central place theory is a result of the economic rational way of thinking in geography and planning in the 1960s. In our opinion this cannot be disconnected from the image of man which was the consequence of this way of thinking. The assumptions of central place theory are a clear illustration of the image of man in an economic, rational, way of thinking. The following two chapters will go into the image of man in western scientific thought in general and in central place theory in particular. The application of central place theory in the Friesland settlement policy and the effects of this policy for the settlements in Southwest Friesland will be discussed in three subsequent chapters. The social friction which eventually led to the abandonment of the key-village policy is the subject of the last but one chapter. In the conclusion some suggestions will be given for an alternative approach to a policy framework for the settlement pattern.

The image of man in western scientific thought

To trace the materialistic-mechanistic way of thinking in western scientific thought we have to consult the history of human thought. Two outstanding scientists, namely Galileo Galilei (1564–1642) and René Descartes (1596–1650), can be considered as the founding fathers. Natural scientific thinking was the only way of thinking for both. Relationships were only cause-and-effect relationships which have to be transferred into mathematical symbols and formulas. True science is quantitative and naturalistic.

According to Descartes, animals react as machines and human beings do likewise. But he did not know how to treat the human mind. Though Descartes recognized a certain dualism between body and mind, his contemporaries, the Englishman Thomas Hobbes (1588–1679) and the Frenchman Jean Offray de la Mettrie (1709–1751), regarded the human body as nothing more than a complicated machine. Body and mind are of material substance and thus have to be studied according to the method of the natural sciences. And it is in this issue that the naturalistic, quantitative and reductionist scientific attitude of thinking is rooted today. As scientists, mostly unconsciously, we have reduced man to the status of an object of lifeless nature.

We do have a conception of man, although mostly implicit, at least if we, as social scientists, confess that man has to be part and parcel of our science. In any case we have an intellectual duty to ask ourselves in which manner we consider man in practising science, especially social science which has to do with man. But what then is the explicit image of man? Or, to put it differently, are body and mind only of a material substance? Do body and mind function as a machine, robot or computer, in a mechanical way? We do not believe this but we often treat man in this way. At present we attempt to reproduce man's mental capacity in a computer. But research has shown that the so-called computer-analogon does not hold (Lopes da Silva and van der Tweel 1982). Human action is always anticipated, guided and stimulated by a spiritual element, an element which cannot be imitated by a mechanical switchboard. Therefore, in human action, a component of thinking and decision always plays a crucial part. In view of this component of thinking and decision, a natural science approach is highly questionable in the social sciences. But, because of the dominant natural scientific method of thinking in western scientific thought, we consider man mostly as already said, unconsciously, as a thing in human geography, sociology and other social sciences.

The hidden assumptions concerning man
in Christaller's central place theory

From what has been said above about the image of man it can be concluded that even in the social sciences the mechanistic natural-science view of man is dominant. But, having made it more or less explicit now, we can elaborate on it.

In rural settlement planning we can acknowledge that elements of Christaller's theory, though unmentioned in nearly every report, have been applied. A crucial question then presents itself: which assumptions does this theory hold about man?

Without enumerating all assumptions of this theory, concerning man, the theory assumes that all consumers are identical, that means that they all have the same needs and thus have a similar consumer pattern (Buursink 1980, Timmermans 1980). In other words, consumers are considered as research objects, as things, to which the same attribute of an identical consumer pattern is attached. But as similarity is essential in physics, that is physical reactions, it is not essential in social science and in human action (Poincaré 1979). Therefore, this theory does not break away from the natural science view of man. In spite of this serious objection we have to wonder how far this theory (model) is applicable in settlement planning.

In the Netherlands, central place theory was applied for the first time to planning the settlement pattern in the IJsselmeerpolders. These are polders newly reclaimed from the sea, initially only for agricultural purposes. It meant a great opportunity for planners to create a new settlement pattern in an unoccupied area based on recent social science research. Takes (1948) and Constandse (1960, 1972) can inform us in detail.

In the planning of settlements in the Northeast Polder, one of the oldest IJsselmeerpolders, a hierarchy of material provisions (one of the other assumptions of Christaller's model) has been taken into account, but the assumption considering man has not been applied. Contrary to this, a variable consumer pattern has been considered in planning these settlements. Attention has been paid to the composition of population in the settlements and to non-material 'needs' such as church and school (thus not biological but spiritual 'needs') have been taken into account. In general, we can say that some principles of Christaller's model have been applied in the IJsselmeerpolders (the hierarchy of material provisions) on a macro-scale, but on a micro-scale the principles of a 'thingified' man have been neglected. For empty space, therefore, the Christaller-model with some modifications can give us a frame of reference of how to plan settlements.

In already-occupied space things are much more complicated. Planning the settlement pattern means an interference in existing social structures. This makes the application of central place theory with its pure economic materialistic background risky. In the remainder of the paper we will go into the Friesland settlement policy which represents a clear example of the application of central place theory in rural settlement planning in the Netherlands.

Government settlement policy in the province of Friesland

A policy based on the central place theory was implemented in Friesland from 1966 to 1975. We want to examine the role of this theory in rural settlement planning. One of the basic characteristics of central place theory is the assumption that rural settlements occur as part of a hierarchical pattern with the ensuing planning objective that the operation of this hierarchy should be upheld by supporting nodal points within it. The policy in the province of Friesland has been put into words in a research note by the Provincial Planning Agency which appeared in 1966. This research note was approved by the Provincial Council as a guideline in policy-making for municipalities and the provinces. In the Village Plan, which has been formulated in this note, we recognize as we stated above, the basic assumption of hierarchy and the objective of concentration.

In this section we describe the context in which central place theory was adopted, in order to make its application understandable. After that we will go into the policy of the province of Friesland in more detail.

Friesland lies in the north-eastern part of the Netherlands and is one of the most rural provinces. In 1966, it had 500,000 inhabitants of which, according to the Provincial Planning Agency (PPA) division, about 60% lived in rural settlements. In 1960, 23% of the population was employed in agriculture. The attention in this paper will be directed to the south-western part of this province (Figure 31).

Cloke (1983) describes in what he calls a heterodox view of planning, seven variables which affect plan preparation: resource availability, survey and analysis, government advice, theory, planning vogue, ruling political group's requirements and the planners' and politicians' perception of the world. It will become clear in the following that these variables favoured the adoption of central place theory for Friesland.

In the first place, there were the results of research done by the Provincial Planning Agency. These are summarized in the above stated research note (PPA Friesland 1966, p. 107) and are decreasing employment in agriculture and in the service sector; increasing employment in industry which concentrated itself in the towns; rising mobility and the rising expectations of the rural population with respect to the service level, concentration of services in the bigger villages, population decrease in the smaller villages which did not reach the necessary population threshold for services, and increase of population in the bigger villages with increasing commuting from these villages to the towns. Tendencies of concentration were present and likely to continue.

National government at that time was hardly concerned with rural areas. The problem of the settlement pattern in rural areas was viewed as a problem of transition to a more widely-spaced settlement pattern with bigger villages and more efficient provision of services. The policy of dispersal of economic activities to the peripheral part of the country was directed to nuclei of industrialization. In this way the higher order centres were supported.

Other theoretical concepts supported the use of central place theory. Cloke (1983) quotes three concepts which play a role in rural settlement planning in Britain: the threshold concept, economies of scale and the growth centre concept. The growth centre theory found its application in the Netherlands in the nuclei of industrialization policy. Threshold theory was strongly interwoven with central place theory. The idea that thresholds rise continually was general among planners and led to a policy of concentration. In the Friesland Village Plan, too, we can trace this idea. The pre-supposed economies of scale to be gained from bigger service outlets also stimulated concentration policy.

In the field of resources, there was more money to be spent on public services at the start of the 1960s (for example on swimming pools). This created the planning problem of where to locate new services.

These circumstances favoured the adoption of central place theory. Decisive, however, was the attitude of planners and the political context in which they had to work. Cloke (1983, pp. 55–56) saw in post-war Britain a period of intensive co-operation and integration between geography as a discipline and planning as a profession. The same can be said for the Netherlands. We have already seen this for the IJsselmeerpolders. This project influenced settlement planning in the remainder of the Netherlands. Thijsse (1963) admits that the theory is not directly suitable for implementation because it is based on a homogeneous area. "But the pattern may be used as a yardstick. As such it has indicated that the existing pattern in the north-eastern part of the Netherlands is quite rational as regards the situation of the large industrial developments. It also indicates that the number of villages in this area is far too high and that the existing pattern of settlements is far from rational." (Thijsse 1963, p. 136) In the Frisian Village Plan the standards for the desired minimal size of villages are based partly on research done for the planning in the IJsselmeerpolders (PPA 1966, p. 121).

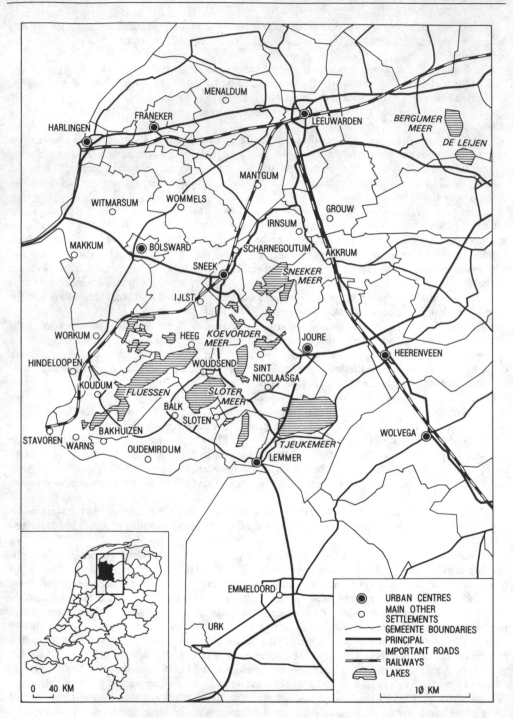

FIGURE 31 *The research area: Southwest Friesland*

In the political field, there was a strong integration between the Provincial Planning Agency and the Provincial Government. The distinction between planner and politician was far from clear. In the Village Plan we see a strong mix-up of expectations based on research and policy objectives. Van Rijn (1975) examined earlier stages in the plan-making process. He concluded that the plan preparation stage was dominated strongly by the Provincial Planning Agency. The Provincial Government approved the policy objectives formulated by the PPA almost without any discussion, and thus there were great opportunities for the planners to apply their theoretical ideas.

Equally important was the attitude of local government, the *gemeente*. In the Netherlands the local authorities have substantial power in spatial planning. They are initiators of plans for housing and services. The province has to judge these plans on directives and programme of actual regional plans, town planning design and structure, land use directives and the financial scheme. In Friesland most *gemeentes* have more than one settlement. Local government is inclined to concentrate its plan-making efforts in the biggest settlement of the *gemeente*. The establishment of modern public services becomes possible by this. As a consequence, the status of government staff rises and career opportunities grow. Moreover, the budget of the *gemeente* is dependent upon population size. Groenendijk (1984, p. 3) concludes that: "Inter-jurisdictional growth concentration planning policies of the provinces are jeopardized by every *gemeente*'s eagerness for growth. Intra-jurisdictional concentration, however, is a policy in which *gemeente* and province easily find each other." In Friesland the Village Plan could be connected largely to the administrative territorial organization, so that there was a great deal of consensus about settlement policy between *gemeente* and province.

There was also consensus about the perception of planners and politicians of the wishes and needs of the public. The opinion was that there was a deficit of 'liveability' in the small villages and that for that reason young people wished to live in the bigger villages with more services. This betrays the image of man the planner-politician of that time had. Man, essentially, has the same needs and wishes and shows the same behaviour. The PPA admitted that 'liveability' is a subjective concept (PPA 1966, p. 75–76) but says at the same time that there is an 'average of values' which appeals to most people.

So we see that central place theory did not appear out of the clear blue sky but that it was a logical policy. At that time a policy of concentration seemed to be the only alternative to cope with such problems as net migration loss, decline in the number of service outlets, decrease in employment in agriculture. Faber and van Rijn (1978, p. 18) concluded that "The leading thread running through the Village Plan is the opinion that concentration of employment, services and populations in the bigger settlements was an irresistible and irreversible process."

Contents of the Village Plan

Now we will go into the contents of the Village Plan itself. The main objective of the plan was to direct the process of concentration in such a way that, in the future, the countryside as a whole would have a reasonable level of provision (PPA 1966, p. 123). This implied the construction of a settlement hierarchy with goals for each settlement category (Figure 32). Although the plan is called the Village Plan the country towns have their own role it it. Five of them were selected to form 'the basic pattern for urbanization of Friesland'. The economic growth necessary to compensate the loss of employment in agriculture would have to take place in these towns. Three types of villages were discerned:

1. The key-villages are those which function as a centre in their surroundings in the provision of non-daily goods and services. The minimal population size is about 2,500. Housing and services should be concentrated in these villages to prevent a strong diminishment of the service level in the countryside. They have to guarantee the provision of non-daily services when the country towns are out of reach.

2. The independent villages are those with a service level tuned to the provision of daily services. The population size lies between 1,500 and 2,500 inhabitants. The task of these villages is to guarantee the service level for daily goods and services on a local scale.

3. The dependent villages are more or less dependent upon bigger villages for services. In general they have less than 1,500 inhabitants.

10 KM

☆   URBAN AREAS
◇   KEY-VILLAGES
○   INDEPENDENT VILLAGES
∘   DEPENDENT VILLAGES

FIGURE 32 *Southwest Friesland: Settlement hierarchy in the Village Plan*

Key-villages and independent villages were selected by such criteria as population size, service level, distance of the village to villages of the same and higher order and potential for growth. A distinction has to be made between villages which already had sufficient population and service level to act as a key-village or an independent village and potential key- or independent villages which were selected because there was no alternative within a reasonable distance. For the selection of these potential villages standards were developed for the distance that the rural population would have to travel to places of higher order. The maximum distance for the rural population to travel to key-villages was put at ten kilometres and to independent villages at four kilometres. In areas beyond the reach of existing independent or key-villages, settlements were assigned to be developed to independent or key-villages.

Essentially, these are the contents of the Friesland Village Plan. We clearly recognize the influence of central place theory with its image of man as a person wishing to live in settlements with material provisions, that is the bigger settlements. We have also seen that circumstances to implement a central place theory in Friesland seemed extraordinary favourable. This caused frictions as a result of a neglect of the non-material needs of the rural population, namely the value people attached to the community life in small villages.

The effects of the Village Plan

In this section we will trace the consequences of the Village Plan with data for the south-western part of Friesland. The Village Plan was actually in effect from 1966 to 1975. We will consider here the period 1960 to 1980 to see if there were already concentration tendencies present before 1966 and to see if there was a fundamental change after the concentration policy had been dropped.

In Figure 33 we see that concentration of population had taken place mostly in the country towns, then in the key-villages and least of all in the independent villages. We can also conclude that growth gradually moved temporarily from the bigger to the smaller settlements. The country towns grew fast in the 1960s but growth diminished slowly in the 1970s. The key-villages and independent villages grew moderately in the 1960s but their growth accellerated in the 1970s. The dependent villages show a gradual decline over the whole period, except the second half of the 1970s. The figures suggest that, after the implementation of the Village Plan, growth of the key- and independent villages accelerated and the already existing tendency of decline in the dependent villages continued. When the policy of concentration had been dropped after 1975, the decline of the dependent villages stopped while the higher order villages continued to grow. Thus a decline of population growth in small villages did not occur at the expense of the bigger villages.

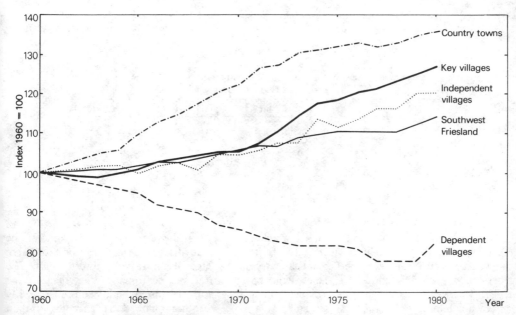

FIGURE 33 *Changes in the spread of population over the settlement categories in Southwest Friesland*

The question which arises now is how far were these developments the result of the implementation of the Village Plan? In the preceding chapter we found that the Village Plan was strongly connected to existing natural tendencies. Does this mean that if there was no Village Plan the same would have happened?

To trace this, we have to analyse the influence of other variables on the changes in the spread of population over settlements. We suppose that two variables are important apart from the Village Plan: suburbanization and the position a settlement occupies in the local jurisdictional territories. To detect the effect of these variables the linear regression between population size in 1960 and the population growth from 1960 to 1980 has been computed. The correlation between these variables was moderate (0.55), but the regression line gives a measure for average growth for a settlement with a given population size. By analysis of the residuals of regression, one can detect whether a settlement grew faster or slower than average for its size.

Table 19 shows the average residuals for each settlement category and by position of the settlement in the *gemeente*. We see here that key-villages and independent villages grew more than

TABLE 19

AVERAGE RESIDUALS OF REGRESSION BY SETTLEMENT CATEGORY AND
POSITION IN THE GEMEENTE

	One-settlement *gemeente*	Poly-settlement *gemeente* Principal	Other	Total
Country towns	− 11.4	29.7	−	2.3
Key-villages	− 7.8	23.5	1.3	15.9
Independent villages	17.8	29.2	14.2	16.5
Dependent villages	−	−	− 3.3	− 3.3
Total	5.8	25.2	− 2.0	0.0

Source: Provincial Planning Agency

TABLE 20

RESIDUALS OF REGRESSION BY SETTLEMENT CATEGORY
AND DISTANCE TO REGIONAL CENTRE SNEEK

	Less than 10 km	10 to 20 km	More than 20 km	Total
Key-villages	−	26.3	8.0	15.9
Independent villages	28.4	11.3	11.0	16.5
Dependent villages	6.8	− 5.7	− 10.7	− 3.3
Total	8.9	− 2.9	− 4.1	0.0

Source: Provincial Planning Agency

settlements with the same population size which were not key-villages or independent villages. The same is true, and to a much stronger degree, for the principal villages in *gemeentes* with more than one settlement. Within every settlement category these villages are the fastest growers. This can be explained by the possibilities that these villages have to attract people from the other villages in the *gemeente*. Key-villages in *gemeentes* of one settlement did not have this possibility and consequently grew much less. The position of a settlement in a *gemeente* appears more decisive for growth than assignment as a key-village.

Suburbanization occurs in peripheral rural areas around the regional centres, although to a substantially lesser degree than in peri-urban rural areas. Table 20 shows that villages near the regional centre grew faster than villages of the same size and settlement category further away. Suburbanization concentrated itself especially in the independent villages around the regional centre but also some dependent villages near the regional centre received some growth. This means that the dependent villages further away declined more than suggested in Figure 33.

In conclusion we can say that the Village Plan stimulated concentration of population in key- and independent villages but it was not the only factor stimulating concentration. Position in the

TABLE 21

CHANGES IN THE NUMBER OF SERVICES

	1964	1972	1980
Educational services	134	120	154
Daily retail services	746	555	363
Non-daily retail services	403	511	747
Private services	90	97	124
Medical services	124	83	127
Socio-cultural services	141	216	252
Southwest Friesland	1,638	1,582	1,767

TABLE 22

DEVELOPMENT OF THE NUMBER OF RETAIL SERVICES
FOR EACH SETTLEMENT CATEGORY 1964–1980

	Daily retail services			Non-daily retail services		
	1964	1972	1980	1964	1972	1980
Country towns	242	171	120	317	319	375
Key-villages	131	105	71	43	73	143
Independent villages	130	101	73	42	64	102
Dependent villages	243	178	99	0	53	126

gemeente and suburbanization contributed to the concentration of population and consequently to the decline of small villages. Changes in the spread of services over the settlement categories have been analysed for 1964, 1972 and 1980 for 36 services split into six groups: educational services, shops for daily goods, shops for non-daily goods, medical services, private services and socio-cultural services. Table 21 shows that the total number of service elements in Southwest Friesland increased in all groups except the shops for daily goods. The increased prosperity is responsible for this. Spectacular is the development in the number of retail outlets for non-daily goods. The contrast that this group makes with the decline of shops for daily goods suggests that some concentration has taken place, for shops for daily goods occur more in the smaller settlements and shops for non-daily goods more in bigger settlements. Figure 34 gives some evidence for this. In 1964, there were only a few settlements with non-daily services and a big group of settlements with only daily services. In 1980, the number of villages where only daily services were offered was much smaller. A group of intermediate villages came into existence with a limited number of non-daily services. This intermediate group consists mainly of key-villages and independent villages (Table 22). It is remarkable that the number of non-daily services grew rapidly in the dependent villages. This growth concentrated itself, however, in a minority of the bigger dependent villages. Although

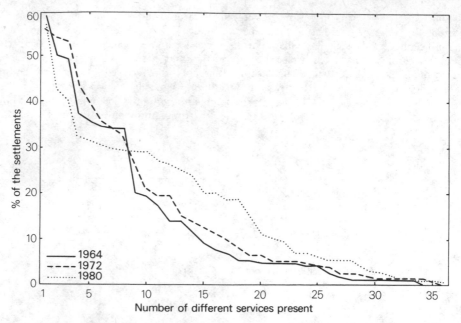

FIGURE 34 *Southwest Friesland: The changing distribution of all 124 settlements according to the number of services present*

there are some tendencies towards dispersal, most small villages did not profit from the overall increase of services. It is difficult to say to what degree this can be ascribed to the Village Plan. At most we can suppose that the process of concentration of population which has been stimulated by the Village Plan accelerated the decrease of services in small villages.

Frictions

In the 1970s, the social frictions which were brought about by the decline of population and services gave rise to an opposition against concentration policies. On a national scale, research done by Groot (1972) was very important in this respect. He found that the 'liveability' in a village community was dependent not only on the degree in which material provisions like services and employment were present but also on immaterial needs like the attachment of the population to the village.

Influenced by this line of thought and more general 'small is beautiful' ideas, the appraisal of small villages rose. As a result of this, the self-consciousness of village inhabitants grew. They began to organize themselves into local unions for village interest. These local unions associated themselves in regional organizations and a national association for small settlements which undertook action for the case of the small villages on the level of regional and national government.

In Friesland actions of this small village movement led to a rejection of the Village Plan ideas. In the preparation stage for the new Regional Plan draft, versions appeared for the sections living, working and recreation. These drafts were held for public participation. In the first draft about living (the *Nota Wonen* 1975) a desirable distribution of population over the settlements was proposed. The policy laid down in the *Nota Wonen* was very much in the line with the ideas in the Village Plan: concentration of housing in the key-villages and country towns to optimize the service level in a regional scale. It was a little less rigid because it permitted small villages to build houses for the local population only. The Frisian population disagreed with this proposal to such a strong degree that the province was forced to adapt the plan. In an answer note (1976) the goal of optimalization of the service level was relaxed. The new policy for the distribution of housing became allocation proportional to population size. With slight changes, this became the formal policy in the new Regional Plan which was approved in 1982.

Conclusion

In this paper we analysed the effects of the application of central place theory for the settlement development in Southwest Friesland. The application of central place heory stood here as an example of the consequences of a materialistic way of thinking among planners and politicians. The settlement pattern in Southwest Friesland stood as an example of a settlement pattern in a peripheral rural area in the Netherlands. We saw that in the early 1960s, circumstances favoured the adoption of central place theory for the preparation of a key-village plan for Friesland. Key-village policy appeared to be one of the major factors responsible for the decline of the unselected villages, although it must be remarked that it was not the only factor. Consequently, it took a substantial part in the decline of shops for daily goods in unselected villages. Most small villages did not profit from the overall increase of other services. Key-village policy must have been a stimulating factor in this. As a whole it can be concluded that key-village policy has been a major force in reshaping the Friesland settlement pattern.

The frictions in the mid-1970s were brought about by the continuous decline in small villages. Key-village policy was one of the greatest targets of criticism because it did not recognize the value of community life in small villages. This raises the question of whether Christaller's model should be rejected completely for rural settlement planning. Cloke (1983) describes a number of alternative planning frameworks which allow mostly for greater resource dispersal. An interesting alternative is the one based on the concept of functional interdependence. The idea is to shape units of five or six contiguous settlements each providing services and facilities for the others. Protagonists of this alternative doubt the existence of a hierarchy on the scale of rural settlements. They stress the fact that most villages, however small, make some service contribution to the surrounding area. In Friesland we saw in the dispersal of non-daily services over the countryside; some empirical support for this alternative. The problems of this approach, however, are twofold. In the first place there is a practical problem of how to recognize functional interdependence units. Secondly, there is the problem of creating a transport network within the cluster and between the cluster and higher-order settlements.

Alternatives should be carefully weighed up against continuing with an adapted version of the hierarchical framework, such as for example in the IJsselmeerpolders where Christaller's model was applied on a macro-scale, but on a micro-scale the principles of a 'thingified' man were neglected. In the Friesland regional plan (1982) we find an adapted version of the hierarchical model. In this plan, hierarchy is no longer a goal in itself but a means to analyse changes in the rural settlement system. This model provided a context of discovery for a policy which advocated dispersal.

Bibliography

BAKKER, R. (1977) *De geschiedenis van het fenomelogisch denken* (A History of Phenomenological Thought), (Utrecht/Antwerpen: Het Spectrum Aula 174, 5e druk).

BAKKER, D. H. DE (1982) *Rationalisatie nederzettingenpatroon: literatuurverkenning en onderzoeksopzet* (Rationalization of the Settlement Pattern: Survey of Literature and Research Design), (Stepro rapport no. 22a, Utrecht: Geografisch Instituut Rijksuniversiteit).

BELD, A. VAN DEN (1982) *Filosofie van het menselijk handelen* (A Philosophy of Human Action), (Assen: Van Gorcum).

BUURSINK, J. (1980) "De centrale plaatsentheorie; misplaatst en misverstaan" (Central Place Theory; Mistaken and Misjudged), *Geografisch Tijdschrift* 14, no. 2: 151–157.

CLOKE, P. (1979) *Key-Settlements in Rural Areas,* (London: Methuen).

CLOKE, P. (1983) *An Introduction to Rural Settlement Planning,* (London and New York: Methuen).

CONSTANDSE, A. K. (1960) *Het dorp in de IJsselmeerpolders* (The Village in the IJsselmeerpolders), (Zwolle: Tjeenk Willink).

CONSTANDSE, A. K. (1972) "The IJsselmeerpolders. An Old Project with New Functions", *Tijdschrift voor Economische en Sociale Geografie* 63, no. 3: 200–210.

DESSAUR, C. I. (1982) *De droom der rede. Het mensbeeld in de sociale wetenschappen* (The Dream of Reason. The Image of Man in the Social Sciences), ('s-Gravenhage: Martinus Nijhoff).

FABER, S.—RIJN, G. VAN (1978) *Provinciaal beleid op Friese leest?* (Regional Policy, the Frisian Way), (Leeuwarden: Fryske Akademy).

GROENENDIJK, J. G. (1984) "A Key to Settlement Growth in Rural Areas; Local Administrators, Their Scope and the Size of Their Territories". In: *The Changing Countryside* (eds.: Clark, G.—Groenendijk, J.—Thissen, F.), (Norwich: Geobooks): 283–296.

GROOT, J. P. (1972) *Kleine plattelandskernen in de Nederlandse samenleving. Schaalvergroting en dorpsbinding* (Small Rural Communities in the Dutch Society. Scale Enlargement and Village Attachment), (Wageningen: Veenman).

HOOFDCOMMISSIE VOOR DE INDUSTRIALISATIE (1951) *Landelijke spreiding der industrialisatie door regionale koncentraties* (National Dispersal by Regional Concentration), ('s-Gravenhage: Staatsdrukkerij- en uitgeversbedrijf).

KUGEL, J. (1982) *Filosofie van het lichaam. Wijsgerige beschouwingen over het menselijk gedrag* (Philosophy of the Body. Philosophical Considerations about the Human Behaviour), (Utrecht/Antwerpen: Het Spectrum Aula 701).

LAAN, L. VAN DER—PIERSMA, A. (1982) "The Image of Man: Paradigmatic Cornerstone in Human Geography", *Annals of the Association of American Geographers* 72, no. 3: 411–426.

LANDMANN, M. (1964) *Philosophische Anthropologie,* (Berlin: Walter de Gruyter).

LEWIS, G. J. (1979) *Rural Communities: A Social Geography,* (London: David and Charles).

LOPES DA SILVA, F. H.—TWEEL, L. H. VAN DER (1982) "Informatieverweking in de hersenen" (Data Processing in the Human Mind), *Intermediair,* 5 maart.

POINCARÉ, H. (1979) *Wetenschap en hypothese* (Science and Hypothesis), (Meppel: Boom). (Original Title: La science et l'hypothèse. Paris, 1902)

PROVINCIAL PLANNING AGENCY FRIESLAND (1966) *De ruimtelijke ontwikkeling van het Friese platteland* (The Spatial Development of the Frisian Countryside), (Leeuwarden).

PROVINCIALE PLANOLOGISCHE DIENST FRIESLAND (1975) *Streekplan Friesland: Nòta Wonen* (Regional Plan Friesland: Report on Living), (Leeuwarden).

PROVINCIAL PLANNING AGENCY FRIESLAND (1976) *Antwoordnota op inspraak en overleg over de Nota Wonen* (Answer Note after Public Participation on the Report on Living), (Leeuwarden).

SCHOUTEN, B.—WITMER-OOR, E. (1982) *Openbaar vervoer en fysiek bereik in Zuidwest Friesland, 1964–1980* (Public Transport and Physical Access in Southwest Friesland, 1964–1980), (Utrecht: Geografisch Instituut).

TAKES, C. A. P. (1948) *Bevolkingscentra in het oude en het nieuwe land* (Population Centers in Old and New Areas), (Alphen a/d Rijn: Samsom).

THIJSSE, J. P. (1963) "A Rural Pattern for the Future in the Netherlands", *Regional Science Association. Papers and Proceedings* 10: 133–141.

TIMMERMANS, H. (1980) "Functionele hiërarchie en ruimtelijk keuzegedrag van consumenten: een theoretische uiteenzetting en een empirische toepassing van een ruimtelijk preferentiemodel" (Functional Hierarchy and Spatial Behaviour of Consumers: a Theoretical Elaboration and an Empirical Application of a Spatial Preference Model), *Geografisch Tijdschrift* 14, no. 3: 182–193.

LOCAL GOVERNMENT
AND SMALL VILLAGES
IN PERIPHERAL RURAL AREAS
A Survey of Municipal Policy-Making

TJEBBE F. DE BOER AND JAN G. GROENENDIJK

KEY-WORDS: *concentration* in dominant village; *IJsselmeerpolders; policy,* concentration ∼, demand type of ∼, dispersal ∼, key-settlement ∼, municipal ∼, supply type of ∼; *policy-making* behaviour of local authority; *size of the municipal apparatus; socio-cultural* accommodation.

Introduction

Conditions for the well-being of localized human groups are in these days exposed to the hazards of events and processes in society, taking place largely beyond local influence. These events and processes are the outcome of decisions taken by various actors in numerous specialized domains. The effects converge in a particular mix, in some accordance to local geographical structure upon a locality.

As geographers we may look for patterns in these events and processes. We may, in our view, look as well into local government, into how far it can hold itself responsible for the well-being of the inhabitants of its territory and have instruments to improve favourable conditions. This makes us interested in the workings of local government—within the broad spectrum of public authority agencies—in their particular geographical milieu.

In this paper we look into the workings of Dutch local government bodies — referred to here as municipalities—in peripheral rural areas, especially in relation to the evolution of the settlement patterns. To what extent is the differential growth of settlements influenced by municipal policies? Do these policies vary between municipalities of variable population size, territorial extent and aim? The second chapter looks into the influence of municipalities on the differential growth of settlements as one aspect of the evolution of the settlement pattern. While we are able to show the imprint of the discontinuity of political spaces on the evolving settlement pattern, we have to allow for the fact that municipalities, acting on behalf of different communities, differ in their outlook of how well-being is connected with a particular size structure of a settlement pattern. We typify municipalities according to the degree of concentration in their largest (dominant) village which has been reached in a certain time interval. In the third chapter we follow notions of organization theory to formulate questions concerning the use that municipalities, acting in a complex network of governmental agents, can make of their authority. A fourth chapter summarizes the results of a survey of a selected population of municipalities into municipal policies, with respect to housing and socio-cultural accommodation in peripheral rural areas.

Differential growth of settlements and local government

Peripheral rural areas are characterized by the thinning out of functions. Modernization of agrarian life, cutting heavily the employment levels of farms and enlarging the scale of the agricultural produce industry, had, together with the advent of the motorized age, the effect of concentrating functions into fewer nodes with good accessibility.

Public authorities are confronted with a situation in response to which they have to find new instruments to promote conditions for well-being. This situation differs widely from peri-urban rural areas where new housing and recreation functions are arising and may tend to fill the gap left by the retreat of other functions.

The deliberate planning of a settlement pattern in peripheral areas was not entirely new to Dutch governmental agencies. Concerning the spacing of servicing nodes (Takes 1948) and the location of farm labour (Groeneman 1946) in the IJsselmeerpolders, the advice of social scientists had been asked. The retreat of farm labour largely outdated this expertise; it is to be noted, however, that Christaller's *Zentralen Orte* concept has been applied to this task.

Concentration policies in different guises have been introduced to cope with an outdated settlement pattern. Cloke (1979) shows that a 'key-settlement' policy has been applied under the rather different circumstances prevailing in peripheral and peri-urban rural areas, having to promote business on one hand and control urban encroachment on the other. Cloke (1983) has reviewed the planning notions from which criteria have been derived to select settlements for growth. Taking for granted that one rural centre will be able to perform functions for a large rural area, larger villages were to be selected for growth.

Leaving aside the relevance of these notions for rural planning, we may search the factual evolution of settlement patterns for traces of the application of planning theory. The fact that several governmental agencies with their own domain of authority perform functions in this respect means that we have to specify which governmental body is under scrutiny. As we limit ourselves to local government we ask whether the differential population growth of villages coincides with the pattern of municipal territories.

That larger settlements grow rather than smaller ones—as may be deduced from the application of planning theory—is confirmed by Figure 35. Settlements in the larger-size classes all tend to be in the category of more than 10% growth. Only a few of the settlements smaller than 5,000 inhabitants grew by more than 10%. Seen from the other side, however, small villages even in peripheral areas do grow occasionally at a considerable rate. In what respects do they differ from declining villages? It has been shown for the northern provinces that they do not cluster around an urban node, but are scattered over almost all municipal territories (Groenendijk 1984).

When the selection of settlements for growth (and decline) is being done by municipalities, population living in declining settlements will be found in many municipalities. Figure 36 shows that this is indeed the case and their occurrence is not confined to peripheral areas. Table 23 shows that the relationship between overall growth of municipalities and the percentage of their population living in declining settlements is rather weak, and becoming more so over time, which underlines the growing importance of selection.

Municipal territories in the Netherlands differ widely in their extent (as can be seen from Figure 36) and settlement structure (as defined by the relationship between size of settlements, especially the degree of dominance of the largest, or dominant, village). Assuming that application of planning principles with respect to municipal territories will lead the local authorities to choose their largest settlement to perform functions for the entire municipality and concentrate new housing accordingly, the selected settlements may fall in rather different size classes. The dominant settlement will outstrip the non-dominant percentage growth in any size class.

Scatter diagrams (Figure 37) relating population change rates to size of dominant and other settlements separately, indeed show different percentage growth between the groups, notwithstanding the considerable spread within the groups. By aggregating the cases in size classes for the provinces separately (Table 24) the figures are made more clear for interpretation. Differences between the two categories of settlements is most obvious outside the central provinces—in already rather high density built-up spaces dominant settlements will often be constrained in their growth. Most clear is the difference between the two categories in the peripheral provinces, especially in

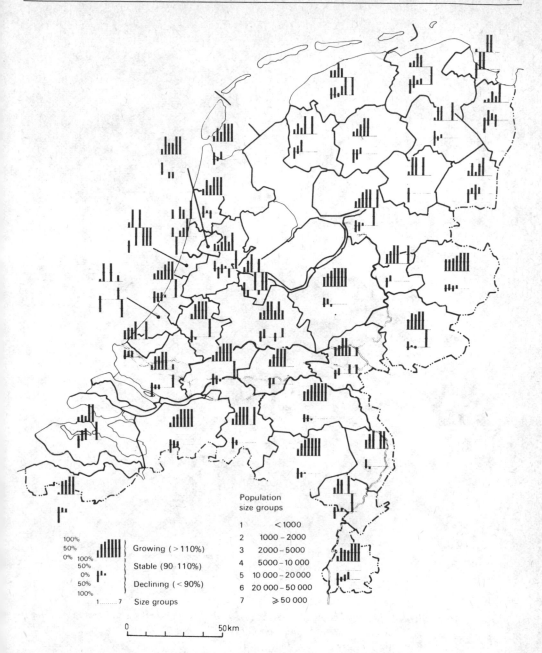

FIGURE 35 *Settlements in COROP-regions by population size groups and 1960–1971 change rates*

FIGURE 36 *Percentage of municipal population living in declining settlements (which lost more than 10 per cent of their population between 1960 and 1971)*

TABLE 23

POPULATION CHANGE RATES OF MUNICIPALITIES AND THE PERCENTAGE OF POPULATION
LIVING IN DECLINING SETTLEMENTS

Population change rates (%)	1947–1960							
	Percentage of population living in declining villages							
	0	< 5	5–10	10–15	15–30	30–50	> 50	Total
< 11	39	7	14	17	45	27	18	167
11–24	72	14	17	9	31	9	1	153
24–41	80	16	18	9	5	3	0	131
> 41	80	13	14	4	5	0	1	117
Cramer's v = 0.3032								568

Population change rates (%)	1960–1971							
	Percentage of population living in declining villages							
	0	< 5	5–10	10–15	15–30	30–50	> 50	Total
< 11	18	15	16	13	32	24	11	129
11–24	46	13	20	17	30	15	3	144
24–41	61	24	24	9	22	5	2	147
> 41	78	15	16	11	19	8	1	148
Cramer's v = 0.2186								568

small size groups: growth of settlements in these classes is not very likely unless they belong to the dominant category.

These results confirm to some degree our inferential statement concerning the application of concentration as a planning principle within municipal boundaries. While 'dominance' of a settlement discriminates between growth classes, the influence of local government on the evolving settlement structure is clearly present.

By measuring the degree of concentration, however, considerable differences between municipalities have been shown (Groenendijk 1983). Figure 38 summarizes these differences in a typlogy; type 4: all difference in growth between the settlements is entirely 'benefiting' the dominant village; in type 3, to a large degree; type 2 municipalities disperse differences in growth over a number of settlements; whereas in type 1 municipalities, the largest villages are losing out to others. Concentration in the dominant settlement proves to be the rule in rural municipalities, but one with many exceptions. These differences make us interested in the diverging policies that might be found to be their explanation.

Differences in policy between municipalities

Municipalities, as with all types of local authority, do not perform their functions entirely upon their own but have some form of dependence-relationship (be it for money or for approval of the policy chosen) with other authorities. (For the performance of rural municipalities towards their small settlements in this respect, see VNG 1979). Elkin (1975) devised a theoretical strategy to analyse local authorities through an inter-organizational approach. The local territorial unit studied is seen as the focus of a network of governmental organizations (other agents could also be studied as part of the network). Each of the organizations in the network has a domain, a sphere of competence, which they seek to protect or expand. One could assume that the prevailing concentration policy aims at autonomy—to have one large settlement with modern public facilities in the municipal

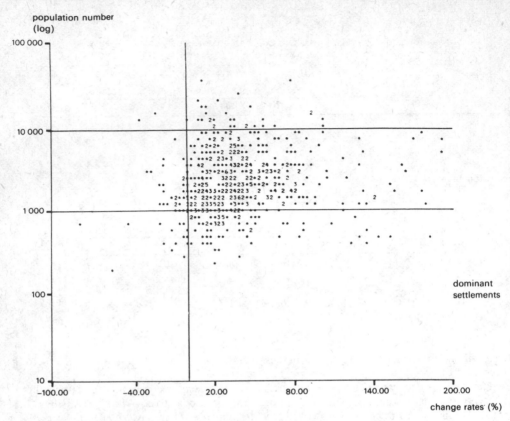

FIGURE 37 *Population change rates 1960–1971 of settlements according to size 1971*

territory makes it less dependent on decision-making by other authorities. Our analysis, however, is to cover both the concentration and the non-concentration municipality type.

To structure our survey of peripheral municipalities' policy-making we have to specify our problem. Essentially, we are interested in the policy-making behaviour of local authorities with respect to the specific settlement structure of their areas. Young and Kramer (1978) discern three aspects of this behaviour. *In the first place*, they make use of Elkin's notion of managing dependence behaviour in such a way that the domain-margins within which decisions are taken are optimally extended. *Secondly*, the striving for autonomy towards outside public bodies in managing dependence has a complementary aspect in that local governments tend to look to their territory as a self-contained unit. In their policy-making activities the municipal administrators will have a specific understanding of local world within the municipal boundaries. *Thirdly*, the local policy-makers try to develop their bounded environment in the direction of a preferred state of affairs. They will try to do so especially in response to exogenous or indigenous hazards that may jeopardize the local preferences.

With regard to policy-making in municipalities in peripheral rural areas, the spatial distribution of public goods (services) over a rural territory that consists of several spatially-defined communities is an issue of crucial importance. We confine our survey to the policy with respect to the distribution aspects of housing and socio-cultural services. As we were limited in the number of

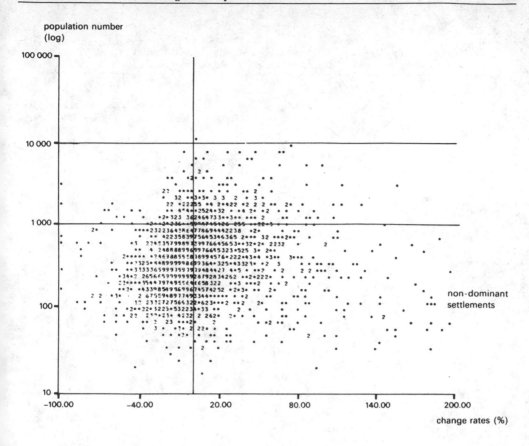

population number
(log)

municipalities to be surveyed, our approach had to provide us with the criteria to choose our objects of study.

First and foremost we set out to picture the range of difference in policies and instruments chosen. The degree of concentration as typified in the first chapter gives us the opportunity to select municipalities that differ in the amount of concentration of population in the dominant village, probably as a result of deliberate policy. We selected municipalities of the opposing types 4 (concentration) and 2 (dispersion). The selection is confined to 'semi-peripheral' and 'peripheral' areas as defined by Engelsdorp Gastelaars et al. (1980).

Secondly, as regards the understanding of the policy-makers of their local world with respect to the distribution issue, the scheme that they have in mind for the settlement pattern within their territory will be the pre-eminent influence on their policy. We chose municipalities with a great number of settlements (from a class of six settlements and over, according to the Central Bureau of Statistics classification) and with a small number.

Finally, with respect to the damage that can be done to a local well-being policy, the distribution of services in rural areas is of course threatened by the prevailing scale enlargement tendencies. Two reactions—schematically opposed to each other—seem possible. One policy is concerned especially with the provision within the municipal territory of specific services at the highest possible level. This 'supply type' policy will try to reach (threshold) conditions in at least one of the villages.

TABLE 24

POPULATION CHANGE RATES OF DOMINANT (d) AND NON-DOMINANT (nd) SETTLEMENTS
IN MUNICIPALITIES OF VARIOUS SIZE GROUPS BY PROVINCES 1960–1971 (%)*

Province	0–999		1000–1999		2000–3999		4000–9999	
	d	nd	d	nd	d	nd	d	nd
	(8)	(230)	(21)	(27)	(10)	(2)	(6)	(3)
Groningen	5,41	−7,33	15,03	0,17	31,77	53,89	41,22	−2,20
	(10)	(325)	(9)	(35)	(14)	(2)	(6)	(0)
Friesland	13,23	1,57	16,49	13,26	24,95	44,41	25,83	–
	(6)	(229)	(15)	(13)	(6)	(8)	(2)	(2)
Drenthe	49,66	−0,76	43,91	16,58	59,22	4,28	43,52	15,26
	(6)	(114)	(10)	(13)	(13)	(7)	(13)	(1)
Overijssel	22,81	15,36	40,71	19,15	56,08	9,90	38,60	−6,74
	(17)	(225)	(28)	(40)	(20)	(13)	(25)	(6)
Gelderland	33,62	15,03	54,36	28,30	46,39	34,10	45,66	57,67
	(6)	(91)	(11)	(14)	(16)	(4)	(7)	(2)
Utrecht	20,42	62,15	48,84	26,85	58,92	44,80	29,43	49,37
	(18)	(202)	(22)	(23)	(19)	(9)	(22)	(5)
Noord-Holland	33,19	24,66	36,62	12,15	40,06	19,59	55,51	19,69
	(37)	(224)	(30)	(17)	(32)	(12)	(27)	(8)
Zuid-Holland	49,38	19,77	51,40	29,95	61,80	14,34	86,38	78,90
	(2)	(132)	(16)	(19)	(10)	(6)	(4)	(1)
Zeeland	18,13	2,67	10,01	13,85	13,62	15,83	18,46	40,98
	(10)	(247)	(41)	(50)	(40)	(8)	(31)	(1)
Brabant	27,69	17,55	36,42	25,07	49,54	6,54	43,84	10,85
	(17)	(311)	(37)	(39)	(25)	(9)	(15)	(4)
Limburg	41,47	10,90	40,29	13,89	46,05	62,11	22,29	6,42

* (. .) = N of cases
Source: Central Bureau of Statistics

As opposed to this, we discern a 'demand type' policy which tries to provide at least basic services in all settlements. Examples of these two policy-types might be found in the opposed concentration/dispersion types of municipalities respectively; this choice has already been catered for in our first criterion. With respect to policy-making in municipalities, one criterion cannot be left out of consideration. This is the size of the municipal apparatus—the number of civil servants, the number of politicians in office etc. In the Netherlands this size is directly proportional to the number of inhabitants. Difference in size has its influence in a more or less bureaucratic political structure, degree of explicitness of policy, and degree to which policy options are specified. In larger municipalities, specialized civil servants will influence policy formulations whereas in smaller municipalities the local politicians will be able to formulate policy options more directly. The fact that the mayor is appointed by the Crown, however, makes the civil servants influential, even in small municipalities.

The collection of material for this survey was obtained during a telephone conversation with one of the members of the municipality board. We asked him to send us policy documents which could give us some idea of the question of distribution in settlements. We asked for documents concerned especially with public housing or public welfare or both, especially the distribution of services. Although the possibility cannot altogether be excluded that our respondents have forgotten some important documents, it is our impression that the documents which we received represent the policy pursued until now or for the future policy. Some documents directly answered our questions while others could be used indirectly for our survey. Their diversity reflects the plurality of options

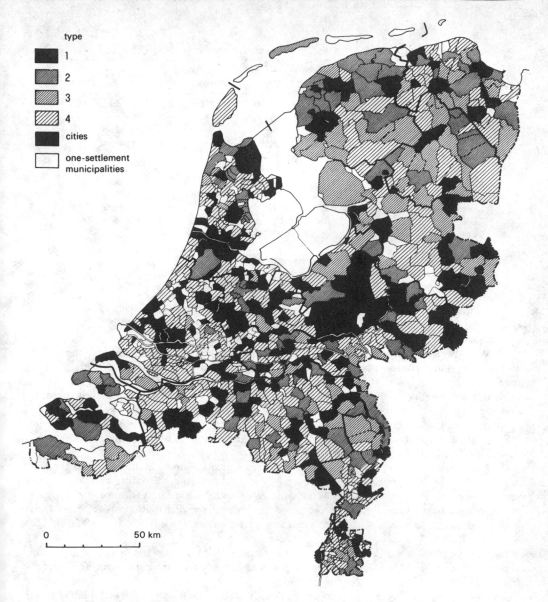

type
1
2
3
4
cities
one-settlement
municipalities

0   50 km

FIGURE 38 *Typology of municipalities according to the degree of concentration in dominant settlement
(for types 1–4, see page 151)*

TABLE 25

SELECTED MUNICIPALITIES

Municipality	Number of inhabitants		Number of settlements	conc./disp.* 1960–1971
	1960	1983		
Vledder	1,767	3,400	6	disp.
Rauwerderhem	2,072	3,000	6	conc.
Roggel	2,781	4,200	6	disp.
Beerta	3,193	3,100	4	conc.
Sevenum	3,646	6,700	6	conc.
Brakel	4,003	6,100	5	disp.
Lichtenvoorde	7,804	17,500	5	conc.
Opsterland	10,652	26,000	16	disp.
Weststellingwerf	15,381	24,000	23	conc.
Deurne	16,098	29,000	11	disp.
Emmen	58,422	90,800	32	conc.

* conc. = concentration in dominant village
  disp. = dispersion over (all) villages

open to the local governments to direct their policy in their own way. The 11 municipalities questioned were selected by the above-mentioned criteria.

The study of the (political) documents was achieved on three assumptions:

(a) We expected that there should be a relationship between the number of inhabitants of the municipality and the degree of explicitness of planning regarding the settlements. We expected that the larger the municipality the more explicit would be the formulation of the policy on behalf of the settlements, expecially the distribution item. The reason for this expectation was that the larger the municipality the more likely it was that specialized civil servants could take care of policy preparation. Closely related to this was the expectation that the larger the municipality the more differentiated would be the local policy regarding the existence of more differentiated local government institutions and instruments.

(b) Our second assumption was that the more settlements a municipality contains the more complex would be the 'scheme' which is used by the local government to distribute housing and services over the settlements. This scheme consists of a schematic impression of the settlement structure and, linked with that, some choosing of priorities. The distribution of—possibly scarce goods and services over many settlements can be expected to be more difficult than over only a few settlements.

(c) The third assumption concerns the policy contents of the selected municipality. One would expect that there should be a continuity in the policy of dispersion or concentration which was to be found in 1960–1971 into the following period.

We also surveyed whether the concentration/dispersion dichotomy showed parallels with 'demand orientation' or 'supply orientation' (Table 25).

The results of the survey

First we can establish that eight of the 11 municipalities did formulate an explicit policy regarding the (small) settlements. Regarding the other three one can conclude that their policy was at least rather vague. The eight 'positive' municipalities make clear that they consist of several settlements and that it is necessary to work within a frame of reference to distribute people, houses and services. It strikes immediately that one can roughly discern two groups. On the one hand there are municipalities which concentrate on the development of one special settlement, which implies that the other settlements 'get a lesser chance'. On the other hand there is a group of municipalities following a more differentiated policy towards all settlements within their territory (in which obviously one or more settlements could have a more pronounced position).

Our assumption that there should be a relationship between municipality size and explicitness in formulating a settlement policy could not be proved convincingly. For Rauwerderhem, for instance, one can conclude that an explicit distribution policy is followed for the settlements. This policy is supported by making special plans for each settlement in the municipality. On the other hand, larger municipalities are more vague on this: in one case policy formulation takes the municipality as a whole (with special attention to the central village); the settlements are handled in the same was as the neighbourhoods of the central village. Otherwise this municipality is 'leaning' heavily on the policy as formulated by the regional authority *(gewest)* in which it participates for settlement policy. On this regional level, an overall settlement plan is formulated in which an integrated policy is suggested for each individual settlement.

Looking at the so-called *dorpenplannen* (integrated plans for one settlement or a group of settlements, usually developed by the municipality) as an expression of explicitness of the local policy, in our sample such plans are available in Rauwerderhem, Vledder (for the main centre only), Weststellingwerf, Opsterland and Deurne (via the regional authority). It seems that the size of municipalities is of hardly any importance for explicitness in policy-formulation. A more determining influence, therefore, seems to be the number of settlements per municipality. One can suggest with some prudence that there is such a relationship: two out of the three municipalities with only a few settlements have no explicit policy because of that; most of the eight other municipalities clearly formulated their settlement policy.

Also, the degree of differentiation in policy—measured by the use of instruments in different sectors of local government—shows only a weak relationship with municipality size. At least this relationship could be traced only with difficulty. Possibly the quality of the received documents creates some bias (incompleteness, for instance). It can surely be concluded that in all municipalities housing is the directive element in local government settlement policy. In most of the municipalities the distribution of services depends on that. Other local governmental instruments are seldom used as instruments in distribution policy. We mention here one positive exception, Rauwerderhem. For the integrated village plans in that municipality, the renewing of the sewerage-system was used as a catalyst for renewing the villages. Other instruments improving the life and work situation were integrated, including the use of funds for the improvement of employment. Such an integrated policy can—in a lesser way—also be seen in Weststellingwerf and Opsterland.

Our second assumption was that municipalities with (relatively) many settlements will operate more complex schemes for the distribution of people, houses and services than the municipalities with relatively fewer settlements. We examined this assumption by making an inventory of the different ways municipalities 'group' their settlements in 'schemes'. That means: how municipalities trace special strategies for individual or groups of settlements within their territory, with respect to
—the distribution of population growth (for instance the measure for the distribution of natural increase or net migration rates over the settlements);
—housing policy: the distribution of houses which can be built during a year (depending on the funds provided by the national government);
—the distribution of services (new ones or a policy to continue existing services).

The survey makes clear that the group of municipalities with few settlements does not 'handle' complex strategies in the distribution policy. Even in the municipalities with many settlements there are some handling a rather simple distribution scheme. Simplicity in this group, however, concerns most municipalities with a dominant centre (Emmen, Sevenum, Vledder, Deurne). It is our conclusion that a slight relationship can be traced between the number of settlements per municipality and the complexity of the (intended) policy, but that the degree of dominance of one centre in the municipality rather than the quantity of settlements is a more important determinator of the complexity of the schemes.

In the second chapter we referred to the concentration or dispersion policy of the municipalities during the period 1960–1971 (as could be determined by population development in parts of the municipality). The documents collected for this survey concern especially the later period. Most papers and documents date from the period 1978–1982. We expected a continuity in the distribution policy during the whole period. The next survey (Table 26) provides an impression of that

TABLE 26

CONTINUITY OF MUNICIPAL DISTRIBUTION POLICY

Municipality	Concentration/ dispersion 1960–1971	Concentration/ dispersion 1971–1978/82
Beerta	conc.	conc./disp.
Sevenum	conc.	conc.
Rauwerderhem	conc.	conc.
Lichtenvoorde	conc.	conc.
Weststellingwerf	conc.	disp./conc.
Emmen	conc.	conc.
Brakel	disp.	disp.
Vledder	disp.	conc.
Roggel	disp.	disp.
Opsterland	disp.	disp.
Deurne	disp.	conc.

continuity. The second column is based on empirical results, the third column is partly empirical, partly policy intentions.

One can conclude that there exists a high degree of consistency in concentration and dispersion, with Vledder and Deurne as exceptions. There, a clear concentration policy can be determined for the 1970s in the central village. The most remarkable change took place in Weststellingwerf. During the 1970s, municipal policy changed (at least in its intentions), partly because of political pressure from the inhabitants of the (small) settlements, especially in the case of housing policy where there should be a more proportional distribution over all the settlements. That was the intention. The facts show, however, that house-building is still concentrated in Wolvega (the main centre). Because of this development, a recent municipal policy document gave the intention of moving towards a policy of increased dispersal.

In this context, it is important to indicate that during the 1970s, the provincial governments made haste in developing *streekplannen* (schemes for physical planning in part of the province). A trademark of most of them was a pronounced policy towards the growth/non-growth strategy of individual settlements. Environmental arguments, particularly, came to the fore in this period. In some cases this led to restriction of population growth in small settlements—or even stopping any growth. The goals of the *streekplannen* are important in leading local governmental planning. Regarding its own responsibility for, and the political discussion about, the future of the local community, it is not surprising that frequent protests are uttered against the detailed exertion of the provinces to the physical and socio-economical planning of the municipality.

However, during that same period, a reverse movement occurred in the rethinking of liveability— the right of existence of the small villages. In some areas this led to blockade on the leading planning philosophy during the 1960s, which was the enlargement of scale, in which small villages were non-efficient entities. This change of opinion gave new scope to the on-going development of the small villages, which often meant stopping further downgrading. In the change of policy in Weststellingwerf, as we mentioned before, one can specifically see an expression of this evolution.

We also surveyed the municipal policy-contents in two other ways. First we examined if a relationship could be traced between concentration or dispersion policy and, respectively, a supply orientation and a demand orientation. The first orientation tries to guarantee the highest possible level for specific services in the municipality. The second tries to provide for at least basic services in all settlements. In Table 27 we give an impression of this.

TABLE 27

MUNICIPAL POLICY ORIENTATIONS

Municipality	Concentration/ dispersion 1960–1971	Concentration/ dispersion 1971–1980/83	Demand/supply orientation	Policy characteristics				
				0	1	2	3	4
Beerta	conc.	conc./disp.	s		1		3	
Sevenum	conc.	conc.	s		1		3	
Rauwerderhem	conc.	conc.	s		1		3	
Lichtenvoorde	conc.	conc.	s		1		3	
Weststellingwerf	conc.	disp./conc.	d		1	2	3	
Emmen	conc.	conc.	s	(0)		2	3	4
Brakel	disp.	disp.	d		1			
Vledder		disp./conc.	s		1	(2)	3	
Roggel	disp.	disp.	d	(0)	1		3	
Opsterland	disp.	disp.	d		1	2		
Deurne	disp.	conc.	s		1		3	

Secondly, we looked into municipal settlement policy. One can distinguish in the following some continuity in policy intentions:

(0) one can imagine that local authorities see villages as non-efficient entities; therefore they intend to allow the 'bleeding to death' of such villages;

(1) the political objective can be the right of existence of each village; therefore local policy has to aim for the liveability of each village;

(2) local government policy can be directed towards creating an intermediate level of main villages within the municipal territory; those villages should have a central function for a part of the municipality;

(3) the municipality can have the 'ambition' of one village functioning as a centre for the whole municipality; for that reason that village is stimulated;

(4) it can be the objective of local policy for the whole municipality—or the main centre within it—fulfilling a central function for a larger territory.

Municipalities can take more than one of these options, such as the guaranteeing of liveability of each village and further development of a nodal village functioning for the municipality as a whole. In the Netherlands, the policy to let villages 'die' is hardly accepted. The definition of 'village', however, then comes into the question. In some municipalities (in our sample Emmen and Roggel) one can distinguish some hamlets or settlements which are not distinguished as such by the local authority. They are not mentioned in the policy documents and, therefore, they are not an object of policy-making. In our opinion, then, a 'hidden starvation' can be traced.

Both surveys are represented in Table 27. For comparison, we repeated whether there has been a concentration or dispersion policy since 1960. Most municipalities combine option 1 and option 3—taking care of each village as such and developing a central village for the municipality as a whole.

Supply orientation and demand orientation correlate somewhat to concentration policy and dispersion policy respectively. The assertion that the central village should offer 'just a little more' to the municipality as a whole is seldom abandoned.

Conclusions

Effects of the territorial pattern of Dutch municipalities can be shown in the evolving settlement pattern. Once more the municipalities show their relevance to rural development by devising their own, rather diverging, spatial distribution policies. These policies show continuity to a large degree while fashions of planning principles went by and provincial policies changed; again stressing that municipalities manage their independence quite well.

Local authorities tend to have a very subjective picture of the settlement structure in their territory. This may not always be to the benefit of all localized groups. An inter-municipal approach as performed in the Helmond-region (Deurne) may force the municipality to confront their images with more objective standards.

From this survey the need for amalgamations of municipalities cannot be concluded. Larger municipalities do not always tend to be more explicit in their distribution policy. On the contrary, some small municipalities do have a deliberately structured policy in which several fields of action are integrated. When central government policies concerning the well-being in peripheral areas are to be implemented properly, the fact that this has to be done in an inter-organizational cadre will influence the effects. In view of this, proper use should be made of the initiative and information that municipalities may provide.

Bibliography

CLOKE, P. J. (1979) *Key-Settlements in Rural Areas*, (London: Methuen).

CLOKE, P. J. (1983) *An Introduction to Rural Settlement Planning*, (London: Methuen).

ELKIN, S. L. (1975) "Comparative Urban Politics and Interorganizational Behaviour". In: *Essays on the Study of Urban Politics* (ed.: Young, K.), (London: McMillan): 158–184.

ENGELSDORP GASTELAARS, R. E. VAN—OSTENDORF, W. J. M.—VOS, S. DE (1980) *Typologieën van Nederlandse gemeenten naar stedelijkheidsgraad* (Typologies of Dutch Municipalities according to Degree of Urbanization), (Monografieën Volkstelling 1971, deel 15B, CBS, The Hague).

GROENENDIJK, J. G. (1983) *Centrumdorpen 1947–1971: beleid op gemeentelijke schaal* (Key-Villages 1947–1971; Policies on the Municipal Level), (Amsterdam: Free University, Geografische en Planologische notities, no. 26).

GROENENDIJK, J. G. (1984) "A Key to Settlement Growth in Rural Areas; Local Administrators, Their Scope and the Size of Their Territories". In: *The Changing Countryside* (eds.: Clark, G.—Groenendijk, J. G.—Thissen, F.), (Norwich: Geobooks): 283–296.

GROENMAN, S. J. (1946) *De verspreiding van de bevolking in de Wieringermeer* (The Distribution of Population in the Wieringermeer), (Directie Wieringermeer).

TAKES, CH. A. P. (1948) *Bevolkingscentra in het oude en het nieuwe land* (Population Centres in the Old and in the New Land), (Alphen a/d Rijn: Samsom).

VERENIGING VAN NEDERLANDSE GEMEENTEN (1979) *Wie het kleine niet eert* . . . . (If You Don't Value Small Things . . . .), (The Hague).

YOUNG, K.—KRAMER, J. (1978) "Local Exclusionary Policies in Britain". In: *Urbanisation and Conflict in Marketsocieties* (ed.: Cox, K.), (London: Methuen): 229–251.

INDEX

Forthcoming

in the REGIONAL RESEARCH REPORTS *series:*

REGIONAL DEVELOPMENT PROCESSES
AND POLICIES

EDITED BY

WILLIAM H. BERENTSEN, DARRICK R. DANTA AND ETA DARÓCZI

The second volume in the series will include contributions from Hungarian and U.S. geographers/economists/planners. Unity of the book's content is achieved by way of a common aim among the authors to analyse contemporary spatio-social problems arising from rapid change in the international economy and the consequent need for re-evaluation of existing regional and urban policies.

From the contents:

METHODOLOGICAL APPROACHES TO REGIONAL ANALYSIS